THE LOV

Edited by S. T. Joshi

No. 15 (2021)

Contents

Abbreviations used in the text and notes:

AT   *The Ancient Track* (Hippocampus Press, 2013)
CE   *Collected Essays* (Hippocampus Press, 2004–06; 5 vols.)
CF   *Collected Fiction* (Hippocampus Press, 2015–17; 4 vols.)
IAP   *I Am Providence: The Life and Times of H. P. Lovecraft* (Hippo-
      campus Press, 2010; 2013 [paper])
LL   *Lovecraft's Library: A Catalogue*, 4th rev. ed. (Hippocampus
      Press, 2017)
SL   *Selected Letters* (Arkham House, 1965–76; 5 vols.)

Copyright © 2021 by Hippocampus Press
Published by Hippocampus Press, P.O. Box 641, New York, NY 10156
www.hippocampuspress.com

Cover illustration by Allen Koszowski. Hippocampus Press logo designed
by Anastasia Damianakos. Cover design by Barbara Briggs Silbert.

Lovecraft material is used by permission of The Estate of H. P. Lovecraft;
Lovecraft Holdings, LLC.

Lovecraft Annual is published once a year, in Fall. Articles and letters
should be sent to the editor, S. T. Joshi, ℅ Hippocampus Press, and
must be accompanied by a self-addressed stamped envelope if return is
desired. All reviews are assigned. Literary rights for articles and reviews
will reside with *Lovecraft Annual* for one year after publication, where-
upon they will revert to their respective authors. Payment is in con-
tributor's copies.

ISSN 1935-6102
ISBN 978-1-61498-344-6

The Acolyte of the Abyss: or, In the Long Shadow of the House at 454 Angell Street

Manuel Pérez-Campos

"I am a part of this milieu—it is mine by natural placement & personal contact—soaked into my subconscious mind & rooted there by a thousand tentacles."
—H. P. Lovecraft to Frank Belknap Long, 27 February 1931

I. The Cogitator

The tall, formative house swirls out its mists
and with stairs deep with myth swirls out its voids
to a hair-pinned daughter and her fey son,
who through whispers to fauns at pretend trysts
offers self-inculpated reparation
to the absent one, the house's negation,
whose touch of winter beyond winter persists
and lulls with odes for Hekate her bleak moods.
Although lured back, she's the house's outcast
and proscribed to him by her sire's letters:
Should he elect hers or the house's disdain?
Where is his future, could it be in her past,
Baptist-bound to deranged locust eaters
or, breaching its laws, face one that's more vast?

II. *The Tempter*

I'm glad you got your bogeys earlier
than I, and may they take you to the moon;
and may you grow anon less of a loner
and as sturdy as time, which roots one in ruin;
and may your toy train plots clank out your wit
and your letter-press pamphlets bold Barnum hype.
You must not not partake of my proud spirit:
Snake River Dam is our house's archetype
and my ticker our house's horologe.
But with my apron, the one with the eye
that sees all, I will build you a great Lodge;
I will be the one who goes on through you
and who whispers through you when I am gone
of those lives not of flesh flesh must not shun.

III. *The Despairer*

To obstruct that house's prejudice that
holds me the antithesis of America,
you've become my apologist: Britannia,
my birthplace, you defend as though your own.
You parade as a redcoat and screech "God
save the King" with pointed tambour and brat
eclat, despite holding forth one's but sod.
I leave never: and your mater, although
courageous, must not be flanked in, lest she
flaunt precedent to you of melancholy.
I, an abomination of blank prospect,
see the house through your young mind, but
neglect you: this cell is walked by a might-have-been,
and I curse the spring that turns the boughs green.

IV. *The Abettor*

He thinks of me, his ardour, and of us
praying in our corner for him, of me
strolling beside him in a dusk that is
dusk still, and of that darkling white veil through
which to turn routes to roots he sang "I thee
wed." He thinks of you too, of the cues he
misread, of not being there to make sense
of you harder, of hugging you back when
you give in to dread, and of not having
your locks shorn by his barber. His absence
denounce not: one needs not have proved anything
to be loved. You belong to one unseen:
He and I brought you out of the infinite,
and now that winter is here is your chance
to find out what this house wants you to omit.

Astronomy with Lovecraft's First Telescope

Horace A. Smith

I bought Lovecraft's first telescope. Well, not Lovecraft's actual first telescope, but an antique telescope of the type that Lovecraft acquired in February 1903. Howard Phillips Lovecraft's enthusiasm for astronomy burgeoned as 1902 turned into 1903. It was natural that the twelve-year-old should want to observe the heavens through a telescope as well as with the eye alone. His first telescope was, however, hardly a splurge. It was an Excelsior spyglass, sold by the New York mail-order firm of Kirtland Brothers & Company for the grand sum of 99 cents.

SPECIAL 60-DAY OFFER TO INTRODUCE OUR LATEST LARGE, POWERFUL ACHROMATIC TELESCOPE, THE EXCELSIOR.

FACE TO FACE WITH THE MAN IN THE MOON!

3½ FT. LONG ONLY 99 CTS

POSITIVELY such a good Telescope was never sold for this price before. These Telescopes are made by one of the largest manufacturers of Europe, measure closed 12 inches and open over 3 1-2 feet in 5 sections. They are BRASS BOUND, BRASS SAFETY CAP on each end to exclude dust, etc., with POWERFUL LENSES, scientifically ground and adjusted. GUARANTEED BY THE MAKER. Heretofore, Telescopes of this size have been sold for from $5.00 to $8.00. NEEDED ON FARM, SEA OR RANCH. Every sojourner in the country or at seaside resorts should certainly secure one of these instruments, and no farmer should be without one. Objects miles away are brought to view with astonishing clearness. Sent by mail or express, safely packed, prepaid, for only 99 cts. Our new catalogue of Watches, etc., sent with each order. This is a grand offer and you should not miss it. We WARRANT each Telescope JUST AS REPRESENTED or money refunded. WANTS ANOTHER: Brandy,Va. Gents,—Please send another Telescope, money enclosed. Other was a bargain, good as instruments costing many times the money.—R. C. ALLEN. Send **99 CENTS** by Registered Letter, Post-Office Money Order, Express Money Order, or Bank Draft payable to our order, or have your storekeeper or newsdealer order for you.

EXCELSIOR IMPORTING CO., Dept. F, 296 Broadway, New York.

A 1901 advertisement for the Excelsior. The Man in the Moon apparently objects to being spied upon.

Excelsior telescopes, made in Germany, were widely advertised at the end of the nineteenth and start of the twentieth centuries by a variety of vendors, with slight variations in construction over time. Astronomy was by no means their only selling point. As one 1901 advertisement stated: "Every sojourner

6

in the country or at seaside resorts should certainly secure one of these instruments, and no farmer should be without one." However, that ad also touted the line: "Face to face with the man in the moon!" I even came across one 1913 advertisement that implied that the *Titanic* might have been saved had it been equipped with a telescope like the Excelsior. Although Excelsior telescopes were sold for decades, after World War I the price increased, usually to between $1.50 and $2.50.

To my knowledge, Lovecraft never explicitly states that his first telescope was an Excelsior, so why do I think it was? He wrote that he bought his first telescope for 99 cents from Kirtland Brothers early in 1903. In the August 1903 issue of his juvenile scientific magazine, the *Scientific Gazette*, Lovecraft wrote that the 99-cent telescope sold by Kirtland Brothers is "a big bargain worth $10.00 named 'Excelsior.'" In the second issue of his *Rhode Island Journal of Astronomy*, dated 9 August 1903, Lovecraft offered to sell a second-hand Excelsior for the reduced price of 50 cents. So, putting two and two together, I think we can have confidence that the Excelsior was the one.

A 1906 Kirtland Brothers & Company ad for the Excelsior, with the price jumped to $1.00 from 99 cents.

In July 1903, Lovecraft (or his mother) purchased a larger telescope from Kirtland Brothers for $16.50. It boasted an objective lens 2¼ inches in diameter, and for the next few years most of the astronomical observations in Lovecraft's self-published science magazines were made with its aid. Lovecraft, however, did not despise his inexpensive starter telescope. The 21 May 1905 issue of the *Rhode Island Journal of Astronomy* carried an article titled "The Cheap Telescope." It begins with the narration of an advertisement for a 99-cent telescope that reads very much like one of the advertisements for the Excelsior. However, Lovecraft continued: "The average reader pays no attention to these ads., thinking such cheapness below his notice. Such, however, is not the case." Lovecraft went on to note that he owned three cheap telescopes, the cheapest of them being his 99-cent instrument. Despite their price, he found that the views of celestial objects his cheap telescopes provided were surprisingly good. This led to the question, what could I see through a telescope like the Excelsior? What better way to answer than to acquire my own Excelsior and give it a try?

Fortunately, since they were widely sold for years, antique Excelsiors can still be purchased today. Mine came via eBay. I didn't need a pristine example, untouched by time or human hand, with a perfect original box and a correspondingly high price tag. Mine does have its original box, but both it and the telescope itself have obvious dings and wear, hence its $20 price. However, my Excelsior is still fully functional. In fact, my $20 in 2019 is not very different from the value of 99 cents in 1903, at least according to some inflation calculators.

My Excelsior telescope with its now somewhat battered original box. The draw tubes are at much less than their full extension. The box features a cap with solar filter that allows direct viewing of solar eclipses and sunspots. That solar cap is detached in the photograph.

What did I get for my $20? As I mentioned, the telescope came in a battered but original Kirtland Brothers & Company cardboard box. The label glued to the box featured the "solar eyepiece," to which it gave a 24 April 1906 patent date. Alas, my Excelsior was therefore made a few years after the one Lovecraft purchased—

so much for fantasies of having the same Excelsior Lovecraft once owned. The label is headlined "'The 'Excelsior' Telescope and Microscope Combined"—more about that microscope bit later. Kirtland Brothers were apparently jealous of their product, because the label on the box claims that unscrupulous vendors were stealing their advertising pictures to sell inferior telescopes.

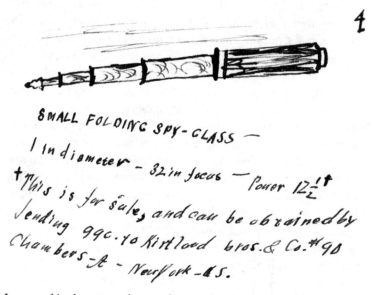

SMALL FOLDING SPY-GLASS —
1 in diameter - 32 in focus — Power 12½
† This is for sale, and can be obtained by sending 99c. to Kirtland bros. & Co. #90 Chambers-St - New York - U.S.

Lovecraft's drawing of a spyglass in his Science Library matches my Excelsior very well. The science magazines that Lovecraft "published" in his youth are now online at the Brown University Digital Repository.

Somewhat oddly, to me at least, the label does not specify the magnifying power of the telescope. Almost all Excelsior advertisements are also silent on that subject. Lovecraft in the *Scientific Gazette* and in the *Science Library* gave the Excelsior a magnifying power of 12½. However, in his "Cheap Telescope" article, he stated that his 99-cent telescope magnified 10 times. To complicate the issue further, I came across one advertisement for the Excelsior that claimed a magnifying power of 16. It is possible, I suppose, that not all Excelsiors were built with exactly the same optics, and that not all had the same magnifying power. I measured the magnification of my Excelsior to be about 10, in good agreement with the Cheap Telescope article.

My Excelsior looks very much like the drawing of the 99-cent Kirtland Brothers telescope that Lovecraft included in the *Science Library*. Inside its cardboard box I found a telescope about a foot long with its drawtubes closed. That grows to three feet when all four pull tubes are extended to full length from the tube holding the objective. Brass caps hold the objective lens and the eyepiece, but the tubes themselves appear to be made of what looks like stiff cardboard, although the label on the box calls them "drawn paper" and Lovecraft stated that his cheap telescopes were papier-mâché. The draw tubes are secured with brass fastenings and are covered with decorative and water-resistant paper. A small cap that can be slid over the eyepiece holds a dark solar filter for viewing sunspots or solar eclipses. The objective lens of my Excelsior is about one inch across, with a focal length of about 32 inches. However, a diaphragm behind it limits the effective aperture to ¾ of an inch. The eyepiece is a three-lens terrestrial one. That is, an extra lens is added to a two-lens eyepiece to make the image right-side-up rather than inverted, as is usual with eyepieces made for purely astronomical use.

Simple single lenses do not focus light of all colors to the same point. This chromatic aberration can produce images that are not sharp in all colors and which appear to have colored fringes. That fault can be partially remedied by using an achromatic objective lens, composed of two different types of glass. My Kirtland Brothers Excelsior label does not claim it to have an achromatic lens, and Lovecraft's writings signify that he believed "cheap telescope" objective lenses to be non-achromatic. However, some, but by no means all, 1899–1910 advertisements call the Excelsior an achromatic telescope. I have not attempted to disassemble the lens mounting of my Excelsior, but the objective looks to me as though it might be a single lens. Nevertheless, as Lovecraft noted, if a small non-achromatic lens has a long focal length compared to its size (a high focal ratio), then chromatic aberration can be reduced so as to be unimportant. That is the case with the Excelsior.

On inspection, my eBay Excelsior appeared to have safely survived shipping, but what kind of images did it actually produce? I took the telescope outside and removed its solar filter. I began by pointing it at some distant trees. I slid the tubes back and forth until I achieved focus. The images of the trees were sharp, and showed little distortion until very near the edge of the field of view. But would I see what Lovecraft wrote that a "cheap telescope" should reveal when I turned the Excelsior on the heavens?

Lovecraft wrote that his 99-cent telescope provided "excellent views of the moon." The moon was in the waning gibbous phase when I first turned my Excelsior toward it. The image of

This figure illustrates the detail that can be seen when the Excelsior is pointed at the moon (but it is not actually a photograph taken through the Excelsior).

the moon was sharp and revealed only slight chromatic aberration. The gray lunar maria that make up the Man in the Moon were clearly defined. White rays diverged from the bright crater Tycho. Toward the terminator, where shadows were long, many of the larger craters could be recognized. Like Galileo, I could see that the moon was a world rather than just a light in the sky—a promising beginning. On other nights with different phases, I again turned the Excelsior toward the moon. The views were similarly pleasing. Excellent views of the moon? For a telescope of its size, I would check "yes."

On to the sun. I slid the solar filter into place, and it dimmed the sun's image enough to provide a comfortable view. I kept my views brief at first, because I was not sure how well the filter was keeping out the sun's infrared light. I have not experienced any signs of retinal burning, so the solar cap is probably safe enough in that regard. It should be mentioned, however, that eyepiece solar filters can be dangerous. Even if they adequately block light, they heat up as they absorb the sun's radiation. Sometimes that heat can cause them to crack suddenly, letting the solar blaze through and risking the eye. That is less of a risk with so small a telescope as the Excelsior, but I still do not recommend solar observation with an eyepiece filter.

It was approaching minimum in the eleven-year solar cycle when I turned my Excelsior to the sun, and I had to wait a few weeks before any sizable sunspot appeared. When one did, I was able to see it as a well-defined dot on the sun's disk. When sunspots are more plentiful, the Excelsior should do a good job of revealing the larger spots—although I think I will project the sun's image onto paper to look for spots rather than trust the solar filter.

So far so good. However, holding a three-foot telescope steady by hand is difficult. The field of view is small, only about 1⅓ degrees (less than three moon diameters), and unless I prop the tube against a tree or post, the sun and moon are difficult to keep fixed in view. The Excelsior is much more difficult to use than the much shorter modern prism binoculars, which also have a wider field of view (typically around 6 degrees for a 10-power instrument). I soon concluded that I would not have been a good lookout in olden-days, trying to scout out lurking pirates through my hand-held spyglass from the crow's nest atop a toss-ing sailing vessel. Lovecraft eventually made a table stand to hold his cheap telescope, and I could certainly see why. Attach-ing my Excelsior to a sturdy camera tripod helped considerably.

Jupiter was celestial target number three. The image again was sharp. Even at only 10 power, I could see that Jupiter had a tiny disk rather than the point-like appearance of a star. No de-tails on the planet itself could be discerned. However, all four of the Galilean moons of Jupiter could be seen when they were not positioned too near the much brighter planet. A patient Galileo could have eventually measured the orbital periods of the Jovian moons with an Excelsior, but I did not target Jupiter often enough to attempt that feat.

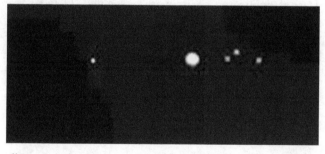

This illustrates the amount of detail that the Excelsior reveals when turned toward Jupiter. The four Galilean moons are visible unless they are close to the brilliant disk of the planet, which shines with greater glare than the figure might suggest.

When the Excelsior was pointed toward Saturn, I could tell that the planet was extended in size along the direction of the long-axis of the rings, but I could not tell that the extension was due to a ring system. By contrast, when Venus was almost be-tween the earth and the sun, I could clearly see its crescent form. As Venus became more distant from the earth, smaller in apparent size, and closer to being full, it became hard to tell what its phase was using the Excelsior.

Lovecraft would have observed from areas around his Providence homes, but urban light pollution has become much worse since 1903. I sought a location with a dark sky for my next trials. When I turned the Excelsior on the stars, I found that its narrow field of view and relatively small aperture limited what I could see. A few double-stars separated by more than about 20 arc seconds (an arc second is 1/3600 of a degree) could be recognized as double. Albireo (blue and yellow stars separated by 35 seconds of arc) could just be seen as two stars, but the blue color of the fainter star was not well shown. Mizar, a double star with components of unequal brightness separated by 14 arc seconds, was not resolved.

The Pleiades star cluster made a pretty target, as the Excelsior brought into view many more stars than could be seen with my eye alone. In seeing these additional members of the Pleiades, I again duplicated a discovery of Galileo. Pleiades stars of the sixth and seventh magnitude were easily seen. None of the nebulosity surrounding the stars of the Pleiades was visible, but I would not have expected it to be with such a small telescope.

Galileo's drawing of the Pleiades, with additional stars revealed by his telescope, from the Sidereus Nuncius. My view was not too dissimilar.

The Great Nebula (M42) within Orion's Sword was a bit disappointing. It was visible, and more stars could be seen around it than the eye alone revealed, but the gaseous nebula itself was not bright or detailed. Galileo also saw additional stars around M42, but he made no note of its nebulosity in the Sidereus Nuncius. The brighter globular star clusters, such as M3 and M13, were fuzzy spots in the sky—nothing to write home about. The Andromeda Nebula (not yet confirmed as a galaxy separate from the Milky Way when Lovecraft first observed) was an elongated glow, brighter toward the center, that stretched across the entire width of the field of view. Overall, I would not recommend the Excelsior to today's deep sky observers, who want to tease out the faintest glows of distant galaxies, but it performed as well as one would expect given its small aperture.

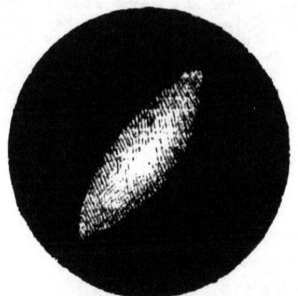

Gt Neb in Andromeda

The drawing of the Andromeda Nebula in R. A. Proctor's Half-Hours with the Telescope (1878 edition) resembles my view with the Excelsior, although in my case the nebula stretched across the entire field of view.

Now what about that statement on the label that the Excelsior was both a "telescope and microscope"? If the final draw-tube of the Excelsior, holding the optics for the terrestrial eyepiece, is removed, it can be used as a low-power microscope. One looks through the end of the tube as usual, and moves the tube toward or away from the subject until a magnified image comes into focus. Voilà, microscope as well as telescope.

Overall, I saw through the Excelsior enough to confirm Lovecraft's conclusion that such instruments are not to be despised. However, will I continue to use my Excelsior? I must admit that the answer is not often. Its small field of view and unwieldy length make it too inconvenient compared to modern binoculars, especially those capable of image stabilization. However, in 1903 the Excelsior was much cheaper than a good pair of binoculars. Lovecraft wrote of spending the fabulous sum of $55 around 1907 on a pair of Bausch & Lomb prism binoculars. That would be the equivalent of more than a thousand dollars in 2019. Opera glasses or field glasses lacking prisms were cheaper, but still cost several dollars and typically had magnifying powers a third or a half that of the Excelsior. One can see why the inexpensive Excelsior successfully sold for decades.

The opportunity has not yet arisen for me to make all possible tests of my Excelsior. I have, for example, not yet ventured to Dunwich to confirm the Excelsior's effectiveness in delineating the features of any unearthly Whateley who happens to be momentarily puffed into view while climbing Sentinel Hill. The stars haven't yet been right for such an experiment. Maybe next year.

Briefly Noted

The John Hay Library, repository of most of H. P. Lovecraft's surviving manuscripts, recently acquired his letters to Frank Belknap Long. The sizable cache will probably constitute the final two volumes of Lovecraft's *Collected Letters*.

The Detestation of Mammon in Lovecraft

Duncan Norris

Even in his own time H. P. Lovecraft was a gentleman of the truly "olde Skool," as the youth of today might characterize it, and as such gave no real consideration or effort to the significant acquisition of money, outside the necessities which life requires. Such pursuits were somewhat vulgar and beneath his status in his own self-perception and worldview.[1] It is curious fact that, for all his vaunted and very genuine love for New England, Lovecraft had no interest in the commerce and the ethic espousing the virtue of hard work that was one of the region's defining characteristics. Given this noted subversion of his cultural norm, in combination with his focus as a writer having almost no interest in the mundane, realistic, and ordinary, it should come as no surprise that money thus makes very little impact on his fictional writings. This is not to suggest that Lovecraft viewed money as unimportant. His frugal habits to extend his always meager reserves and exuberant happiness at being paid a decent commission—such as for "Under the Pyramids" ("ONE HUNDRED BERRIES! No spoofin'" [*Letters to James F. Morton* 67])—shows he understood its necessity and appreciated it. It was just that he saw many other things in life as vastly more important than the accumulation of filthy lucre. Yet it is an amusing, and occasionally enlightening, aside to examine the relative few instances of the intrusion of money into his fiction and see the distinctly uniform themes and connections that stem from these sparse usages.

---

1. Numerous citations could be produced to this effect, but his own slow, life-long decline further into poverty speaks to the fact far more elegantly.

17

In one of his earliest extant writings, composed sometime in 1898 when he was about eight years old, Lovecraft shows his understanding of money in the wider scheme of life, and offers a poignant disdain for the rather useless value it often holds. In the extremely short "The Secret Cave," the ten-year-old protagonist goes on an adventure against the wishes of his parents when they go out. Ultimately a success, in the sense of discovering a hidden treasure, the expedition causes the death of his sibling Alice, and the tale concludes: "The funeral of Alice occupied so much time that John quite forgot about the box—but when they *did* open it they found it to be a *solid gold* chunk worth about $10,000 enough to pay for any thing but the death of his sister" (CF 3.484).

This idea of the ultimate futility of money, or the evils associated with pursuing it, will gently echo throughout the wider body of Lovecraft's work, although rarely as pointed or poignantly as in his distinctly and paradoxically adult yet childish expression in "The Secret Cave." Ten thousand dollars was clearly a symbolically large sum for the precocious Lovecraft, as he uses the identical amount for the ransom demanded in "The Mystery of the Grave-Yard," written in the same year. Yet in a curiosity young Lovecraft utilizes both pounds and dollars as current units in the same story. This may be merely an unintentional error, which only highlights Lovecraft's dismissal of such minutiae concerning mere cash at a young age. Yet allowing that the tale is set in England, as the reference to Kent and Newgate prison (still extant and in use as a prison at the time Lovecraft wrote the story) imply, and the protagonist King John being "a famous western detective" who "sports a brace of revolvers" (CF 3.485) is likely an American, King John's citation of dollars instead of pounds in the offer to the hackman may have been a deliberate clue as to his identity, as he is otherwise unnamed in the passage, although identified in an authorial footnote.

Hidden gold will be a main motivating factor in the comedic parody "Sweet Ermengarde," but this uncharacteristic work is hardly a good basis for examination of anything in Lovecraft save that he was quite capable of broad humor if he so desired. There are hints as Lovecraft's disdain for the mercantile, and the money that is its lifeblood, in "The Doom That Came to Sarnath" (1919). The titular city, with its great economic power reduced in a single night to absolute desolation, is simplistic in its message of the dangers of the disdaining of the mystic and magical in ignoring and eventually forgetting the scrawled warning of the high-priest Taran-Ish in favor of eating from "golden platters set with rubies and diamonds" with the food "prepared by the subtlest cooks in all Mnar, and suited to the palate of every feaster" (CF 1.129). The endless descriptions of the gaudy and ostentatious nature of the inhabitants of Sarnath only highlight its true worthlessness against the inevitable destruction that is the fate of all temporal works. It is tempting to make a cheap Freudian analysis and relate this back to the sudden disappearance of his own family fortune as a tender age child, but this is mere conjecture.

Not at all conjectural is the implication that desire for money is distasteful in "The Terrible Old Man" (1920). The three robbers, whose profession has been upgraded in modern parlance to the term "home invaders," are very clearly the epitome of the degradation money instills. For its acquisition they are quite prepared to torture and if necessary kill a "very old and very feeble" (CF 1.141) man, and their own brutal fate as a direct consequence of this is clearly designed to evoke in the reader a sense of justice and karmic "serves you right." Yet the Terrible Old Man (there is a less than subtle clue in the name) himself has "Spanish gold and silver minted two centuries ago" (CF 1.142) as his sole currency. This, in conjunction with a career (probably euphemistically elevated to respectability) as a sea captain and characters named "Jack, Scar-Face, Long Tom, Spanish Joe, Peters, and Mate Ellis" (CF 1.141), naturally invokes ideas of pirates and their treasure hordes. The Terrible Old Man seems to have either access to a store of such ill-gotten booty or a supernatural means of acquiring it. As such, although he is a more sympathetic character than our three extremely ethnic robbers, he too seems to have been one who has trod down dark paths for the mere gain of wealth, and lives in isolation and as pariah in consequence.

"The Tree" (1921) likewise presents the desire for riches, in this case intermixed with renown,[2] as a malignant motivating force. Musides murders his best friend Kalos in an attempt to obtain the Tyrant's contract, and suffers a nameless fate as a result. Interestingly, his perfidious behavior is never brought to light, and the townspeople raise him a temple in honor of his "gifts, virtues, and brotherly piety" (CF 1.150). This adds an additional darkness to the tale, showing the corruption of even the noble values of the Greeks by the intrusion of desire for money causing the ignorant townsfolk thus to honor a murderer. Yet this means naught to him for whom the temple was raised. Musides indeed got much of what he desired, but was not in a position to enjoy it, in the best ironic manner so beloved of classical Greek writings and tales.

Wealth as a sign of stigma of character is heavy-handedly drawn in the nameless man in "Celephaïs" (1920), who takes over the ancestral home of Kuranes, Trevor Towers. He is solely described as "a notably fat and especially offensive millionaire brewer" (CF 1.191). Additional to his patently odious physical and personal traits is his occupation. Lovecraft had a low opinion of alcohol and thus even more so of those who sell it, as encapsulated in the description of both sellers and imbibers in "The Shadow over Innsmouth," and he uses the word "especially" as a pejorative with precision here. As "Celephaïs" was written after the implementation of Prohibition in America, this small note of character[3] doubles to add emphasis to the fact of such business as deeply sordid.

Yet, as he often did, Lovecraft recrudesced and expanded his ideas into a second fictional usage. "The Moon-Bog" (1921) features a wealthy but somewhat insatiable and mercenary character as the inciting cause of the events in the story. Denys Barry's "gold from over the sea" (CF 1.256) is enough to allow him to purchase anew his ancestral lands in Ireland, but his greed sets him to draining the great bog for further profit, insensible to the

---

2. Kleos is "the fame that does not decay" as the ancient Greeks would have understood it, and which will survive the death of its author, such as Achilles sought (and received) at Troy, and ultimately that which HPL himself has achieved.

3. Or anti-character, in the moral rather than literary understanding.

warnings of the locals. This actually reflects the prevalent practice in the later nineteenth and early twentieth centuries of
temporary migrants to America known as "birds of passage."
These were generally male laborers who emigrated temporarily
in order to take advantage of the greater employment opportu-
nities the expanding United States offered, and who would return with the profits of their labors to enrich their natal
communities, or at least their position inside them. They were
not always positively viewed, especially by those with strong na-
tivist sentiments on both sides of the arrangement, and this attitude may help explain the generally negative portrayal of the
character of Denys Barry. As do most who pursue wealth in
Lovecraft, doom naturally supervenes, and again there is the
conflation of those who pursue wealth being somewhat deaf to
the mystic and supernal. It is worth noting that this tale, counted among "the most conventional supernatural" (Joshi 64) in
Lovecraft's output, was created at short notice to be read at a
party in celebration of Irish heritage, and this rather prosaic
trope of the rich interloper ignoring the protests of locals to revive a lurking menace would again be eventually transmuted into literary brilliance in "The Rats in the Walls" (1923). It is in
part the prosaic nature of the elder de la Poer as a "stolid Yankee . . . merged into the greyness of Massachusetts business life"
(CF 1.376) that allows him to ignore local knowledge and his
own experiences and continue to use his commercially obtained
wealth to rebuilt the ancestral home that will be his undoing.

The residents of Teloth are presented most unfavorably given
their fixation on toil in "The Quest of Iranon" (1921). For all the
celestial afterlife promises awaiting them as described in the tale,
their financial interest also motivates and compels their actions.
The idea that a desire for wealth excludes the finer emotions and
a true appreciation of art is never more blatantly on display in a
Lovecraft work. For all his cosmic outlook Lovecraft's roots in Puritan New England occasionally show through. Thus it would
come as no surprise that in the story Lovecraft co-wrote with his
future wife, Sonia H. Greene, "The Horror at Martin's Beach"
(1922), the main character, Capt. James P. Orne, who in exhibit-

ing his unusual marine catch "with typical Yankee shrewdness . . . reaped a harvest of admission fees" (CF 4.38), comes to a terrible, poetically fitting end. He is dragged to his death on a line in a dark parody of the manner in which he had made his fabulous catch, yet being a Lovecraft tale the innocent, helpful, and unlucky suffer in the uncaring world along with the truly guilty.

"The Horror at Red Hook" (1925), set mainly in great mercantile metropolis of New York so detested by Lovecraft, has financial gain as a root cause of the evil that befalls Detective Malone, albeit as a by-product. It is to be remembered that his being drawn into the Suydam "case"[4] occurred as a result of that gentleman's relatives seeking to have him committed. Ostensibly this is for Robert Suydam's own welfare, but viler motives concerning a potentially lost inheritance are heavily implied given that "the court action revealed that he was using up his income and wasting his principal in the purchase of curious tomes" (CF 1.487). Even if the reader ascribes pure motives to the Suydams, Corlears, and Van Brunts who investigated their kin, it is Robert's wealth that allows for his interest to go from the academic to the truly horrific. While it is occasionally a lack of money that condemns a person to negative experiences—for example, the necessity of Frank Elwood lodging in Arkham's notorious Witch House—it is rarely as dangerous as having an excess.

The Dream-Quest of Unknown Kadath (1926–27) again espouses the dangerous and corrupting nature of desire for wealth. The inhabitants of Dylath-Leen, with its "dark and uninviting" streets and "dismal sea-taverns" (CF 2.109), openly trade with the noisome black galleys of obviously evil nature for no other reason than to obtain the rubies of which "no mine in all earth's dreamland was known to produce their like" (CF 2.110). Their callous nature in emphasized by their engagement in the slave trade and willful ignorance of the patent fate of the "fat black men of Parg" (CF 2.110). They are willing to be a main link in a mercantile

---

4. The word *case*, so familiar to the modern audience with the saturation of police procedurals across all fictional and nonfictional media, appears in quotation marks in HPL's original tale. The Old Gent was not one to use slang without qualification.

trade in human beings that ultimately ends (perhaps at best) in anthropophagy, for mere pretty stones. That the inhabitants of Dylath-Leen readily believe Carter when he warns them of the nature of the rowers of the black galleys and their noxious masters, but are degraded enough by the lure of these precious gems such beings provide to continue the trade, truly lays bare the toxic dangers of avarice. While it is always treading upon treacherous ground to read too much into the artist from his art, the connection between the slave trade at Dylath-Leen, wherein the good and respectable citizens turn a deliberately blind eye to its evils, and the historical slave trade practiced from New England is quite a biting condemnation, especially noteworthy given the tendency of some revisionists to characterize Lovecraft's personality and actions as a caricature of excessive racism.

It is significant that the ghouls, who are simpler creatures, do not take the valuable stores of rubies they find at the moon-beasts' island after discovering "they were not good to eat"; as such, "they lost all interest in them" (CF 2.189). Carter likewise refuses this bounty, "since he knew too much about those which had mined them" (CF 2.189) and had earlier, upon seeing idols of clearly unwholesome aspect of the same materials, "took the trouble to hammer five of them into very small pieces" (CF 2.188). By contrast, the merchants of the galleys specifically take gold as their only (presumably) non-consumable trade good.

The association of such evil beings with gold's acquisition only highlights the pernicious nature of desire for the metal, which was fundamentally only of ornamental and fiscal rather than practical value until the advent of modern electronics: the evil Khephren is naturally wearing a "golden pshent" (CF 1.448) as he lords over the nightmarish creatures under the pyramids in "Under the Pyramids" (1924). It is worth noting that the gold standard was not officially abolished in the United States until 1971, and that for the majority of Lovecraft's life paper money was exchangeable for gold upon demand. The gold standard was a controversial issue that long lingered in the public consciousness. William Jennings Bryan's Cross of Gold speech advocating bimetallism is still considered one of the great classics of Ameri-

ca politics, and the satire upon it in *The Wizard of Oz,* Dorothy's
silver slippers dancing upon a road of gold, still resonated
enough that they were changed to Judy Garland's now iconic
ruby slippers. A final comment on gold in the context of *Dream-
Quest* is metaphorical, on the unreality on the locale Carter
seeks. His city, "all golden and lovely" (CF 2.98), exists only as a
fevered fantasy in his own transmuted remembrances.

This dangerous power of money and the damning evils of
greed make themselves interestingly known in several different
yet juxtaposed ways in *The Case of Charles Dexter Ward* (1927).
In a pettier way is the manner in which Ward Senior uses money
to pacify the rodent-featured property owner possessing the
Curwen portrait so as not to have to get involved in extended
"unctuous haggling" (CF 2.274) with him; the landlord's short
and ill-favored character shows clearly in the sordid nakedness
of his implied greed. Yet Ward Senior's own hereditary wealth—
quite possibly derived from the very New England occupations
of cotton manufacturing that the poet William Blake infamously
characterized as "dark Satanic mills," or the more sordid nature
of the Triangular Trade in chattel slavery—allowing the easy
purchase of the eidolon is a major factor that dooms Charles, as
is the minor inheritance that allows him to travel to the horrors
he uncovers in Europe and to buy the Pawtuxet farmhouse.

But it is the behavior of Joseph Curwen and his connections
with Mammon that lay bare its deeper dangers under a greater
scrutiny. In his own time Curwen is clearly suspected of being up
to unnatural and dangerous actions, but is able with remarkable
ease to effect changes, "necessarily slight" thought they might
have been, through judicious and public-spirited spendings for
"such is the power of wealth and of surface gestures" (CF 2.235).
Paradoxically, though to the same point, it is his wealth that
dooms Curwen: knowing he is in danger and under scrutiny, he is
nonetheless unable to flee due in no small part to his investments
and mercantile interests that fund his experimentation. In an interesting and likely deliberate parallel, in his modern guise Curwen's undoing is begun by his inability to forge Charles's signature
on checks and navigate the modern banking system. It is money,

as much as any other factor, that ultimately dooms him.

Continuing Lovecraft's usage of gold (again quite literally) from an unnamed but certainly nefarious source used for evil purposes are the Whateleys of Dunwich. Like some kind of backwoods New England version of infamous Colombian drug kingpin Pablo Escobar, Wilbur and his grandfather before him are able to maintain their freedom and buy silence for a series of heavily implied murders through a combination of bribery and the threat of violence, *plata o plomo*.[5] Likewise, this gold pays for the feeding and maintenance of Wilbur's brother, and should the plan have come to fruition would have been part of the foundation that destroyed the world. As the character of Gregori Rasputin,[6] after buying an artefact to bring about the destruction of the earth, states in a voice dripping "with serene brutality" in noted Lovecraftian director Guillermo del Toro's *Hellboy* (2004), "Enjoy the bright metal you've earned." As a final coda on the transient worthlessness of gold, it is this substance, rather than any of the actually cosmically important events occurring, that is the focus of the stories in the *Boston Herald* and *Arkham Advertiser*. This highlights the preoccupation of the city folk with money over the critically important events that are actually occurring.

Again, it is the quest for riches that dooms so many of the characters in "The Mound" (1929). Ed and Walker Clay encounter their individual but equally horrific fates as a result of wanting to dig into the Mound and commit grave robbery to obtain the supposed gold of the murdered Indian maiden which was in legend buried with her. His lust for gold is what initially leads Zamacona to his hideous experiences in the nightmare cities of K'n-yan, and it is his still unquenched greed in trying to decamp with some of said riches that foils his initial escape. Interestingly, the city of gold here is not merely a fable, misunderstanding, or imaginary locale as in *The Dream-Quest of Unknown Kadath*, but an actual physical reality. That it is inhabited by

---

5. Spanish for "silver or lead," referring to the traditional choice of the Colombian cartels for the hearer to take a bribe (silver being slang for money) or be murdered (lead in the form of a bullet).

6. Distinct from the historical figure from which he is fictionalized.

such beings of malevolent decadence only further reinforces the connection between the venal nature of the pursuit of wealth and deeper evils.

The subtle connection betwixt money and the malevolent is reinforced by the aforementioned "easily, although not cheaply obtained" (CF 3.185) illegal hooch to be found in Innsmouth, a foreshadowing of the entire town, which had fallen into the basest of miscegenation initially started in order to have access to the fish and (once again) gold provided by the Deep Ones. Along with—and probably more so given its relative economic stability—the now perennial fish, it is this gold and its associated refinery that allow the town to maintain its veneer of normal existence while secretly inculcating horrors. In fact, the entire trip of the protagonist to Innsmouth was precipitated by the desire to avoid the high cost of the train to Arkham. The ticket seller, not being a local and thus ignoring their warning tales in favor of fiscal pragmatism, inadvertently dooms[7] the protagonist by advocating putting financial interest above all else. The pawning of the Innsmouth jewelry by a drunken sailor, with its mixed beauty and repulsion, serves to draw the protagonist back into the siren's call of his return to his unknown origins in Innsmouth and beyond, and it is implied that this rash act of greed was the cause of the sailor's death as well.

In the revision text "The Horror in the Museum" (1933) the greed and perfidy of the priest of Ghatanothoa are the cause not only of T'yog's unimaginable suffering but of the enslavement of the whole populace of K'naa for endless generations, so that each priest would have, among other luxuries, "a chest of gold" (CF 4.413). It is certainly the greed of Randolph Carter's cousin, Ernest B. Aspinwall, in trying to secure the former's estate that precipitates the meeting that is the setting for "Through The Gates of the Silver Key" (1932–33), and it is the unmasking of Carter in the body of Zkauba that causes Aspinwall's death. Again it is "an odd bit of gold bullion" (CF 3.323) that is brought from Yaddith and cashed by Carter as Swami Chandra-

---

7. Or perhaps saves, depending on one's view of being a cultist fish monster. It behooves us not to judge.

putra upon his return to Earth in Zkauba. Here, in an unusual case for a Lovecraft character, it is not greed but rather necessity that drives the protagonist's requirement of gold, and Carter suffers no ill-effects as a result of his modest accumulation of treasure. Yet in an oblique way the reliance on gold condemns Carter just the same: his insufficiency of funds leads to a lack of the suppression drugs that keep Zkauba at bay, and allows him to be bodily hijacked into an unknown destination.

The repeated blackmail aspects that recur in "The Thing on the Doorstep" (1933) are acts perpetrated for the acquisition of money, but they have deeper consequences. Had Derby's presence at certain affairs been brought to his father's notice instead of being used to extort him for money, it is quite likely the later events leading to his death might have been forestalled or even averted entirely. Had the Innsmouth servants (perhaps anonymously, given their own secrets) gone to the police instead of resorting to blackmail, the discovery of Asenath's body might have led to a different final conclusion of events. In a like manner, the possession of money insulates the wealthy of Arkham from the seasonal depredations of Keziah Mason and her ilk in "The Dreams in the Witch House" (1932) and allows the "fine folk up in Miskatonic Avenue" (CF 3.243) a pretense of ignorance concerning the known endless seasonal murdering of children rather than confronting the horrid reality. In one of Lovecraft's final stories, the collaboration with Kenneth Sterling "In the Walls of Eryx" (1936), the desire for wealth is the entire point of the narrator's expedition and the cause of his death. The more cosmic aspect of the dangers of greed in reaching out beyond man's true domain are wonderfully summed up in part of the narrator's dying words expressed in his diary, and make a fitting conclusion to our examination:

> I believe we have violated some obscure and mysterious law—some law buried deep in the arcana of the cosmos—in our attempts to take them. Who can tell what dark, potent, and widespread forces spur on these reptilian things who guard their treasure so strangely? . . . But it may be that these scattered deaths are only the prelude of greater horrors to come. (CF 4.579)

Works Cited

Hellboy. Columbia TriStar, 2004. Directed by Guillermo del Toro. www.imsdb.com/scripts/Hellboy.html.

Joshi, S. T. *A Subtler Magick: The Writings and Philosophy of H. P. Lovecraft.* San Bernardino, CA: Borgo Press, 1996.

Lovecraft, H. P. *Letters to James F. Morton.* Ed. David E. Schultz and S. T. Joshi. New York: Hippocampus Press, 2011.

Briefly Noted

One of the most peculiar discoveries in recent years (brought to our attention by an Italian journalist and novelist, Adriano Monti-Buzzetti) is the appearance of a person named Howard P. Lovecraft in the city directory of Los Angeles for 1917. His employment is given as boilermak[e]r:

```
CITY DIRECTORY                    1293

LOVE—Continued
  "  Waldo W dept mgr Ville de Paris h 1548
       3d  av
  "  Walter A foremn Weaver Rof Co h 1018
       E 57th
  "  Walter C r 631 W 45th
  "  Wilbur W clk r 1548 3d av
  "  Wm J clk h 3920 Budlong av
Loveall Amanda M wid Abram r 224½ S
       Burlington av
  "  Frank appr r 559 Stanford av
Loveberg Godfrey contr 2025 Ellendale av
  "  Nels h 1248 N Westmoreland av
  "  Nels H electr h 1252 N Westmoreland av
Lovecraft Howard P boilermkr r 2033 E 4th
loveday Geo 1st eng L A Gas & Elec Corp
       h 3484 Lanfranco
  "  Geo R driver r 2912½ Raymond av
  "  Richd H clk r 3484 Lanfranco
Lovegreen Agnes C bkpr Elmer L Woods r
       1163 W 24th
```

What to make of this? The address given for this person (2033 East 4th Street) is now an apartment building—presumably not the same building that Howard P. Lovecraft occupied in 1917. If any readers have a solution to this mystery, we would be gratified to hear it.

Lovecraft and the Irish

Ken Faig, Jr.

In the early historic period the peoples of Britain & Ireland were very much alike—& very much like the Gauls of the Continent. Ireland probably surpassed Britain in settled folkways & arts, but the condition was hardly what one would call an actual civilization. It probably paralleled the advanced barbarian-cultures of Gaul & Spain—which of course included settled town-dwelling & considerable artistic craftsmanship.

—H. P. Lovecraft to Elizabeth Toldridge, mid-March 1930
(*Letters to Elizabeth Toldridge* 140)[1]

When it came to debates over history and culture, H. P. Lovecraft and Robert E. Howard were often on opposite sides. While Lovecraft admired the Romans and their empire, Howard forcefully took the side of their barbarian opponents. While Lovecraft considered the Teutons (i.e., Anglo-Saxons) the supreme race of humanity, Howard took the side of the Celts. Lovecraft wrote to his correspondent F. Lee Baldwin on 16 February 1935 that Howard was "so fond of his Celtic heritage that he has Gaelicised his middle name Ervin into EIARBIHN—as the fanatics of Ireland nowadays Gaelicise theirs" (*Letters to F. Lee Baldwin* 128).

The Irish literary figure most admired by Lovecraft was undoubtedly Lord Dunsany (1878–1957), whom he saw lecture in Boston in 1919 (*IAP* 335–37). Lovecraft liked best Dunsany's early fantasies and was lukewarm toward his more nuanced later work. Lovecraft placed his discussion of Dunsany under the chapter heading "Modern Masters" in his treatise "Supernatural Horror in Literature" and remarked upon Dunsany's "Celtic wistfulness" (*SHL* 90). Although he divided his time between

---

1. This letter is dated 1 April 1930 in *SL*.

Dunsany Castle in County Meath and Dunstall Priority in Kent,
Dunsany was wholly aligned with England in opposition to the
Irish rebellion of 1916. Earlier Irish literary figures in the domain
of the spectral influenced Lovecraft less significantly. Irish-born
Bram Stoker (1847–1912), who used Irish folklore to advantage
in his work, moved to London upon his marriage in 1878. Joseph
Sheridan Le Fanu (1814–1873), by way of contrast, spent his entire life in Dublin. Irish novelist Regina Maria Roche (*née* Dalton)
(1764–1845) wrote many Gothic novels over her long career.
Stoker (*SHL* 74), Le Fanu (*SHL* 48), and Roche (*SHL* 42) receive
only brief mentions in "Supernatural Horror in Literature." However, even apart from literary influences, Ireland and persons of
Irish descent played a significant role in Lovecraft's own life.

Lovecraft was not without a component of Irish blood—his
five times great-grandfather Thomas Casey, who died about 1719
in Newport, Rhode Island, was an emigrant from Ireland.[2] Thomas Casey's grandson John Casey (1723–1794)[3] of Kingstown,
Rhode Island, had for a brother the noted silversmith Samuel Casey, who was freed by his neighbors after being sentenced to death
for counterfeiting in 1770 and was believed to have escaped to
Canada. Lovecraft loved to regale his correspondents with the
story of Samuel Casey.[4] Lovecraft's great-grandmother Roby
Rathbun (1797–1848) was the daughter of John Rathbun (1750–
1810) and John Casey's daughter Sarah Casey (1755–1813).

After Lovecraft's maternal grandfather Whipple V. Phillips
(1833–1904)—the son of Jeremiah Phillips (1800–1848) and Roby
Rathbun (1797–1848)—established himself at 454 Angell Street[5]

---

2. For the descent of immigrant Thomas Casey, see Thomas Lincoln Casey,
"Early Families of Casey in Rhode Island," *Magazine of New England History* 3,
No. 2 (April 1893), reprinted by Higginson Books.

3. John Casey's wife was long identified as Mercy Dyer and through her HPL
claimed descent from the Quaker martyr Mary (Barrett) Dyer (d. 1660). However, more recent research indicates that John Casey's wife was born Mercy
Babcock and only assumed the surname Dyer after her mother took Richard
Dyer as her second husband (Faig 24).

4. See for example HPL's letter to Wilfred B. Talman dated 19 March 1929
(*Letters to Wilfred B. Talman* 108–10).

5. Originally numbered 194 Angell Street before the renumbering of the street
in 1896. The house, demolished in 1960, stood on the northwest corner of

on the East Side of Providence about 1881, Irishwomen customarily provided domestic service in his household. By the time the U.S. census was enumerated on 1 June 1900, the servant staff at 454 Angell Street had been reduced to one person—Maggie Corcoran, age twenty-three, single, born April 1877 in Ireland to Irish-born parents, who emigrated in 1895. In fact, the female servants in the household were customarily called "Maggie," regardless of their actual given names.

Photograph of Joseph Banigan (1839–1898)

Angell Street and Elmgrove Avenue.

One of Rhode Island's most illustrious Irish-born citizens was a near neighbor of the Phillips family. Michael Joseph Banigan (more commonly known as Joseph Banigan in later life), was born 17 June 1839 in County Monaghan, Ireland, to Bernard (1799–1867) and Alice (1811[6]–1889) Banigan. After leaving Ireland, he and his family spent two years in Dundee, Scotland before arriving in Providence, Rhode Island in 1847. He received only one year of formal schooling and as early as 1856 was working at the New England Screw Company in Providence. In 1858, Bernard Banigan, laborer, resided at 8 Winslow Place in Providence.[7] His sons Michael, a jeweler, and Patrick, a tailor, boarded at the same address. The 1860 U.S. census captured Bernard Banigan and his family in the Sixth Ward of Providence: Bernard, age fifty-nine, laborer, born Ireland; Alice [wife], age forty-five, born Ireland; Patrick [son],[8] age twenty-three, tailor; Michael [son], age twenty, born Ireland, jeweler; Margaret [daughter],[9] age fourteen, born Ireland; Mary A. [daughter],[10] age four, born Rhode Island.

Joseph early became interested in the rubber industry. By the time the 1865 Rhode Island census was taken, Joseph Banigan had his own household in Smithfield: Joseph, age twenty-five, born Scotland, rubber worker; Margaret [wife],[11] age twenty-

---

6. Year of birth also given as 1813.

7. Bernard continued to reside at 8 Winslow Place until his death on 21 December 1867. He was the son of Patrick and Alice (———) Banigan. His widow Alice continued to reside there until she removed to 50 Lester Street in 1874 and to 59 Dean Street in 1875. Her son Patrick continued to reside with her until he removed to 189 Angell Street in 1882. By 1903, he had removed to 244 Angell Street.

8. Patrick T. Banigan (b. 1829 Ireland, d. 28 February 1909 Providence) spent most of his life working as a merchant tailor on Westminster Street in Providence. He married Catherine J. Brophy (1850–1923) and had sons Joseph Henry Banigan (1879–1970) and John Bernard Banigan (1880–1943). His son John was associated with him in business as a merchant tailor.

9. Margaret Theresa Banigan married James Finnigan on 17 January 1869 in Providence. She died 30 July 1875 in Providence.

10. Mary Ann Banigan was born in Providence on 5 February 1857. She died on 12 April 1939.

11. Joseph Banigan married (1) 26 December 1860 (Providence) Margaret J. Holt (b. 31 August 1843 Manchester, England, d. 4 April 1871 Rhode Island), the daughter of John Francis Holt (1824–1896) and Margaret Lowry (1825–

one, born England, housekeeper; Mary A. [daughter],[12] age three, born Massachusetts; John J. [son],[13] age two, born Massachusetts; William B. [son],[14] age eight months, born Massachu-

---

1901). He married (2) 4 November 1873 Maria Theresa Comary (b. 1847 Ireland, d. 16 January 1901 Illinois). However, the passport application of Mrs. Joseph Banigan dated 9 January 1900, indicates that she was born on 17 October 1844 in New York City. Bayles (2.682–84) calls Banigan's second wife "Maria T. Conway of New York City."

12. Mary Ann Banigan was born 24 December 1861 in Roxbury, Massachusetts. On 7 November 1882 in Providence she married William Bartholomew McElroy (b. 7 June 1857 Rhode Island, d. 8 March 1914 Providence). When William B. McElroy applied for a U.S. passport on 30 April 1902, he resided in Baltimore, Maryland, and stated his occupation as capitalist. He and his wife had children: (1) Margaret Mary McElroy (b. 1883 Providence, d. 1929), who married Hugh M. Blair (1875–1953); (2) Joseph McElroy (b. 16 February 1884 Providence, d. 27 September 1885 Providence); (3) Alice Helen McElroy (b. 10 May 1890 Providence, d. 27 Dec. 1918 Brookline, Massachusetts), who married 28 November 1916 (Rhode Island) Leo Henry Leroy (b. 6 November 1883); (4) Robert Bernard McElroy (b. 7 July 1886 Colchester, Connecticut, d. 22 December 1953 Los Angeles, California) (he was working as a Christian Science practitioner in Los Angeles when he registered for the World War II draft); (5) John H. McElroy (b. 26 November 1892 Providence, d. 10 May 1944 East Providence), who married Ruby H. Williams. The name John Stanislaus McElroy, with date of birth 10 November 1892, is also found for the fifth child. The date of birth 7 July 1885 is found in the California Death Index for the fourth child. Mary Ann (Banigan) McElroy died on 13 February 1923.

13. John Joseph Banigan was born on 6 July 1863 in Roxbury, Massachusetts. He married 20 July 1887 (Providence) Mary Catherine Davis (b. August 1863 Rhode Island, d. 22 June 1936), the daughter of Richard Davis (b. 1825/26 Ireland, d. 6 January 1886 Providence) and Bidelia Carmody (b. March 1829, Ennis, County Clare, Ireland, d. 9 November 1877 Providence). They had sons Joseph Banigan (born June 1888), Richard Davis Banigan (born May 1890), and John J. Banigan Jr. (born July 1894), and a daughter Mary Banigan, who died 23 April 1897, age less than one year. By the time the U.S. census was taken on 1 June 1900, John J. Banigan was head of household at 468 Angell Street in Providence. In the 1901–06 Providence Directories, he also reported having a residence in Westerly, R.I. In the 1908 Providence Directory, he was residing in the Crown Hotel, while his wife Mary C. Banigan continued to reside at 468 Angell Street. He died on 30 December 1908.

14. William Bernard Banigan was born on 12 December 1864 in Roxbury, Massachusetts, and died on 25 February 1901 in Providence. He married 4 October

setts. By 1866, Joseph and his partners Lyman A. and Simeon S.
Cook had formed the Woonsocket Rubber Company, which grew
into an enterprise of worldwide significance. Joseph lived in
Woonsocket from 1867 to 1873, but by 1874 transferred his residence to the East Side of Providence, where he lived at 276 Angell Street in 1874–75 and at 214 Angell Street[15] thereafter.

The Rhode Island 1875 census recorded the Banigan household at 276 Angell Street in Providence: Joseph [head], age
thirty-seven, born Ireland, rubber manufacturer; Maria [wife],
age thirty-three, born Ireland, housekeeper; Mary A. [daughter],
age thirteen, born Massachusetts, at Catholic school; John J.
[son], age eleven, born Massachusetts, at Catholic school; William B. [son], age nine, born Cumberland, Rhode Island, at
Catholic school; Alice [daughter],[16] age seven, born Woonsocket,

---

1893 (Washington, D.C.) Emma Plumb Tyree (b. 24 March 1867 West Virginia,
d. 12 December 1954). (She married (2) —— O'Connor.) The 1887 Providence
Directory reported that he had removed to Illinois. When the 1900 U.S. census
was enumerated, William was a real estate broker residing in Cranston, R.I., with
his wife, their daughter and four servants. He was survived by his wife and by
their daughter Margaret ("Madge") Tyree (Banigan) L'Engle (b. 14 August
1894 Rhode Island, d. 1988), the wife of Philip Fatio L'Engle (1887–1967).
Margaret and her husband had daughters Elizabeth L'Engle (1916–2002), who
married Arthur Tufts (1911–1996), and Margaret Fatio L'Engle (1919–2010),
who married Nathaniel Arnold Hardin (1917–1993). The L'Engles and their
daughters lived in Georgia.
15. This home was moved to 9 Orchard Avenue in the early 1890s. The 1896
and 1897 Providence House Directories listed Joseph Banigan as householder
at 3 Orchard Avenue; in 1897, Susan Maher, widow, was co-householder. By
1900, Joseph's son John Joseph Banigan (1863–1908) was householder at 468
Angell Street, the house immediately east of 454 Angell Street. Perhaps John
Joseph Banigan erected a new house at this address after his father moved the
house where he and his family had dwelled since 1876 (originally numbered 214
Angell Street, renumbered 468 Angell Street in 1896) to Orchard Avenue.
16. Alice Margaret Banigan was born on 14 September 1866 in Smithfield, R.I.
She died on 28 September 1909. She married 4 November 1885 (Providence)
James Edward Sullivan (b. October 1849 Ireland, d. 8 October 1920 Provi-
dence). Alice and her husband Dr. Sullivan had children: (1) Robert Joseph
Banigan Sullivan (1887–1929), (2) John E. Sullivan (1889–1889), (3) Cathe-
rine Ellen Sullivan (1890–1890), (4) Edmund James Gibbons Sullivan (1893–

Rhode Island, at Catholic school. The 1880 U.S. census recorded the Banigan household at 214 Angell Street (renumbered as 468 Angell Street in 1896) in Providence: Joseph [head], age forty, owner (felt mill), born Ireland of Irish-born parents; Maria [wife], age thirty-eight, born

Ireland of Irish-born parents; Mamie [daughter], age eighteen, born Connecticut, at school; Johnnie [son], age sixteen, born Connecticut, at school; Willie [son], age fifteen, born Rhode Island, at school; Allie [daughter], age fourteen, born Rhode Island, at school; Maggie [brother's daughter], age fifteen, born Scotland of Irish-born parents, at school. There were also a coachman and a domestic servant in the household.

Joseph Banigan was eventually bought out by the United States Rubber Company. As a wealthy man, he was well known as a philanthropist. Pope Leo XIII created him a Knight of St. Gregory the Great. In 1897, he built a magnificent mansion at 510 Angell Street. However, he was not to occupy this home for long, as he died on 28 July 1898, age fifty-nine, of a gall bladder ailment—just nine days after Winfield Scott Lovecraft (1853–1898) died at Butler Hospital. The mansion at 510 Angell Street became

Posthumous painting of Joseph Banigan owned by Brown University. Painted 1901.

the home of Joseph's daughter Mary A. Banigan (Mrs. William B. McElroy). It remained in the family until it was sold and torn down to facilitate the construction of Wayland Manor, which opened in 1927. Joseph Banigan and many of his close family were originally

1936), (5) William Banigan Sullivan (1901–1911), and (6) James B. Sullivan (1905–1970). The 1893 home of Dr. Sullivan and his wife is still preserved at 254 Wayland Avenue in Providence.

entombed in the Banigan Chapel constructed on the grounds of St. Francis Cemetery in Pawtucket, Rhode Island. The chapel was torn down when the expenses connected with its maintenance became too great, and the Banigans are now memorialized by medallions in the basement of the cemetery administration building.

In any case, Lovecraft was early admitted to the precincts of the Banigan home at 468 Angell Street, where he became the playmate of John Joseph and Mary Catherine Banigan's sons Joseph,[17] John Joseph,[18] and Richard Davis Banigan.[19] He told the story of his re-

---

17. Joseph Banigan was born on 20 June 1888 in Blackstone [Millville], Massachusetts. He removed to Canada on 10 September 1911 and married 22 April 1912 (Toronto, Canada) Olive Juanita Loudon (b. 18 March 1886 Picton, Ontario), the daughter of John Samuel Loudon (banker) and Sarah Wilson. At the time of his marriage, Joseph Banigan stated his occupation as social worker. When he registered for the draft on 8 June 1917, he stated his legal residence as 176 Medway Street, Providence. However, he was residing in Toronto, Canada, with his wife and two children and employed as a architect by the firm of Banigan, Mathews & Johnson. He and his wife Olive arrived at La Guardia airport for a visit to Danielson, Connecticut, on 14 April 1944. In 1957, he was an advertising manager (with wife Marguerite) residing at 59 Chestnut Hill Parkway in York West, Ontario. He died in Canada in 1962. He and his first wife Olive had children (both born in Toronto): Elizabeth Banigan (b. 17 September 1913) and Joseph Banigan Jr. (b. 18 November 1915).
18. John Joseph Banigan [Jr.] was born on 10 July 1894 in Providence.

Grandson John J. Banigan,
1916 passport application.

He resided in his mother's household at 248 Waterman Street in Providence

lationship in his letter to Robert E. Howard dated 4 October 1930:

> Another Celtic sidelight of my youth was still nearer home—
> my next-door neighbours and best playmates being three broth-
> ers whose relation to the Irish stream might be said to be your
> own, *reversed*—that is, they were descended from a line of
> Irishmen given to marrying Rhode Island Yankees, so that alt-
> hough they were about 80% Anglo-Saxon, they considered
> themselves heirs to the Irish tradition through descent in the

---

when the 1910 U.S. census was taken. When he registered for the draft on 5 June 1917, he was a single man residing at 176 Medway Street in Providence, employed as secretary by the M.B. Tool Company in Danielson, Connecticut. He married (1) Eleanor Criddle (b. 1899, d. 18 January 1926) and (2) Julia A. Carroll (b. 1894, d. 8 January 1968). The 1924 Providence directory listed him at 349 Lloyd Avenue; the 1930 and 1931 directories, at 21 Harwich Road. He died on 3 October 1967 and was survived by daughters Jean Eleanor Banigan Parker (b. 31 October 1920 Rhode Island, d. 1973), Kathryn J. Vassett (1921–1995), and Phyllis L. Hawkins (1925–2013) and a son, John Joseph Banigan (b. 7 January 1926, d. 18 April 2007 Venice, Florida).

19. Richard Davis Banigan was born on 29 May 1890 in Blackstone [Millville], Massachusetts. He was a member of Brown University's class of 1916. He resided with his widowed mother at 468 Angell Street in Providence through at least 1916. When he registered for the draft on 5 June 1917, he was a single man residing at 176 Medway Street in Providence and was employed as treasurer by the M.B. Tool Company in Danielson, Connecticut. He served as a sergeant in Motor Truck Company 473 (Motor Supply Train 418). He departed Newport News, Virginia, on the *Aeolus* on 14 August 1918 and departed Brest, France, on the *Mt. Vernon* on 28 June 1919, arriving in Hoboken, New Jersey, on 5 July 1919. He married 1 October 1919 (Manhattan, New York City, New York) Eileen E. O'Connor (b. 1892 Rhode Island, d. 8 August 1949). The 1930 and 1940 U.S. censuses enumerated Richard and his wife Eileen in Killingly (Danielson), Connecticut. Richard was listed as a filling station manager in the 1930 census and as president of a petroleum company in the 1940 census. When he registered for the draft in World War II, he resided on Peckham Lane in Danielson, Connecticut, and was employed by the Danielson Oil Company, 7 Railroad Street, Danielson, Connecticut. He named his wife of the same residence address as the person who would always know his address. The 1942–47 Pawtucket, Rhode Island, directories listed him as president of the Atwood Crawford Company, residing at Danielson, Connecticut. In 1950, he married Mary G. L. —— in Lawrence, Massachusetts [60:1]. Richard Davis Banigan died on 12 May 1973.

male line and the possession of the name of Banigan. Their family always made a point to travel to Ireland as often as possible, and were great collectors of Celtic antiquities. Their grandfather [Joseph Banigan] had a veritable museum of prehistoric Irish artifacts—indeed, I wish I knew what has become of that collection now that the family has left Providence and the brothers are all dispersed! Observing my admiration for these reliques of unknown yesterdays, they gave me two little greenish figures which they held to be of vast antiquity, but concerning which they admitted very little was known. Some seem to be metallic, whilst others are clearly carved of some light sort of stone. Their average length is only an inch and a half, and they are all overlaid with a greenish patina. They are grotesque human figures, sometimes in conventional poses and with curious costume and headdresses. Their vast age is held to be indicated by the prodigious depth at which they are found in ancient peat-bogs. My two—one stone and one metal—have always appealed prodigiously to my imagination, and have formed high spots of my own assortment of curiosities. I think I will try to sketch them here, and see if your Celtic researches can throw any light on them. My friend Bernard Dwyer—pure Irish and 3 generations from the old sod—cannot explain them, but it is very possible that actual archaeologists have long known and described such things. Their outlines and features, unfortunately, are exceedingly chipped and worn down. But here they are—exact size and all. What are they? Were they ancient and buried and forgotten when Patholan first sighted Iërne's strange green shore? Did some Atlantean colonist, remembering strange secrets from hoary Poseidonis, fashion them in the light of primordial dawns? It's a wonder that I haven't asked museum authorities about them long ago—but perhaps I dread being disillusioned and told that they are either fakes or something relatively recent! Sooner or later I shall probably get one or two tales out of them—for they certainly possess the most fascinating possibilities. (A Means to Freedom 74–75)[20]

---

20. The two figures were traced too faintly in the Arkham House Transcripts to be reproduced in A Means to Freedom. HPL's original letters to Howard were lost.

Grandson Robert B. McElroy,   Granddaughter Margaret
1909 passport application   Tyree Banigan (1894–1988).

In fact, Lovecraft's mother and aunts had known the Banigans, particularly Joseph's daughters Mary and Alice, years before Lovecraft was born.[21] They were next-door neighbors—the Phillipses at 454 Angell Street and the Banigans just to the east across Elmgrove Avenue at 468 Angell Street (addresses reflect 1896 renumbering). Both Banigan daughters attended Elmhurst Academy on Smith Street—Mary in 1874–80 and Alice in 1878–84 (Faig 79). The poet-to-be Louise Imogen Guiney (1861–1920) attended Elmhurst Academy in 1873–79 and visited frequently thereafter. She probably met Sarah Susan Phillips on one of her visits to the Banigan household at 468 Angell Street.

In the succeeding years, the Banigan grandsons dispersed, and Lovecraft lost track of them. (He knew that Richard had served in the armed forces in World War I.[22]) He wrote to Alfred Galpin of his acquaintance with the various Banigan grandsons:

---

21. "My mother and aunts have known the daughters [of Joseph Banigan] from childhood, and found them worthy in every respect." (HPL to the Gallomo, 30 September 1919; *Letters to Alfred Galpin* 54.)

22. See his letter to Rheinhart Kleiner of 5 June 1918 (*Letters to Rheinhart Kleiner and Others* 116). HPL described the visit of Cardinal Mercier in his letter to Kleiner of 27 September 1919 (*Letters to Rheinhart Kleiner and Others* 142). An aunt (most likely Annie E. P. Gamwell) attended the honorary de-

The grandchildren were my earliest playmates, though it made me shudder in my British soul to know "Dicky Banigan," "Robert McElroy,"[23] "Edmund Sullivan,"[24] etc. However, there is some consolation in the fact that Dick, Joe, and John Banigan, who lived nearest me (next house to #454 Angell)) were only a quarter Irish. Their father had followed the example of his own father and married into an old American family.[25] Still, I wished they could have been solidly Saxon! (*Letters to Alfred Galpin* 54)

The home of Mrs. William B. McElroy at 510 Angell Street was the focus of attention in late September 1919 when its served as the headquarters for Cardinal Mercier, who was in town to receive an honorary degree from Brown University. Lovecraft described the occasion in his letter to the Gallomo dated 30 September 1919:

This neighbourhood is quite honoured today, His Eminence Cardinal Mercier of Belgium being entertained in the McElroy mansion only four houses west of Castle Theobald [598 Angell Street] on Angell St. My aunt is now there at the reception being given in his honour. The extensive grounds are all fenced off to deter curious crowds, and awnings cover the long drives whereby the mansion is reached from the street. ... The McElroy house is the only local stronghold of Hibernianism. It was built by the late Joseph Banigan, sometimes called "The Rubber King," who was Mrs. McElroy's father. He was a poor Irish peasant who succeeded in business and lived to found a family whose innate good qualities gave them a definite social standing hereabout. He married an American lady, and gave his children the best education obtainable, so that they are rather influential in the community. ... The Banigan or McElroy

gree conferral at Brown and the reception at the home of Mrs. William B. McElroy; HPL himself did not.

23. Robert Bernard McElroy (1886–1953), son of William B. McElroy (1857–1914) and Mary A. Banigan (1861–1923).

24. Edmund James Gibbons Sullivan (1893–1936), son of Dr. James Edward Sullivan (1849–1920) and Alice Margaret Banigan (1866–1909).

25. In fact, John J. Banigan's wife Mary Catherine Davis was the daughter of Irish-born parents.

Mansion, where Mercier is now receiving the homage of local society, is one of the "show places" of the neighbourhood, and excited Klei's vast admiration when he was here. It is a Gothic manor house of brick and stone, such as its peasant builder may have seen and admired at a distance in his boyhood in Ould Oireland. The grounds are extensive and beautifully kept, with hedges, trees, and stables of pleasing architecture. It lies almost exactly half way between the house where I was born [454 Angell Street] and that which I inhabit [598 Angell Street]. Altogether, I fancy the Irish have helped rather than harmed the locality! (*Letters to Alfred Galpin* 54–55)

The domestic servants at 454 Angell Street were not the only working-class Irish Lovecraft met early in his life. In April 1914, Edward F. Daas recruited him for the United Amateur Press Association, and by November of the same year Edward H. Cole introduced him to the newly formed Providence Amateur Press Club,[26] whose leaders were Victor L. Basinet (1889–1956), of French-Canadian ancestry) and John T. Dunn (1889–1983), of Irish ancestry). Of the club members, Peter Joseph McManus (1888–1971) had actually been born in Ireland. Other club members with probable Irish ancestry included Frederick Aloysius Byland (1894–1967), Edmund Leo Shehan (1891–1972), and William Aloysius Henry (1884–1950). The club was originally formed primarily from evening high school students in Providence. Lovecraft was unlike most of the other club members in that he was not holding down a "day job"—a circumstance that was the origin of some resentment among the other members.

The stiff, formal Lovecraft inevitably generated some laughter as well, and Sarah "Sadie" Henry (1879–1957), the elder sister of member William A. Henry, even called the Lovecraft residence to ask for a date. Club member John T. Dunn recalled that Lovecraft told Miss Henry that he would have to ask his

---

26. For the Providence Amateur Press Club, see Kenneth W. Faig, Jr., *The Providence Amateur Press Club: 1914–1916* (Glenview, IL: Moshassuck Press, 2008). An enhanced electronic edition of this text was later published by David Haden.

Banigan Rubber Co., Woonsocket RI.

mother for permission.[27] After producing two issues of the *Providence Amateur* the club had largely lapsed into inactivity by 1916. Dunn, who worked as a plumber, ardently supported the Irish rebels against British rule in 1916. Along with his refusal to register for the draft—for which he served two years in prison—Dunn's support of the Irish rebels spelled the end of his relationship with Lovecraft.[28] After his release from prison, Dunn eventually entered a Maryland seminary and was ordained a Catholic priest in 1930. He served most of his long career as a hospital chaplain in Ohio.

Lovecraft's connection with the amateur journalism hobby persisted after the failure of the Providence Amateur Press Club. He served as president of the United Amateur Press Association in 1917–18 and as interim president of the National Amateur Press Association in 1922–23. He was later a member of the National's Bureau of Critics in 1931–35, serving as chairman in 1933–35. He had served one term as a National Executive Judge in 1923–24, but served another term—a taxing one on account of disputes dividing the association—in 1935–36. He more or less refrained from most amateur activity—other than through the mails—after his return to Providence from New York City in

27. Dunn's recollections of this incident can be found in L. Sprague de Camp, "Young Man Lovecraft," in Joshi and Schultz, *Ave atque Vale* 172–74.
28. HPL's surviving letters to John T. Dunn, edited by S. T. Joshi, David E. Schultz and John H. Stanley, were published in *Books at Brown* 38–39 (1991–92): 157–223.

1926 until his attendance at the National's Boston convention in 1930. The years 1914–23 were undoubtedly his busiest as an amateur journalist. In 1924–25 Lovecraft and his wife presided over the sad decline of the so-called Hoffman-Daas faction of the United, which expired a year later in 1926. Lovecraft's Hub Club visits in 1919–23 probably represented the peak of his social activity in the hobby. He attended Hub Club meetings in Boston with some regularity during this period. At the meeting held to celebrate St. Patrick's Day on 10 March 1921 (one week in advance of the actual holiday), he read his Irish-set story "The Moon-Bog" and was applauded by his fellow club members.[29] Significantly, Lovecraft set his story in County Meath, which is also home to Dunsany Castle. The protagonist Denys Barry plans to drain the peat-bog adjoining his recently acquired ancestral residence. While the amulets or figurines the Banigans had given him were reportedly recovered deep below peat-bogs, there is no direct reference to amulets or figurines in "The Moon-Bog." The story did not see publication until June 1926 in *Weird Tales*. The Hub Club included a fair share of persons of Irish descent, of whom the most devoted Hibernophile was probably J[oseph] Bernard Lynch (1879–1952), born in Boston of Irish-born parents and composer of "On a Starry Irish Night" (1936).[30] Other club members teased member Laura Anna "Laurie" Sawyer (*née* Moody) (b. 1865) over her refusal to enter a Protestant church.

The last of the Banigan grandsons died in 1973, and Joseph Banigan's mansion at 510 Angell Street in Providence fell to the wrecker's ball to allow the construction of Wayland Manor, opened in 1927. The houses at 9 Orchard Avenue (home of Joseph Banigan before the completion of 510 Angell Street) and 254 Wayland Avenue (home of his daughter Alice Margaret Banigan and her husband Dr. James Edward Sullivan) remain as reminders of the Banigan clan. Lovecraft's own boyhood home at 454 Angell Street fell to the wrecker's ball in 1960, while his later residences at 598 Angell Street, 10 Barnes Street, and 66

29. For HPL's reading of "The Moon-Bog," see *IAP* 314–15 and 384–85.
30. For Lynch, see Kenneth W. Faig, Jr., "Lovecraft's 1937 Diary," *Lovecraft Annual* No. 6 (2012): 169n24.

College Street (moved to 65 Prospect Street) remain. The site of the Banigan home at 468 Angell Street is now occupied by a Starbucks. Lovecraft's equivocating over the Anglo-Saxon component of the Banigan's heritage is difficult to read in more tolerant times. That he did admire the Banigans' allegiance to the best of their Irish cultural traditions is to his credit. Lovecraft was not an easy fit with the working-class majority of the Providence Amateur Press Club and he had especial conflict John T. Dunn, who supported the 1916 Irish rebels and resisted the draft. By the time of his association with the Hub Club in 1919–23, he could more readily navigate social, cultural, and economic differences. That the club reacted with approval to the reading of his only Irish-set story "The Moon-Bog" is heartening. All told, Lovecraft's favorable opinion of ancient Irish culture, as expressed in his letter to Elizabeth Toldridge quoted at the beginning of this paper, redounds to his credit. A master of the supernatural could hardly deny all merit to a culture which had produced legends like the fairy folk and the banshee.

Banigan Mortuary Chapel, St. Francis Cemetery, Pawtucket RI. Demolished.

Works Cited

Bayles, Richard M. *History of Providence County, Rhode Island.* New York: W. W. Preston & Co., 1891. 2 vols.

Faig, Kenneth W., Jr. *The Unknown Lovecraft.* New York: Hippocampus Press, 2009.

Joshi, S. T., and David E. Schultz, ed. *Ave atque Vale: Reminiscences of H. P. Lovecraft.* West Warwick, RI: Necronomicon Press, 2018.

Lovecraft, H. P. *The Annotated Supernatural Horror in Literature.* Ed. S. T. Joshi. 2nd ed. New York: Hippocampus Press, 2012. [Abbreviated in the text as *SHL*.]

———. *Letters to Alfred Galpin.* Ed. S. T. Joshi and David E. Schultz. New York: Hippocampus Press, 2003.

———. *Letters to Elizabeth Toldridge and Anne Tillery Renshaw.* Ed. David E. Schultz and S. T. Joshi. New York: Hippocampus Press, 2014.

———. *Letters to F. Lee Baldwin, Duane W. Rimel, and Nils Frome.* Ed. David E. Schultz and S. T. Joshi. New York: Hippocampus Press, 2016.

———. *Letters to Rheinhart Kleiner and Others.* Ed. S. T. Joshi and David E. Schultz. New York: Hippocampus Press, 2020.

———. *Letters to Wilfred B. Talman and Helen V. and Genevieve Sully.* Ed. David E. Schultz and S. T. Joshi. New York: Hippocampus Press, 2019.

———, and Robert E. Howard. *A Means to Freedom: The Letters of H. P. Lovecraft and Robert E. Howard.* Ed. S. T. Joshi, David E. Schultz, and Rusty Burke. New York: Hippocampus Press, 2009.

Molloy, Scott. *Irish Titan, Irish Toilers: Joseph Banigan and Nineteenth-Century New England Labor.* Durham, NH: University of New Hampshire Press, 2008.

Following *The Ancient Track*

David E. Schultz

In mid-March of 1937, less than a week following the unexpected death of H. P. Lovecraft, August Derleth wrote to R. H. Barlow asking what he knew of various of Lovecraft's writings. Derleth was beginning to amass Lovecraft's work for publication in a book—three books, actually—and had only just begun seeking items he did not have. It is clear that he considered Barlow far more knowledgeable than himself when he told Barlow that Lovecraft "wrote on one occasion of a story or poem (?) entitled THE ANCIENT TRACK; do you know anything of this?"[1] At the time, Barlow was in Providence to obtain and save Lovecraft's manuscripts. He first saw Lovecraft's papers—in his own study—the previous summer, when he spent thirty-five days with Lovecraft in Providence. One supposes that Barlow was able to examine Lovecraft's papers carefully, under Lovecraft's eye and guidance. Barlow's new-found familiarity with Lovecraft's manuscripts surely earned him the position of Lovecraft's literary executor, which he now attempted to fill. It is clear that in the weeks following his friend's death, Barlow considered himself to be collaborator and peer in the preservation of Lovecraft's work, acting in accordance with Lovecraft's wishes, but he was denied recognition in the two large books that emerged.[2]

In something of a frenzy, Derleth repeated his question to other

---

1. AWD to RHB, 21 March 1937 (TLS, Wisconsin Historical Society [hereafter abbreviated WHS]). (Because AWD was uncertain as to where best to reach RHB, he composed and sent two separate letters.)

2. The third volume was intended to contain a selection of HPL's letters, but the sheer volume of text obtained made such an inclusion impractical. Eventually, Arkham House published HPL's *Selected Letters* in five volumes (1965–76).

correspondents, trying to find the elusive item. Howard Wandrei had responded: "Neither Long nor I [both in New York City at the time] have ever heard of THE ANCIENT TRACK."[3] Barlow's own reply is something many readers of Lovecraft would find most unusual: "The Ancient Track [consists of] about 25 varied poems which he assembled & gave to me in MS."[4] Lovecraft's poem "The Ancient Track" is well known. He wrote it on 26 November 1929, at the beginning of a spate of poetry writing over a forty-day period that concluded with *Fungi from Yuggoth*. It is not a sonnet, as are thirty-seven other poems he wrote at that time, but a poem of 44 lines in 11 quatrains written, not in heroic couplets such as Lovecraft's earliest verse—his favorite form for a very long time—but in iambic tetrameter. Derleth could perhaps be forgiven his unfamiliarity with the piece, given that Lovecraft's death was a profound shock to him. But he had been rereading Lovecraft's letters to him, and he surely would have come across Lovecraft's several mentions of the piece and what it was: "I'm glad you regard my metrical vagaries kindly. Wright has just taken two—'The Ancient Track' & 'Recapture'" (*ES* 235). And again: "I just received an $11.00 cheque for 'The Ancient Track'" (*ES* 249), the low payment clearly indicating it was for verse rather than fiction—25¢ a line.

It is uncertain, from the first of these comments, whether Lovecraft sent the poem to Derleth. Perhaps Derleth's kindly comments were merely blanket praise for Lovecraft's poetry in general. "The Ancient Track" appeared in *Weird Tales* shortly thereafter, in the March 1930 issue, which Derleth surely saw, and not merely because he was a regular reader of the magazine. His story "The Pacer" (co-written with Mark R. Schorer) appeared in the issue. Inexplicably, Derleth asked Barlow once again about the unknown item despite Barlow's reply (though perhaps their furiously exchanged letters crossed before Derleth learned the answer): "HPL also spoke or rather, wrote, at one time of a tale or poem, The Ancient Track—what do you know of this? That may be Smith's, my reference is not clear."[5]

3. Howard Wandrei to AWD, 25 March 1937 (TLS, WHS).
4. RHB to AWD, n.d. [c. 23 March 1937] (ALS, WHS).
5. AWD to RHB, 25 March 1937 (TLS, WHS). There is no surviving discus-

But what is the manuscript that contained "about 25 varied poems" of which Barlow writes? By way of reply, Barlow wrote "The Ancient Track is a 44-line poem and the title poem of a collection Howard compiled for me last year, including Nemesis &c. I have [the] Ms. given me last summer. Fungi (36 sonnets) A. T.—(about 25 miscellaneous) and three or four Providence poems are all he wished to keep."[6] Clearly this was intended to be a booklet of some kind, containing only what Lovecraft considered his best poetry. Lovecraft compiled the material in the summer of 1936, but there is no such manuscript among the papers Barlow scrupulously deposited at the John Hay Library of Brown University, Providence. Lovecraft letters to Barlow shed a little light on the matter. On 4 June he wrote:

> Now about this matter of The Collected Poetical Works of H. P. Lovecraft—I'll consider it when I have a finished copy of Klarkash-Ton's "Incantations" in my hands. One thing at a time! But even then there won't be much to add. Most of my verse was utter tripe, as you'll see when I shew you some of the old-time specimens for fun. I wouldn't have it printed again for the world! "Nemesis", "Recapture",[7] "The Ancient Track", & "The Outpost" are all right for inclusion—& I'll give a verdict on "The Nightmare Lake" when I have time to burrow for it in my files. It is in Cook's Dec. 1919 *Vagrant*—the one that got rain-soaked before issuance, & of which only 100 copies were mailed. [. . .] I have a lot of other old weird verse—some of which I shall let Wollheim & other kid editors reprint in their magazines—but I don't think I'd want it in a collection. However, I'll see when I exhume it. Of non-weird verse perhaps 3 or 4 items are worth preserving—but they ought not to go in a collection predominantly weird. Well—we'll see after "Incantations" has been safely issued. I'm more interested in *finishing* jobs than in *starting* them!" (*O Fortunate Floridian* 338–39)

---

sion of the poem in the AWD–Smith correspondence.

6. RHB to AWD, Easter Sunday [28 March 1937] (ALS, WHS); written from the YMCA in New York City. RHB later cautioned Derleth, much as HPL had once urged him, against allowing publication of any of HPL's verse beyond that contained in the two books HPL planned with RHB.

7. "Recapture" was integrated into *Fungi from Yuggoth* shortly afterwards.

Even this is somewhat confusing. At the time, Barlow was bursting with ideas for book projects. He had been setting type for *Fungi from Yuggoth* and printing some pages, but abruptly stopped and began planning a collection of Clark Ashton Smith's verse, to be titled *Incantations.* Work on that book got no further than Smith preparing a manuscript for it, to which he added a few more poems after having submitted it. Barlow did not even commence typesetting. Instead he was quickly distracted by yet another project—the supposed collected poetical works of H. P. Lovecraft.

Despite Lovecraft's pique at Barlow's jumping from uncompleted project to uncompleted project, he obliged the boy by preparing a list of potential titles for a book of his poetry that he provided in his letter to Barlow of 13 June.

Fungi from Yuggoth
and Other Verses

———————————

H. P. Lovecraft

———————————

Fungi From Yuggoth, I–XXXVI

Aletheia Phrikodes ?

The Ancient Track
Oceanus ?
Clouds ?
Mother Earth ?
The Eidolon ?
The Nightmare Lake ?
The Outpost
The Rutted Road ?
The Wood
Hallowe'en in a Suburb ?
The City
The House

Primavera
October

To a Dreamer
Despair ?

Nemesis

Barlow mounted the list on a larger sheet of paper, on which he wrote in the upper right-hand corner "TENTATIVE LIST." But this is simply a list of titles, not a complete manuscript. A bit later, Barlow wrote to Derleth: "I have sent F. W. the Ancient Track group—or, at least, those W. T. hasn't used. ¶ He must not get hold of junk & use it."[8] So Barlow took the initiative to submit Lovecraft's unpublished work to Farnsworth Wright of *Weird*

———————————

8. RHB to AWD, 6 May 1937 (ALS, WHS).

Tales.[9] But was there a manuscript of *The Ancient Track*?

Among Lovecraft's papers at the John Hay Library, there is a 34-page typescript apparently prepared by R. H. Barlow. For the most part the untitled typescript follows Lovecraft's letter enclosure listing his "collected poetical works." The typescript comprises the following eighteen poems (not "about 25"): "Aletheia Phrikodes,"[10] "The Ancient Track," "Oceanus," "Clouds," "Mother Earth," "The Eidolon," "The Nightmare Lake," "The Outpost," "The Rutted Road," "The Wood," "Hallowe'en in a Suburb," "The City," "The House," "Primavera," "October," "To a Dreamer," "Despair," and "Nemesis." It omits *Fungi from Yuggoth,* from which *Weird Tales* published ten sonnets from 1930 to 1932. The typescript also omits "The Ancient Track," which *Weird Tales* had published, but includes "To a Dreamer" and "Nemesis," which *Weird Tales* had published years before, and "The Outpost," which it had previously rejected as too long. None of the poems in Barlow's submittal was accepted. But this document is not the "collection Howard compiled for me last year"—at least not a physical manuscript that Lovecraft himself prepared. What became the collection Lovecraft compiled?

The answer lies in those of Barlow's papers that did not find their way to John Hay Library. Barlow had deposited many of Lovecraft's papers and his own with the library during his lifetime. It is known that some items were not, such as the draft manuscript of "The Shadow out of Time," which Barlow had given to a friend. Following Barlow's death in January 1951, George T. Smisor microfilmed papers that remained in Barlow's possession, such as drafts and manuscripts of his own fiction and poetry, correspondence from others, and Lovecraft's letters and postcards to him. Among the items microfilmed is a set of type-

---

9. As material was obtained for *The Outsider* and *Beyond the Wall of Sleep,* AWD followed Barlow's lead and submitted more unpublished work to *Weird Tales,* including five sonnets from *Fungi from Yuggoth,* with payment therefor sent to HPL's surviving aunt.

10. I.e., the long part of the poem "The Poe-et's Nightmare" but omitting the comic beginning and ending and retaining only cosmic central portion. *Weird Tales* inexplicably published the poem only in July 1952.

scripts of Lovecraft poetry as prepared by him long ago. Many are old enough that his typed return address was given as 10 Barnes Street, sometimes revised by hand to 66 College. These sheets are prefaced by a number of pages explaining the makeup of a proposed book: *The Ancient Track*. The cover or title page reads as follows:

Copy sent AWD   FOR FUTURE PUBLICATION UNIFORM
All poems but Aletheia   WITH FUNGI FROM YUGGOTH (1936).
submitted to Wright
4/23/37

THE ANCIENT TRACK
By H. P. Lovecraft

file copy—
sent to AWD

The Dragon-Fly Press

It would seem that the simple title page was typed by Barlow, including his note about "uniform publication with Fungi from Yuggoth," but when? Perhaps upon receipt of the various typescripts from Lovecraft in the summer of 1936. It surely was before Barlow visited Lovecraft in Providence in August 1936. The note on the upper left, as well as the note mid-page about Derleth, were written in April 1937, as indicated, confirming that Barlow had already submitted verses to *Weird Tales*. The page that follows the title page (too poor to reproduce here from the microfilm) is handwritten by Lovecraft, mounted by Barlow on a letter-sized piece of paper. It is clearly a draft of the copy on p. 49 later provided to Barlow. Balloons around and pointing lines toward certain titles are the poems flagged with question marks on the fair copy. The sheet bears the same title, which differs from the typed title page Barlow made for *The Ancient Track*.

Fungi from Yuggoth
and other verses
By H. P. Lovecraft

Fungi from Yuggoth

I–XXXVI

Aletheia Phrikodes

The Ancient Track

Oceanus

Clouds

Mother Earth

~~Nemus~~   The Eidolon   Probably not good enough
~~Avernale~~

The Nightmare Lake

The Outpost

The Rutted Road

The Wood

Hallowe'en in a Suburb

The City

The House

Primavera

October

To a Dreamer

Despair   Last moment. I think this
                                     is pretty bad. Better count
                                     it definitely out.

Nemesis

Both drafts of the contents contain what seem to be intended groupings of poems, such as "Primavera"/"October" and "To a Dreamer"/"Despair." The significance of these groupings is unclear. Lovecraft had considered a section title "Nemus Avernale" ("The Grove of Avernus") for the largest group but ultimately cancelled it, probably when he had second thoughts about eight poems in the group, the deletion of which would leave only three.

Yet another untitled page, also mounted on a larger sheet of paper, survives pertaining to *The Ancient Track*. It is written in Lovecraft's hand and is first rough draft of titles.

———————

The City (Vagrant Oct 1919)
The House (Philosopher Dec 1920)
Oceanus ⎤
Clouds ⎬ Tryout July 1919
Mother Earth ⎦
Nightmare Lake (Vagrant Dec. 1919)
The Wood (Planeteer) [†]
~~The Cats (revise)~~
~~Astrophobos (U. A. June 1918)~~
Despair ?
~~Revelation (Tryout Mar 1919)~~
Primavera (Bklynite Apr. 1925
Hallowe'en in a Suburb (Planeteer) [†]
Alethia Phrikodes (Tryout July 1918)—prob too long
October
To a Dreamer (WT [Nov. 1924])
Rutted Road (?)
The Eidolon
Nemesis
Ancient Track
Outpost

non-weird
To an Infant
Brick Row
Ave atque Vale
Providence (Bklynite)

[†]only known & available copies in possession of Wm. Miller, Jr., 69 Halsted St., East Orange, N.J., awaiting publication in *The Planeteer*

———————

The listed items (except those crossed out) are preceded with something like a checkmark, presumably to indicate that they were acceptable for inclusion. Note that *Fungi from Yuggoth* is not on the list.

Besides the individual typescripts of certain poems, there is a running typescript of pages that appears to be the typescript at John Hay Library, but there are some minor differences between the two sets. It does not seem that one is merely a carbon of the other. For example, the typescript on the microfilm has the poem "Oceanus" alone on a page, whereas the typescript at John Hay library has seven lines from the poem "The Ancient Track" above the text of "Oceanus." It would seem that Barlow had typed the sheaf of poems more than once.

From all this we can ascertain the following. Even though Barlow had begun printing a booklet to be called *Fungi from Yuggoth,* he ultimately abandoned it and sought to establish a book of modestly broader scope—Lovecraft's "best" poetry. Lovecraft thrice prepared lists of proposed contents, ultimately settling on the title *Fungi from Yuggoth and Other Verses.* (His title *The Collected Poetical Works* etc. is merely jocular.) Although Lovecraft had doubts about whether to include nine poems, Barlow kept them in the fair copy he typed of the proposed book. Even so, that fair copy did not include *Fungi from Yuggoth* and a few other poems—not that he intended to omit them, but because his copy was meant to offer *Weird Tales* unpublished poems. August Derleth received a slightly different version of that fair copy—possibly Barlow's own file copy—and consulted it when he published Lovecraft's poetry. It is not clear when the title *The Ancient Track* came into being. Barlow was not one to override Lovecraft's wishes, but he did not balk at making suggestions to Lovecraft, such as when Lovecraft accepted his idea at the eleventh hour to assume "Recapture" into *Fungi from Yuggoth.* Presumably it was Barlow who suggested the title—a completely natural choice[11]—and Lovecraft acceded. Rather than mar or discard a page of Lovecraft's handwriting, Barlow prepared a new cover sheet with the new title, but did not cancel it on Lovecraft's list of proposed contents. Not only did Lovecraft prepare that list; he ultimately provided a ragtag sheaf of typed

---

11. Indeed, so thought the editor of *The Ancient Track: The Complete Poetical Works of H. P. Lovecraft* (Night Shade Books, 2001; Hippocampus Press, 2013), who knew nothing of the edition discussed in this essay.

poems culled from his files. Those pages may no longer survive, although images of them can be seen on the microfilm prepared George T. Smisor, copies of which are held at the John Hay Library.

In the end, neither *Fungi from Yuggoth* nor *The Ancient Track* ever appeared from the Dragon-Fly Press. However, much of *The Ancient Track* appeared in *Beyond the Wall of Sleep*, Arkham House's second Lovecraft omnibus, although the poems therein are not labeled as such. Indeed, *Fungi from Yuggoth* (with "Recapture" included) appeared toward the end of the grouping of poems rather than at the fore, and "Oceanus," "Clouds," "Mother Earth," and "The House" were passed over; only "The House" was included in Lovecraft's *Collected Poems* (Arkham House, 1963), along with all the others. In fact, the poems as presented there are more tightly grouped (but not exactly) as they were on Lovecraft's list, although *Collected Poems* also contains many other poems as well.

Works Cited

Derleth, August. Wis Mss WO; Micro 923; M2004-152. Wisconsin Historical Society. Box 4, Folder 5 contains correspondence of Derleth and R. H. Barlow.

———, and Clark Ashton Smith. *Eccentric, Impractical Devils: The Letters of August Derleth and Clark Ashton Smith.* Ed. David E. Schultz and S. T. Joshi. New York: Hippocampus Press, 2020.

Kenneth W. Faig, Jr. Archive on Robert H. Barlow (Ms.2018.019), John Hay Library, Brown University, Providence, R.I. George T. Smisor's microfilms of Barlow's papers are in Box 2.

Lovecraft, H. P. ["Alethia (*sic*) Phrikodes."] Ms., John Hay Library, Brown University, Providence, R.I. Box 24, Folder 1. The T.Ms. itself is untitled, though identified as such by the library, based on the first item in the T.Ms.

———. *Beyond the Wall of Sleep.* Collected by August Derleth and Donald Wandrei. Sauk City, WI: Arkham House, 1943.

———. *Collected Poems.* Sauk City, WI: Arkham House, 1963.

———. *O Fortunate Floridian: H. P. Lovecraft's Letters to R. H. Barlow.* Ed. S. T. Joshi and David E. Schultz. Tampa: University of Tampa Press, 2007.

———. *The Outsider and Others.* Collected by August Derleth and Donald Wandrei. Sauk City, WI: Arkham House, 1939.

———, and August Derleth. *Essential Solitude: The Letters of H. P. Lovecraft and August Derleth.* Ed. David E. Schultz and S. T. Joshi. New York: Hippocampus Press, 2008. 2 vols. [Abbreviated in the text as *ES*.]

Briefly Noted

Horace A. Smith and Edward Guimont are at work on a book about Lovecraft's devotion to astronomy. Smith, aside from his article in this issue, has previously contributed an essay on the subject, "Lovecraft Seeks the Garden of Eratosthenes" (No. 13 [2019]), that will no doubt find its way into the book; Guimont has written an article on a related subject, "An Arctic Mystery: The Lovecraftian North Pole" (No. 14 [2020]). This topic has been the focus of considerable scholarly attention in recent years: issue 13 also contained Fred S. Lubnow's article "The Lovecraftian Solar System," while issue 2 (2008) included T. R. Livesey's immense study "Dispatches from the Providence Observatory: Astronomical Motifs and Sources in the Writings of H. P. Lovecraft." Work on this subject has been substantially added by the digitization of Lovecraft's early astronomical writings (still extant in manuscript at the John Hay Library) as part of the Brown Digital Repository.

Lovecraft's Presentiment: Taphonomy as a Narrative and Horrific Element in the Tales of H. P. Lovecraft

Raphaël Hanon

"The nethermost caverns," wrote the mad Arab, "are not for the fathoming of eyes that see; for their marvels are strange and terrific. [. . .] For it is of old rumour that the soul of the devil-bought hastes not from his charnel clay, but fats and instructs the very worm that gnaws; till out of corruption horrid life springs, and the dull scavengers of earth wax crafty to vex it and swell monstrous to plague it. Great holes secretly are digged where earth's pores ought to suffice, and things have learnt to walk that ought to crawl."—H. P. Lovecraft, "The Festival" (October 1923) (CF 1.417)

"Archaeology is still too incomplete to afford an answer, hence imagination is free to speculate over the whole of Mesopotamia, Persia, India, and kindred regions."—H. P. Lovecraft to Robert E. Howard (12 September 1931; MF 207)

Introduction

Taphonomy (from the contraction of the ancient Greek τάφος ["burial"] and νόμος ["law"]) is the study of "burial laws." It is a scientific field of palaeontology and archaeology, defined in 1940 by the Russian palaeontologist Ivan Efremov as the "the study of the transformation of animal remains from the biosphere into the litho-sphere, i.e., the study of the process in the upshot of which the organisms pass out of the different part of the biosphere and, being fossilized, become part of the litho-sphere" (81–93). Koch has refined the definition of taphonomy as "a process or chain of events that begins just before the death of an organism, and proceeds through decomposition, desarticulation, burial, fossilisation, exposure, and collection. At each stage of this process, various taphonomic agencies intervene to obscure, bias, and add to the information that is available from the resulting collection" (85). The epistemological syntheses of Dodson, Olson, Cadée, Lyman, Denys and Patou-Mathis have retraced the development of taphonomy as a discipline since its first definition by Efremov. However, very few of these historical syntheses were interested in the beginnings of "taphonomic concepts" before the end of the first half of the twentieth century (Cadée; Lyman; Denys and Patou-Mathis). In addition, there is no mention of the use of taphonomy or taphonomic approaches in fiction. Nevertheless, some fictional texts written before the 1940s used archaeology as well as taphonomy as central elements of narratives. We are particularly interested here in the weird tales of the American author Howard Phillips Lovecraft, who used taphonomy as a recurring element in his horror tales.

This paper presents the first analysis of the use of "pre-taphonomic" concepts in Lovecraft's fiction. Before outlining our observations, we must define what taphonomy is and what it was in Lovecraft's time. After a brief historical and methodological review of taphonomy, we attempt to understand the construction of reasoning and to establish the origin of the inspirations for Lovecraft's work through the analysis of his writings and his correspondence.

Historical and Methodological Background

The strict definition of what is or what is not taphonomy is still under debate among specialists, leading to some confusion and misunderstanding about the concept of taphonomy. According to Lyman, the original definition of taphonomy "concerns the transition from living to non-living and geological, so includes both natural and cultural formation processes as either biasing or information laden and of research interest."

Based on this definition, Leonardo da Vinci is regularly cited as the very first taphonomist (Cadée) by virtue of drawings he made in his notes of bivalves found at the top of a mountain. By applying taphonomic reasoning, he shows how the bivalves naturally decomposed and fossilized, proving that they lived at the place of their fossilization, thus refuting the biblical version of the Flood (Cadée; Denys and Patou-Mathis). Taphonomic observations are as old as palaeontology (Cadée). Many palaeontologists and archaeologists who predate Efremov made some taphonomic observations and interpretations, such as Cuvier (1812) in volume 4 of the *Recherches sur les ossemens fossiles de quadrupèdes*, Buckland (1823) in *Reliquae diluvianae*, or d'Orbigny (1849) in his *Cours élémentaire de paléontologie et de géologie stratigraphiques*. For an exhaustive early history of taphonomy, closely linked to the history of palaeontology, the reader should refer to Cadée. According to this author, Weigelt's monograph published in 1927 is the first large-scale taphonomic study in the history of science. He also studied the decomposition processes of several animal carcasses and also the role of insects at different stages of decomposition. In that sense, Weigelt could be the earliest accomplished taphonomist, applying an actualistic approach based on experimental data in order to infer the origin of archaeological or palaeontological bone accumulations and to recognized differences in post-mortem degradations (Rattenbury).

Modern taphonomy is based mostly on experimental studies. To understand how fossils accumulated, taphonomists use different analytical scales. At the assemblage scale, the composition of the bone accumulation in terms of spatial distribution and orientation, taxonomy, skeletal part representation, or the age of the individual at death could provide useful information about the origin of the assemblage. For example, a bone assemblage found in an ancient cave and composed of only carnivore species represented by several juvenile individuals is characteristic of a carnivore den assemblage. A monospecific ungulate bone assemblage found in fluviatile sediments, with a mortality profile similar to what we can expect in a living community, could be characteristic of a catastrophic event.

At the specimen scale, it is possible to observe bone surface modifications (by Scanning Electron Microscopy or binocular) and identify post-mortem and post-depositional phenomenon causing these injuries (using photogrammetry, geometric-morphometric coupled with machine learning, or multivariate statistics), or both. Using experimental data and an actualistic approach, it is possible to infer the cause of the death, post-mortem treatments, or preservation conditions by observing bone surface modifications (e.g., carnivore tooth marks, insect damage, anthropic cutmarks or percussion marks, water abrasion, disarticulation).

By consolidating all the information at different analytical scales, it is possible to propose or exclude different accumulation scenarios for archaeological or palaeontological bone assemblages.

Taphonomy in Lovecraft's Early Tales

It appears that Lovecraft used the scientific knowledge of his time to improve the immersion experience of the reader. Indeed, it has long been established that Lovecraft used scientific knowledge as a narrative tool for his weird tales (Beherec; Joshi; Gorusuk). As noted by Gorusuk, the "weird science" category of science fiction demarcates a pronounced attachment to the archaeology and palaeontology developing through American readers' interest for the science of the past, as highlighted by important discoveries of the time publicized by the press. This is particularly clear in Lovecraft's case. For an exhaustive review of Lovecraft's use of science, the reader should refer to Gorusuk's recent work.

Concerning taphonomy, the first tales of Lovecraft are not convincing. In the short story "The Beast in the Cave" (1905), a creature is wounded by the narrator. He does not describe the injury or bone modification induced by the gunshot. The deaths of ancestors are enumerated in "The Alchemist" (1908), but no detailed description of wounds or injuries is given. The narrator provides physical details of the body of Charles Le Sorcier but not in relation to a taphonomic observation.

"The Tomb" (1917) contains the first recorded description of what we can call a taphonomic process: "Several faces I recognised; though I should have known them better has they been shrivelled or eaten away by death and decomposition" (CF

1.49). The description is not detailed, and it is surpassed by a powerful oneiric scene of the narrator's delusional episode. This is not comparable to what Lovecraft will develop in later texts, in which taphonomy is more deep-rooted in reality from a scientific point of view.

"Dagon" as a Turning Point

The first use of taphonomic description as a horrific element in Lovecraft's work can be found in the short story "Dagon," written in 1917 and published in *Weird Tales* in October 1923. After a typical Lovecraftian opening, in which the narrator explains that writing this text will be the last thing he will do before killing himself, he describes how his merchant ship has been attacked by sea-raiders. He escapes his captors and drifts in a small boat, alone. After several days, he wakes up in a "slimy expanse of hellish black mire": "The region was putrid with the carcasses of decaying fish, and of other less describable things which I saw protruding from the nasty mud of the unending plain" (CF 1.53). This is the first detailed description of the decomposition processes of an assemblage of organic remains used for horrific purposes. Just afterward, the narrator uses a taphonomic reasoning by this sentence: "Nor were there any sea-fowl to prey upon the dead things" (CF 1.54). This observation answers to an underlying question: what is the origin of the assemblage of fish carcasses? He explains the accumulation of the assemblage by eliminating seafowls as the taphonomic agent, which seems to be the most reasonable explanation (i.e., parsimonious hypothesis). The fact that the expected accumulating agent is absent in the surrounding region, thus making the origin of this abnormal accumulation unexplained, creates a feeling of discomfort and horror in the reader.

Finally, the narrator describes a scene of a creature killing a whale visible on the monolith. This creature is interpreted by the narrator as a god of a prehistoric human tribe, older than the Piltdown man[1] or the Neanderthal. In this story, there is not yet

---

1. The Piltdown man is a world-famous archaeological hoax. It was a pseudo-

a link between an ancient prehistoric past and the taphonomic observations. However, these are the first steps. Thus, "Dagon" can reasonably represent the first occurrence of the use of the science of taphonomy as a horrific element by Lovecraft, associated with archaeological concepts and knowledges.

After the presentiment of "Dagon", there is just one brief mention in "The Transition of Juan Romero" (1919) about the death of Juan Romero himself: "No direct cause was evident, and an autopsy failed to shew any reason why Romero should not be living" (CF 1.103). This last sentence is closer to what we can read in Edgar Allan Poe's texts and not as characteristic as what we will see in Lovecraft's later work.

Subsequently, there is a notable absence of taphonomic observations in Lovecraft's tales. I have not found any reference in "Beyond the Wall of Sleep" (1919), "The Temple" (1920), or "Nyarlathotep" (1920). There is what we can define as a forensic reasoning in "From Beyond" (1920), when at the end of the story the police arrest the narrator because of the revolver in his hand, next to Tillinghast's dead body, but they release him after they identify apoplexy as the cause of death. However, this is not what we can call a taphonomic approach, even less in an archaeological or paleontological context. Despite the presence of mummified creatures from an ancient past in "The Nameless City" (1921), there is no true description of the decomposition process or a taphonomic approach of the accumulation. Even if we can easily find all the ingredients for the use of taphonomy in an archaeological context for a horrific purpose, no link or description can be found. This absence is also true for "The Music of Erich Zann" (1921) and "Azathoth" (1922).

---

fossil composed by a medieval human skull associated with an orangutan mandible in order to create a chimera of anatomical characters. It was used as a proof of the European human origins at a time when this unfounded statement was questioned by some archaeologists describing earlier hominid species around the world such as *Pithecanthropus* (i.e., *Homo erectus*) in Asia by Eugène Dubois, or *Australopithecus africanus* in Africa by Raymond A. Dart.

Refining the Taphonomic Observations

Taphonomic observations for a horrific purpose re-emerge in
"The Hound," written in 1922 and published in 1924 in *Weird
Tales*. The narrator describes the occult museum he creates with
his friend St. John. In this place of horrors, he notes: "Niches
here and there contained skulls of all shapes, and heads preserved in various stages of dissolution" (CF 1.341). He makes a
direct reference to the process of decomposition. Moreover, it
seems that he identifies several "stages of dissolution," which is a
methodological approach used in the taphonomic field today.

But the real taphonomic approach appears later in the tale,
when the narrator and St. John travel to Holland to unearth the
corpse of an ancient ghoul. They arrive in the cemetery and the
narrator describes the terrible ambience of the place, particularly
the barking they hear. Upon finding the grave, they dig into the
ground: "Then we struck a substance harder than the damp
mould, and beheld a rotting oblong box crusted with mineral
deposits from the long undisturbed ground" (CF 1.342). This is
a remarkable description from an archaeological point a view.
The narrator focuses his attention on the texture of the sedi-
ment and the preservation of the artefact (i.e., mineral coating
on the coffin). He defines the deposit as "undisturbed," an accurate archaeological term. Indeed, it is primordial to define the
disturbance of an archaeological deposit and it is an important
step of a taphonomic study. The notion is still used in scientific
papers, more commonly described as "in situ" or "ex situ."

Upon the opening of the coffin, the protagonists see the body
of the ghoul: "The skeleton, though crushed in places by the
jaws of the thing that had killed it, held together with surprising
firmness, and we gloated over the clean white skull and its long,
firm teeth and its eyeless sockets that once had glowed with a
charnel fever like our own" (CF 1.342–43). The narrator therefore considers it possible to identify the taphonomic agent, ac-
cumulator, and modifier from the study of the marks observed
on the surface of the bones—i.e., at the specimen scale. These
are the beginnings of the conceptualization of the taphonomic
method, still used today to identify the agent at the origin of the

accumulation of bone assemblages in paleontological or archaeological contexts.

Despite a real potential of the episodic story "Herbert West—Reanimator" (1922) for applying the taphonomic concept in the narration, there is no proof of such use. There are many references to the state of preservation of bodies West used for his experiments, but not much about cause of death, taphonomic processes, and modifications. This is understandable, since the horror emerges from the reanimation and experiment process as West employed. The story, in contrast to its successor, is not based on the discovery of the unknown origin of dead bodies.

Indeed, "The Lurking Fear" (1922) is a story of a reporter who decides to investigate Tempest Mountain, in the Catskills, where the locals have reported numerous attacks. A month after the reporter's arrival, a great storm destroys several houses and he decides to investigate the place of destruction. He observes the presence of much human debris and tries to explain the cause of the multiple deaths rationally by observing the wounds, the modifications of the bodies, and the surroundings. The obvious absence of rational explanation is the basis of the reader's feeling of horror. This method of narration is also found later in the story, when the narrator and the reporter Arthur Munroe are trapped in another storm. The latter is found dead, "and on what remained of his chewed and gouged head there was no longer a face" (CF 1.361). The text is characterized by several instances of scientific reasoning and investigation, sometimes referring to taphonomic concepts. After the storm, the protagonists first search for bodies in caves and dens, both commonly known among archaeologists as being "bone or fossil traps." Later, they find a skull crushed by savage blows. Despite the squatters' statement of the presence of only one skull, the narrator identifies several bony fragments belonging to a second human skull. This is truly a taphonomic study and reasoning.

In "The Unnamable" (1923), little is said about taphonomy. Nevertheless, we can still mention what the narrator found in his ancestor's diary, referring to the identification of anthropoid paws and ape-like claws marks. This observation is later linked with a skull bearing "four-inch horns" (CF 1.403).

An impressive taphonomic modification description is made in "The Rats in the Walls" (1923), where the narrator mentions that "all the bones were gnawed, mostly by rats, but somewhat by others of the half-human drove" (CF 1.393). This sentence comes just after the mention of the Piltdown man, as was the case in "Dagon." It is important to say that rodents are today recognized as significant taphonomic agents of archaeological assemblages (Brain). For example, many Plio-Pleistocene fossils coming from South African caves bear porcupine or even small rodent tooth marks. We can also mention that Gapert and Tsokos quote this specific scene of "The Rats in the Walls" in a scientific paper. It is a taphonomic study of rodent gnaw marks through computed tomography, published in the journal *Forensic Science, Medicine and Pathology*.

There is a notable absence of taphonomic concepts in later texts. I cannot find any reference to taphonomy in "The Outsider" (1921), "The Festival" (1923), "The Shunned House" (1924), "Pickman's Model" (1926), "History of the 'Necronomicon'" (1927), "The Colour out of Space" (1927), *The Case of Charles Dexter Ward* (1927), "The Dunwich Horror" (1928), or "The Whisperer in Darkness" (1930).

However, we can mention the application of forensic taphonomy in "The Horror at Red Hook" (1925): "They found him unconscious by the edge of a night-black pool, with a grotesquely horrible jumble of decay and bone, identifiable through dental work as the body of Suydam, a few feet away" (CF 1.502). It is also the case in "The Call of Cthulhu" (1926): "On April 12th the derelict was sighted; and though apparently deserted, was found upon boarding to contain one survivor in a half-delirious condition and one man who had evidently been dead for more than a week" (CF 2.45). And later:

> Locally, interest was intensified by the obscurity of the cause of death. The professor had been stricken whilst returning from the Newport boat; falling suddenly, as witnesses said, after having been jostled by a nautical-looking negro who had come from one of the queer dark courts on the precipitous hillside which formed

a short cut from the waterfront to the deceased's home in Williams Street. Physicians were unable to find any visible disorder, but concluded after perplexed debate that some obscure lesion of the heart, induced by the brisk ascent of so steep a hill by so elderly a man, was responsible for the end. (CF 2.22)

However, this use of pre-taphonomic concept is far away from what we can find in later texts.

The Taphonomy of Madness

I have shown that Lovecraft gradually inserted pre-taphonomic concepts in his tales beginning in 1917 with "Dagon," and the concept was developed beginning in 1922 with "The Hound" and "The Lurking Fear." The culmination of this presentiment was reached in 1931 with the writing of *At the Mountain of Madness*. In the novel, there is an obvious use of scientific knowledge (Joshi; Gorusuk), especially of geology and palaeontology. For example, when the scientific team approaches the continent, the narrator makes a detailed description of the geology, with special reference to the geological stages, which are still partially used today. Furthermore, taphonomic descriptions are no longer secondary but at the center of the horrific narration in the first part of the text.

The geologist William Dyer, professor at Miskatonic University in Arkham, details the expedition to Antarctica in which he was involved with a complete scientific team. After they discover unknown geological specimens, Professor Lake, from the biology department of the university, begins to drill and explore a new part of the continent. Lake's team discovers an important mountain chain in which they identify strange geological formations and cave entrances. They start to drill into the formation and discover the first fossil remains of ancient life-forms:

> Later. Examining certain skeletal fragments of large land and marine saurians and primitive mammals, find singular local wounds or injuries to bony structure not attributable to any known predatory or carnivorous animal of any period. Of two sorts—straight, penetrant bores, and apparently hacking inci-

sions. One or two cases of cleanly severed bone. Not many specimens affected. Am sending to camp for electric torches. Will
extend search area underground by hacking away stalactites.
(CF 3.36)

Here we witness the first taphonomic report of the text. As a real actual taphonomist, Professor Lake first identifies the skeletal
fragments he finds. He observes the preservation of their cortical
surface and describes "singular local wounds or injuries." This is
the description of the taphonomic bone surface modifications.
Afterward, he raises his initial interpretations, "not attributable
to any known predatory or carnivorous animal of any period."
He not only describes the injuries and the bone breakage patterns but also quantifies them. A taphonomic analysis is used to
create horrific atmosphere and to serve the narration as a "set
up/pay off." We have the first real link between all the elements
cited before: context of an ancient past, scientific knowledge
and methodology, taphonomic concepts, and detailed descriptions and interpretations of the probable terrible origin. This is
the most iconic scene from a taphonomic point of view, but it is
not the only one. Later in the story, the narrator William Dyer
goes to Lake's sub-camp and finds the team and the dogs all
dead. He states: "The crowning abnormality, of course, was the
condition of the bodies—men and dogs alike. They had all been
in some terrible kind of conflict, and were torn and mangled in
fiendish and altogether inexplicable ways. Death, so far as we
could judge, had in each case come from strangulation or lacera-
tion" (CF 3.61). This is quite different from the preceding quotation because this is not an archaeological or palaeontological
case but a forensic one, like a murder scene. However, taphonomic observations are still part of the story. Based on these observations, Dyer interprets the facts and concludes that most of
the tissues in the bodies were cut out and removed by a careful
butcher. It seems that there was no clue, despite the presence of
fossil prints described earlier by Lake.

The observation of the scene permits us to link the origin of
the accumulation to the fossil themselves, through the identification of the prints. I must digress here to serve my demonstration.

One of the most important contributions of taphonomy in archaeology was the characterization of early hominid subsistence behaviors through the study of prehistoric butchery marks. Indeed, in the late 1970s it was shown that the analysis of anthropic bone surface modifications completed by actualistic and experimental data provide information on the carcass foraging strategies. In other words, it is possible to know if the prey was hunted or scavenged and how it was exploited and used (e.g., skinning, dismembering, defleshing, bone marrow extraction). Therefore, it is quite impressive to read the premise of a butchery hypothesis through bone surface modification observations in 1931.

Even if this observation were made in a more forensic context, more observations follow. Dyer and Danforth discover an ancient unknown city in the mountains. By studying the bas-reliefs of the city, they begin to reconstruct the story and life of the Old Ones who lived here: "They hunted game and raised meat herds—slaughtering with sharp weapons whose odd marks on certain fossil bones our expedition had noted" (CF 3.98). This is the observation that brings up all the pieces of the study together. The taphonomic analysis conducted by Lake, and then by Dyer, allow for the identification of the origin of the bone surface modifications and the taphonomic agent that accumulated the fossil assemblage. Through the text of *At the Mountain of Madness*, we face the process of a taphonomic study, before the appearance of the term in the scientific community, and before the methodological and analytical process was constructed and accepted.

From a taphonomic point of view, there are few texts comparable to what we can find in *At the Mountain of Madness*. I was not able to find any pre-taphonomic elements in "The Shadow over Innsmouth" (1931) or "The Shadow out of Time" (1934–35), but some appear in three later stories. In "The Dreams in the Witch House" (1932), after the death of the later tenants in a house, the workmen and then the police find strange things among the rubbish of the ceiling:

> There were bones—badly crushed and splintered, but clearly recognisable as human—whose manifestly modern date con-

flicted puzzlingly with the remote period at which their only possible lurking-place, the low, slant-floored loft overhead, had supposedly been sealed from all human access. The coroner's physician decided that some belonged to a small child, while certain others—found mixed with shreds of rotten brownish cloth—belonged to a rather undersized, bent female of advanced years. Careful sifting of debris also disclosed many tiny bones of rats caught in the collapse, as well as older rat-bones gnawed by small fangs in a fashion now and then highly productive of controversy and reflection. (CF 3.273–74)

Once again, we face a clear taphonomic analysis, even if it is applied to a forensic case and not to an archaeological assemblage. This assertion is also true for the "The Thing on the Doorstep" (1933), in which the narrator describes the discovery of a crushed skull, positively identified as Asenath Waite's, based on dental work. The mention of "dental work" (CF 3.357) as a method for identifying a skull is a reference to an actual bioanthropological and taphonomic methodology.

In "The Haunter of the Dark" (1935), Robert Blake notes a peculiar state of bones, some of them scattered or dissolved at the ends. The latter observation is particularly interesting because today, in the study of archaeological bone assemblages, the absence of bone ends, in the case of long bones (e.g., femur, humerus, tibia, radio-ulna), is characteristic of the hyaena's bone-feeding activity. Blake then mentions the yellow color of the bones, interpreting this as charring. Once again, bone color stages are also used today in archaeology to identify calcination or bone used as fuel for fire in home places.

After *At the Mountain of Madness*, taphonomy was still present in Lovecraft's horror stories, even if not applied to archaeological or palaeontological contexts.

Preliminary Conclusions

As S. T. Joshi observes, Lovecraft is, above all else, a scientific rationalist. This statement is supported by development and use of pre-taphonomic elements in his stories. Indeed, instead of describing an emotional, perhaps poetical, observation of a corpse by the narrator, Lovecraft has developed a rational way to create horror, deep-rooted in reality—so much so that actual scientists use this base of knowledge today to describe a fossil assemblage.

The use of pre-taphonomic concepts could be regarded as an epiphenomenon in the work of Lovecraft, especially because the term and the discipline were not then established. However, I have shown that the use of taphonomy is one of the more constant characteristics of Lovecraftian horror from his early works onward. Even more, there is an evolution and a development of the use of taphonomy in his texts, from its almost total absence ("The Beast in the Cave," "The Alchemist," "The Tomb") to its apogee (*At the Mountains of Madness*), passing through its development ("Dagon"). This evolution is similar to the actual scientific development of taphonomy as a scientific field. Indeed, in the firsts works of Weigelt and Efremov, taphonomy was a conceptual framework applied at a large-scale area such as an entire archaeological site. Over time, taphonomy was applied step by step to more restricted scales of study such as an individual animal carcass (see Behrensmeyer) or even an isolated fossil (see Hanon et al.). From a large-scale observation in "Dagon," Lovecraft finally used a fine observation of individual bone remains or organic corpses in "The Hound" and *At the Mountains of Madness*. Even if these similarities remain speculative for now, our study raises questions about Lovecraft's interest for this uncommon field of study.

Beyond taphonomy, archaeology is more than present in Lovecraft's texts, and it is even one of the main recurring themes that he used extensively in many of his texts (e.g., *At the Mountains of Madness*, *The Case of Charles Dexter Ward*, "The Hound," "Facts concerning the Late Arthur Jermyn and His Family," "The Nameless City," "The Shadow out of Time"). It is therefore not surprising that beyond the common introduction of a scientific dimension in their works, H. P. Lovecraft and I. Efremov—the first an enlightened amateur, the second a recognized palaeontologist—have had the same interest in the transition of individuals from the biosphere to the lithosphere as well as the modifications that this process could leave on the bone remains.

It is difficult to identify the origin of Lovecraft's inspirations in taphonomy for several reasons. (1) The use of taphonomy in his texts, although regular, is far from being developed to the point of citing scientific sources, as is the case for the theory of plate tectonics, for example. (2) Taphonomy was not yet a discipline when Lovecraft published his texts. The sources that may be behind his ideas are too scattered to be identified with certainty. (3) We cannot be sure of all Lovecraft's readings. (4) It is not inconceivable that these are original ideas, nourished by a rich imagination, with inspirations far too complex to be able to identify them.

We can, however, make some assumptions. We know that Lovecraft read the stories of Arthur Conan Doyle and Edgar Allan Poe, and according to Houck, "Holmes's methods presaged many actual techniques for linking physical evidence to the perpetrator of a crime." Of course, the author refers to forensic techniques, but this assertion is also true for taphonomy, in which the physical evidences are numerous (e.g., bone surface modifications), the perpetrator is the mode of accumulation (e.g., natural death-trap, predators), and the crime is the accumulation itself. Concerning Edgar Allan Poe's work, we observe the presence of a detailed description of decomposition of a corpse in *The Narrative of Arthur Gordon Pym*:

> Rogers had died about eleven in the forenoon, in violent convulsions; and the corpse presented in a few minutes after death one of the most horrid and loathsome spectacles I ever remember to have seen. The stomach was swollen immensely, like that of a man who has been drowned and lain under water for many weeks. The hands were in the same condition, while the face was shrunken, shrivelled, and of a chalky whiteness, except where relieved by two or three glaring red splotches, like those occasioned by the erysipelas: one of these splotches extended diagonally across the face, completely covering up an eye as if with a band of red velvet.

This description is close to what we can expect, as a non-expert of the scientific field, in an autopsy report. The observations lead to interpretations. This approach is used, as we have seen, in Lovecraft's tales. In light of these preliminary elements, it is not so speculative to argue that Lovecraft found inspiration in Poe's and Doyle's stories for using factual observations, deep-rooted in reality, to identify—in Lovecraft's case—an unnatural origin. This last characteristic is dear to Lovecraft and is abundantly used in order to create a sense of horror.

It seems indeed that Lovecraft used Doyle's maxim: "Once you eliminate the impossible, whatever remains, no matter how improbable, must be the truth." In that case, the improbable should be replace by the horrifying. Lovecraft once wrote:

> I should describe mine own nature as tripartite, my interests consisting of three parallel and dissociated groups–(a) Love of the strange and the fantastic. (b) Love of the abstract truth and of scientific logick. (c) Love of the ancient and the permanent. Sundry combinations of these strains will probably account for all my odd tastes and eccentricities. (*Letters to Rheinhart Kleiner and Others* 158)

Indeed, it appears that his used of taphonomy as a narrative element is at the convergence of this tripartite nature.

This analysis corroborates the assumption that Lovecraft used tangible descriptions and factual scientific reasoning as bases for his fiction, probably originating from assiduous reading of the works of Edgar Allan Poe, Sir Arthur Conan Doyle, and others. Without knowing it, he applied the taphonomic approach as a facet of scientific logic for revealing the horrifying nature of old secrets.

Acknowledgments

This paper is dedicated to those with whom I had the chance to explore the incredible universe of H. P. Lovecraft: Jérémie Bachellerie, Cécile Guitard, Elisabeth Tribouillard, Chloé Fraillon, Vincent Kerhervé, Corentin Hanon, Pierre Toker, Eléna Tejedor, Marine Le Gall, Louise Gonzalez, Quentin Calonge, and Alexandre Depardieu.

Works Cited

Beherec, Marc. "Lovecraft and the Archaeology of 'Roman' Arizona." *Lovecraft Annual* No. 2 (2008): 192–202.

Brain, C. K. *The Hunters or the Hunted? An Introduction to African Cave Taphonomy*. Chicago: University of Chicago Press, 1981.

Buckland, W. *Reliquiae Diluvianae; or, Observations on the Organic Remains Contained in Caves, Fissures, and Diluvial Gravel, and on Other Geological Phenomena, Attesting the Action of an Universal Deluge*. London: John Murray, 1823.

Cadée, G. C. "The History of Taphonomy." In S. K. Donovan, ed. *The Processes of Fossilization*. New York: Columbia University Press, 1991. 3–21.

Cuvier, G. *Recherches sur les ossements fossiles de quadrupèdes*. Paris: Deterville, 1812.

Denys, C., and M. Patou-Mathis. *Manuel de taphonomie*. Paris: Muséum National d'Histoire Naturelle, 2014.

Dodson, P. "Vertebrate Burials." *Paleobiology* 6 (1980): 6–8.

D'Orbigny, A. *Cours élémentaire de paléontologie et de géologie stratigraphiques*. Paris: Victor Masson, 1849.

Efremov, I. A. "Taphonomy: A New Branch of Paleontology." *Pan-American Geologist* 74 (1940): 81–93.

Gapert, R., and M. Tsokos. "Anthropological Analysis of Extensive Rodent Gnaw Marks on a Human Skull Using Post-Mortem Multislice Computed Tomography (pmMSCT)." *Forensic Science, Medicine and Pathology* 9 (2013): 441–45.

Gorusuk, E. *Science et mythologie dans les œuvres d'Howard Philips Lovecraft*. Grenoble: Mémoire de Master 2 recherche, Université Stendhal, 2013.

Hanon, R., S. Péan, and S. Prat. "Reassessment of Anthropic Modifications on the Early Pleistocene Hominin Specimen Stw53 (Sterkfontein, South Africa)." *BMSAP* 30 (2018): 49–58.

Houck, M. M. "CSI: Reality." *Scientific American* 295 (2006): 84–89.

Joshi, S. T. "Time, Space, and Natural Law." *Lovecraft Annual* No. 4 (2010): 171–201.

Koch, C. P. *Taphonomy: A Bibliographic Guide to the Literature*. Orono: University of Maine, Center for the Study of the First Americans, 1989.

Lovecraft, H. P. *Letters to Rheinhart Kleiner and Others*. Ed. S. T. Joshi and David E. Schultz. New York: Hippocampus Press, 2020.

Lyman, R. L. *Vertebrate Taphonomy*. Cambridge: Cambridge University Press, 1994.

———. "What Taphonomy Is, What It Isn't, and Why Taphonomists Should Care about the Difference." *Journal of Taphonomy* 8 (2010): 1–16.

Olson, E. C. "Taphonomy: Its History and Role in Community Evolution." In K. Behrensmeyer and A. P. Hill, ed. *Fossils in the Making: Vertebrate Taphonomy and Paleoecology*. Chicago: University of Chicago Press, 1980. 5–19.

Rattenbury, A. E. "Forensic Taphonomy." In T. Komang Ralebitso-Senio, ed. *Forensic Ecogenomics: The Application of Microbial Ecology Analyses in Forensic Contexts*. London: Elsevier, 2018. 37–60.

Weigelt, J. *Rezente Wirbeltierleichen und ihre Paläobiologische Bedeutung*. Leipzig: Max Weg, 1927.

The Promise of Cosmic Revelations: How the Landscape of Vermont Transforms "The Whisperer in Darkness"

Dylan Henderson

While writing "The Whisperer in Darkness" in 1930, H. P. Lovecraft did something curious: he inserted several passages from his travelogue "Vermont—A First Impression," which he had written in 1927, thereby transforming his delightful trip to Vermont into Wilmarth's nightmarish journey into the "shunned hills" (CF 2.480) of the Green Mountain State. Even for Lovecraft, whose tales so artfully stitch fact and fiction together, this insertion seems bold, for it all but dissolves the boundary between the author's life and work. Not surprisingly, scholars have rushed to comment on the added passages and the countryside they so lovingly describe (Burleson; Leiber; Schweitzer; Wheelock). And yet, though scholars have studied the origin of these poignant and detailed descriptions, they have paid less attention to their significance within the narrative, viewing them, it seems, as if they provide nothing more than local color.[1] As a result of this omission, crucial questions remain

---

1. Alan S. Wheelock, for instance, refers to HPL's description of Vermont as "a tour-de-force of the picturesque," though he concludes that "it is too much to suggest that the author's highly colorful exploitation of the Vermont landscape accounts" for the story's success (225, 227). Darrell Schweitzer, it seems, would agree, insisting that it "is not so much a story of New England as of outer space" (10). In his re-examination of the story, Fritz Leiber goes one step further. Noting that "the Vermont landscape is described in considerable detail at least four times," Leiber argues that the passages constitute an unwelcome intrusion, which slows down the pace (145).

unasked and unanswered. Why incorporate these lengthy and seemingly gratuitous descriptions into the story? How does their inclusion change it or affect how readers interpret it? And what would the story be like without them?

Lovecraft's description of Vermont, I would argue, is nothing less than the emotional climax of "The Whisperer in Darkness." It is the turning point for both Wilmarth and the reader, the key to the author's subtle yet forceful symbolism, and the answer to the story's most difficult question: why does Wilmarth reject the Outer Ones' offer of transcendence, their proposal, as Wilmarth himself calls it, "to shake off the maddening and wearying limitations of time and space and natural law" (CF 2.505)?

The story, as is well known, begins when the narrator, Albert N. Wilmarth, receives a letter from Henry Wentworth Akeley. A resident of Vermont, Akeley urges the professor of folklore to stop publicly discussing a controversial theory about the nature and origins of the misshapen bodies recently spotted floating in the West River. Though skeptical of Akeley's assertion that these corpses are the bodies of extraterrestrials, Wilmarth agrees, and the two begin to correspond. Akeley's letters and Wilmarth's reactions to them take up most of chapters 2 to 5. Lovecraft so skillfully infuses these early chapters with tension that readers may overlook just how counterintuitive his approach is. Indeed, from a writer's perspective, it defies convention, if not common sense:

> Writing instructors always pound the rule of *show, don't tell* into their students. A conventional story, ideally, contains *no* exposition, and is entirely made up of scenes, action, and dialogue. The purpose of such narration is to take the reader into the story, to make him vicariously experience the events therein. But in "The Whisperer in Darkness" we experience the story only at a distant remove, sharing not Akeley's nightmarish siege in the remote farmhouse as the forces from Outside descend upon him, but the narrator Wilmarth's suspense and uncertainty as, indeed, the facts come together and letters from Akeley arrive by post—or fail to. (Schweitzer 9)

Darrell Schweitzer, in his perceptive analysis of the story, recognizes how innovative Lovecraft's approach is, but he overlooks how it depicts Wilmarth. Despite being the narrator and the protagonist of the story, he lives, as far as readers can tell, in a surprisingly empty world. Of course, Wilmarth mentions that he is an "instructor of literature at Miskatonic University in Arkham, Massachusetts, and an enthusiastic amateur student of New England folklore" (CF 2.468), but this one statement provides readers almost everything they know about him. Readers never actually see the university where he works, nor do they ever see the city in which he lives. When the story begins, Wilmarth does mention several friends, who seek his opinion on folklore, but they seem oddly insubstantial, lacking names as well as distinct personalities. Wilmarth never describes them (though he mentions that one has a mother in Hardwick), nor does he mention any family or provide any details about his home, his career, or his life. Even for a Lovecraft character, Wilmarth is a blank; he is an eyeball, a consciousness, one might say, equipped with a "full sensory and articulate life—albeit a bodiless and mechanical one" (CF 2.522). He lives not in Arkham (an imaginary city Lovecraft would develop in "The Dreams in the Witch House," but which he does not describe here) but in a void, his detachment from the world contrasting sharply with Akeley's immersion in it.

Indeed, the two men are doubles: when Akeley is not Wilmarth's antithesis, he is his doppelgänger. Despite their differences in station, both men share the same passion for "pure scholarship," Akeley having been "a notable student of mathematics, astronomy, biology, anthropology, and folklore at the University of Vermont" (CF 2.474). One might even argue that Wilmarth's description of Akeley, whom he calls a "man of character, education, and intelligence, albeit a recluse with very little worldly sophistication," applies just as well to Wilmarth, who, much later in the text, demonstrates his own lack of "worldly sophistication" (CF 2.474) when he stumbles into the trap the Outer Ones have set for him. Granted, Wilmarth is not exactly a "recluse," but he does seem very alone in the world. The "friends" mentioned above appear briefly in the text and do nothing but argue with

Wilmarth, who views them with amusement mixed with disdain:

> The more I laughed at such theories, the more these stubborn
> friends asseverated them; adding that even without the heritage
> of legend the recent reports were too clear, consistent, detailed,
> and sanely prosaic in manner of telling, to be completely ig-
> nored. Two or three fanatical extremists went so far as to hint
> at possible meanings in the ancient Indian tales which gave the
> hidden beings a non-terrestrial origin. (CF 2.473)

Like Akeley, whose story is believed only by "the ignorant people" (CF 2.499), Wilmarth seems surrounded by inferiors, "stub-
born friends," "opponents," and "fanatical extremists," whose
opinions he must correct or silence (CF 2.473). Being Wilmarth's true equal, Akeley has nothing in common with such
people. In his first letter to Wilmarth, he even claims that "if I
knew as little of the matter as they, I would not feel justified in
believing as they do. I would be wholly on your side" (CF
2.476). Like twins separated at birth, the two share a connection, and as they work together to decipher the black stone
Akeley has discovered, the Vermonter quickly becomes the col-
league that Wilmarth never had. Not surprisingly, as soon as
Akeley appears in the text, Wilmarth's "friends" disappear.

Because of this connection, Akeley knows, despite never
having met Wilmarth, that the academic will accept the not insubstantial risks their joint investigation will incur. In one of the
most important passages in the story, Akeley, who is writing to
Wilmarth for the first time, alerts him to the danger involved
and promises that the knowledge they might gain is well worth
it: "I don't wish to put you in any peril, and suppose I ought to
warn you that possession of the stone and the record won't be
very safe; but I think you will find any risks worth running for
the sake of knowledge" (CF 2.479). Wilmarth agrees. He accepts the devil's bargain that Akeley has offered him, exchang-
ing his safety, perhaps even his "life, soul, and sanity" (CF
2.506), for the promise of knowledge. In Lovecraft's world, it is
always the most sought-after treasure. One recalls the cultists
who worship the Haunter of the Dark not because it grants

them power or riches, but because it "tells them secrets in some way" (CF 3.464). At this point in the story, there is nothing, absolutely nothing, in Wilmarth's empty life that he values more.

In Akeley's second letter, which the reader never sees, he shares his knowledge with Wilmarth, telling him all he knows of the Outer Ones. These are extraterrestrials that, according to legend, resemble a "huge, light-red crab with many pairs of legs and with two great bat-like wings in the middle of the back" (CF 2.470). Though telepathic, they can mimic human speech, their droning voices "like a bee's that tried to be like the voices of men" (CF 2.472). And yet, despite their bizarre appearance and incredible origins, the Outer Ones may be the least alien of Lovecraft's many monstrosities. Unlike Great Cthulhu, whose titanic bulk defies the natural order, or some of the truly outré creatures Lovecraft created, such as the Old Ones of *At the Mountains of Madness* or the Great Race of "The Shadow out of Time," the Outer Ones seem far more animalistic—in part because they are compared to three everyday species: the crab, the bat, and the bee. The Outer Ones, moreover, are not godlike entities: despite their fearsome appearance, they seem wary of Akeley's big-game rifle and scared of his police dogs, which actually manage to kill one of them. Indeed, the animosity the dogs feel for the Outer Ones recalls not just the fear the dog has for the ghost or the spirit, a common trope in weird fiction, but the hatred the dog has for the rabbit or the squirrel. These crab-like creatures, moreover, have come to Earth not to usher in a "holocaust of ecstasy and freedom" ("The Call of Cthulhu" [CF 2.40]) or to open a gate between dimensions, but—according to legend—to mine a stone, the most primitive of building materials.

One might be tempted to laugh at Lovecraft's depiction of the Outer Ones, but there is a pattern here worth noting: Lovecraft uses every opportunity in chapters 1 to 5 to link the Outer Ones to the natural world, which he then in turn depicts as menacing. Unlike Wilmarth, who has lived his entire life in "the mechanised, urbanised coastal and southern areas" (CF 2.508) of New England, the Outer Ones live in caves deep in the forest. As far as we know, they possess no machines or vehicles of any kind. Aside from their claws, they have no weapons, and they even use their powerful wings—as opposed to rocket ships—to travel through space. Devoid, it seems, of possessions, they recall the nomadic and semi-nomadic tribes of the premodern world, specifically the American Indians, who understand them far better than the Puritans and the Scotch-Irish do. Even the ritual Akeley records, which praises "the Lord of the Woods" and Shub-Niggurath, *"the Black Goat of the Woods with a Thousand Young,"* suggests the ancient rites of pagan Europe, as does the "druid-like circle of standing stones on the summit of a wild hill," which Akeley photographs (CF 2.486–87, 481). Here again, Lovecraft juxtaposes the Outer Ones with the American Indians, who in "The Dunwich Horror" and later in "The Thing on the Doorstep" also erect "great rings of rough-hewn stone columns on the hill-tops" (CF 2.421). Indeed, in chapters 2 and 3, the inquisitive Akeley resembles nothing so much as a twentieth-century ethnographer, camera and phonograph in hand, trying to document the secret rites of supposedly primitive peoples.

While the Outer Ones seem to possess nothing that is not made of stone, their antitheses, Akeley and Wilmarth, have access to an array of state-of-the-art technologies, including rifles and poison gas, the twin symbols of the Great War. Akeley's very life depends upon modern infrastructure, those lines that connect his farmhouse to the industrial world: the mail, the railway, the telephone, all linkages the Outer Ones try to sever. As for Wilmarth, the urbanite, he seems to all but loathe the forested hills where the Outer Ones have made their home, referring to them as the "haunted hills," the "lonely green hills," the "shunned hills," the "wild, haunted hills" and "those silent and problematical hills" (CF 2.472, 475, 480, 484, 485). The connection between the Outer Ones and the hills where they live is so strong in Wilmarth's mind that, slipping into metonymy, he twice refers to Akeley's deteriorating situation as his "hill problem" (CF 2.492, 493), as if the hills of Vermont, rather than the monstrosities infesting them, were the real danger. Not surprisingly, Wilmarth, who lives in an imaginary city and teaches at an imaginary university, cannot understand why Akeley, who lives in Windham County near Townshend, Vermont, does not simply abandon his "almost morbidly cherished birthplace" (CF 2.494). He cannot understand his friend, who repeatedly insists that "it is not easy to give up the place you were born in, and where your family has lived for six generations" (CF 2.478), because Akeley has that which Wilmarth has never experienced: what Lovecraft would call, in a letter to Clark Ashton Smith written about six weeks after finishing "The Whisperer in Darkness," a "close correlation with the landscape & historic stream" to which he belongs (*Dawnward Spire* 263).

In chapter 5, a letter—purportedly from Akeley—tempts Wilmarth yet again with the promise of revelation. In it, Akeley, whose house has been under siege, informs Wilmarth that the threat is gone: he has made peace with the Outer Ones, whose only "wish of man," he now claims, "is peace and non-molestation and an increasing intellectual rapport" (CF 2.501). With this goal in mind, the Outer Ones, to whom "the totality of all cosmic entity is only an atom," have shared their secrets with Akeley and promised him that *"as much of this infinity as any human brain can hold is eventually to be opened up to me, as it has been to not more than fifty other men since the human race has existed"* (CF 2.503). Akeley is even planning a "trip *outside*," an experience that will require him to sacrifice his body, for only his brain, carried by the Outer Ones in a fluid-filled cylinder, can make the voyage through the cosmos (CF 2.502). One of the few men who has undertaken such a journey claims that he has "been on thirty-seven different celestial bodies—planets, dark stars, and less definable objects—including eight outside our galaxy and two outside the curved cosmos of space and time" (CF 2.525). As S. T. Joshi notes, "such a thing actually sounds rather appealing" (148). Who would not want to explore the outskirts of the known universe and the wilderness that lies beyond? Who would be so small-minded as to cling to this mortal shell when one could, in exchange for shedding it, learn the secrets of space and time, in the process "transcending everything which we have hitherto been accustomed to regard as human experience" (CF 2.502)? Surely, the writer of the letter is justified when he claims that "what I had thought morbid and shameful and ignominious is in reality awesome and mind-expanding and even *glorious*" (CF 2.501). As Joshi points out, such a voyage would certainly, it seems, have appealed to Lovecraft, who explains again and again in his letters that he does not value an "ordinary life," his strongest desire being to transcend the limitations of time, space, and natural law:

> The crucial thing is my lack of interest in ordinary life. No one ever wrote a story yet without some real emotional drive behind it—and I have not that drive except where violations of the natural order ... defiances and evasions of time, space, and cosmic law ... are concerned. [...] And the only conflict which has any deep emotional significance to me is that of *the principle of freedom or irregularity or adventurous opportunity against the eternal and maddening rigidity of cosmic law* ... especially the laws of *time*. Individuals and their fortunes within natural law move me very little. They are all momentary trifles bound from a common nothingness toward another common nothingness. (*Letters to E. Hoffmann Price* 122)

In a letter written to August Derleth two months after he had finished "The Whisperer in Darkness," Lovecraft is even more direct, claiming that "time, space, & natural law hold for me suggestions of intolerable bondage, & I can form no picture of emotional satisfaction which does not involve their defeat— especially the defeat of time, so that one may merge oneself with the whole historic stream & be wholly emancipated from the transient & the ephemeral" (*Essential Solitude* 288). After a brief moment of doubt, Wilmarth, who in the second chapter had accepted Akeley's claim that "you will find any risks worth running for the sake of knowledge," agrees. Despite the risks, he cannot resist such an adventure:

> My own zeal for the unknown flared up to meet his, and I felt myself touched by the contagion of the morbid barrier-breaking. To shake off the maddening and wearying limitations of time and space and natural law—to be linked with the vast *outside*— to come close to the nighted and abysmal secrets of the infinite

and the ultimate—surely such a thing was worth the risk of one's life, soul, and sanity! (CF 2.505–6)

Fritz Leiber, noting how easily Wilmarth is "hoodwinked into going to Vermont," considers him absurdly naïve, a fool whose credulity defies belief (144). But what, one might ask, does Wilmarth, the disembodied conscious of chapters 1 to 5, have to lose?

Wilmarth is ready, having "slept soundly and long" (CF 2.507) after making his decision, and yet, in the end, he does not go. Long before he discovers the ruse the Outer Ones have perpetrated or overhears their midnight colloquy, he changes his mind, noting on his arrival at Akeley's farmhouse that he "honestly dreaded the coming discussions which were to link me with such alien and forbidden worlds" (CF 2.513). Filled with apprehension, Wilmarth almost screams when he notices the familiar claw-prints in the soil, and when he meets Akeley, he greets his incredible revelations with disgust and horror. His "zeal for the unknown" has evaporated—along with his once ardent desire to be "linked with the vast *outside*." After his conversation with Akeley in the study, he wants only to leave: "One thing was certain—I would not spend another night here. My scientific zeal had vanished amidst fear and loathing, and I felt nothing now but a wish to escape from this net of morbidity and unnatural revelation" (CF 2.527–28). What has changed? What has happened, between chapters 5 and 7, to convince Wilmarth that such revelations are *not* "worth the risk of one's life, soul, and sanity"? What has happened, I would argue, is simply this: Wilmarth saw Vermont.

In chapter 6, Wilmarth, as a body that takes up space and moves through time, enters the story. He is no longer a disembodied voice, a consciousness reacting to stimuli; for the first time, he is a character in the fullest sense of the word, being not just the story's narrator but its protagonist. Previously stationary, he now begins to move through this new world, which is, quite fittingly, the real world. Leaving Arkham, Lovecraft's imaginary city behind, Wilmarth begins a "long westward run out of familiar regions into those I knew less thoroughly. Waltham—Concord—Ayer—Fitchburg—Gardner—Athol—" (CF 2.507). The void Wilmarth occupied in chapters 1 to 5 has been replaced with a world of vivid details and startling beauty, and as Wilmarth's train approaches Vermont, he understands, in a way he did not before, what has been missing from his life:

> I knew I was entering an altogether older-fashioned and more primitive New England than the mechanised, urbanised coastal and southern areas where all my life had been spent; an unspoiled, ancestral New England without the foreigners and factory-smoke, billboards and concrete roads, of the sections which modernity has touched. There would be odd survivals of that continuous native life whose deep roots make it the one authentic outgrowth of the landscape—the continuous native life which keeps alive strange ancient memories, and fertilises the soil for shadowy, marvellous, and seldom-mentioned beliefs.[2] (CF 2.508)

For the first time, we learn of Wilmarth's life, which has been spent in the overcrowded cities of southern New England—a region, he now realizes, blighted by modernity. Like Lovecraft, who so famously claimed that "Providence is part of me—I am Providence" (*Family Friends* 583), Wilmarth realizes that he is a part of *this* world, of this landscape, which has shaped and molded him and which "one remembers from boyhood," the very "roofs and steeples and chimneys and brick walls . . . touching deep viol-strings of ancestral emotion" (CF 2.509). He is experiencing, much as Lovecraft did when he saw Marblehead in 1922 or Vermont in 1927, a revelation, a sudden, overpowering awareness of his place in space and time, which modernity had taken from him. This is, as the sight of Marblehead was for Lovecraft, the "high tide" of his life (*Letters to James F. Morton* 222). Though he is not being carried through the cosmos by the Outer Ones, he has still found a way to transcend time and space, to escape, as Lovecraft so ardently wished to do, an age in which he does not belong and to return to the lost world of his youth:

---

2. The passage quoted above closely resembles the opening paragraph of "Vermont—A First Impression," in which HPL decries the "reservoirs, billboards, and concrete roads, power lines, garages, and flamboyant inns, squalid immigrant nests and grimy mill villages," which "have brought ugliness, tawdriness, and commonplaceness to the urban penumbra" (CE 4.13).

There was a strangely calming element of cosmic beauty in the hypnotic landscape through which we climbed and plunged fantastically. Time had lost itself in the labyrinths behind, and around us stretched only the flowering waves of faery and the recaptured loveliness of vanished centuries—the hoary groves, the untainted pastures edged with gay autumnal blossoms, and at vast intervals the small brown farmsteads nestling amidst huge trees beneath vertical precipices of fragrant brier and meadow-grass. Even the sunlight assumed a supernal glamour, as if some special atmosphere or exhalation mantled the whole region. I had seen nothing like it before save in the magic vistas that sometimes form the backgrounds of Italian primitives. Sodoma and Leonardo conceived such expanses, but only in the distance, and through the vaultings of Renaissance arcades.[3] (CF 2.512)

Just as Lovecraft would come to feel that "these waving grasses & towering elms & brook-threaded valleys & stone-wall'd farmsteads & white village steeples are ME, MYSELF, I, THE CONSCIOUS EGO" (*Letters to James F. Morton* 180), Wilmarth, who has spent his adult life among "billboards and concrete roads," objects to which he had no emotional or aesthetic connection, has found himself in the landscape of Vermont, the only portal still open to the past, to the world before the alienating and disorienting blight of modernity. He has, without ever leaving New England, discovered how to defeat time, how to "merge oneself with the whole historic stream & be wholly emancipated from the transient & the ephemeral." While seeking a link to the "vast outside," Wilmarth has stumbled upon its antithesis, the vast inside, and found that which "I had innately known or inherited, and for which I had always been vainly searching" (CF 2.512).

And then, having encountered Vermont, its "green and cryptical hills" (CF 2.508) so different from the "shunned hills" of his imagination, Wilmarth encounters the Outer Ones, who, like the landscape around them, have also undergone a change. Their transformation actually begins in chapter 5 when readers, for the first time, hear from the Outer Ones directly. Prior to

---

3. Here HPL is quoting almost verbatim from "Vermont—A First Impression."

this moment, their true nature has been hidden behind a series of interpretative layers. Readers encounter them through Akeley's letters and the phonograph he records, which are, in turn, either reconstructed or summarized by Wilmarth. Aside from a brief telegram quoted in chapter 4, their forged letter to Wilmarth (which is later supplemented by the False Akeley's monologue in the study) provides readers with their first clear look at the Outer Ones, at the Outer Ones as they really are or believe themselves to be; their connection to nature, so central to Akeley's depiction of them, is gone. According to this letter, which was composed on a typewriter, the invention Lovecraft hated, not all the Outer Ones can fly through space; some need the help of machines or surgery, which is a specialty of theirs. When they were fighting with Akeley's dogs, the Outer Ones had seemed like animals themselves, but they now seem almost oddly unnatural, the syntax and diction in their letter being unusually formal—far more so than Akeley's, as Wilmarth himself notices. After Wilmarth arrives at his friend's farmhouse, the False Akeley even alludes to Albert Einstein, the living symbol of the modern era. He also reveals that the Outer Ones, who, according to legend, mine only stone, have a surprising penchant for metal and machinery, their colony in the hills containing, presumably, smelters, mills, and factories. Indeed, the False Akeley's instructions to Wilmarth, regarding the operation of their machinery, reek of the industrial age:

> Here—take the three machines I point to and set them on the table. That tall one with the two glass lenses in front—then the box with the vacuum tubes and sounding-board—and now the one with the metal disc on top. Now for the cylinder with the label 'B-67' pasted on it. Just stand in that Windsor chair to reach the shelf. Heavy? Never mind! Be sure of the number—B-67. Don't bother that fresh, shiny cylinder joined to the two testing instruments—the one with my name on it. Set B-67 on the table near where you've put the machines—and see that the dial switch on all three machines is jammed over to the extreme left. (CF 2.523–24)

These are not, as the American Indians and the Druids are believed to be, the denizens of the forest, the inhabitants of an
"unspoiled, ancestral New England," nor, for that matter, are
they futuristic saviors. Their ugly, clumsy machinery, which
Lovecraft, unlike other science fiction writers, makes no attempt
to glamorize, connects them to what Lovecraft considers the
corroding agents of modernism, "the foreigners and factory-
smoke, billboards and concrete roads," and what he calls in
"Vermont—A First Impression" the "menacing tyranny of
mechanism and viceroyalty of engineering which are fast hurrying the present scene out of all linkage with its historic anteced-
ents and setting it adrift anchorless and all but traditionless in
alien oceans" (CE 4.13). One might go so far as to claim that
the Outer Ones are akin to the builders Akeley fears, the "pro-
moters and real estate men flooding Vermont with herds of
summer people to overrun the wild places and cover the hills
with cheap bungalows," being, in a sense, intergalactic real-
estate developers (CF 2.478). They are certainly not native to
New England, their true home being not in the woods or the
hills, but in the city. According to the False Akeley, "there are
mighty cities on Yuggoth—great tiers of terraced towers built of
black stone," through which flow "black rivers of pitch" (CF
2.518). Whereas Vermont, lit by a "supernal glamour," recalls
"the magic vistas that sometimes form the backgrounds of Italian
primitives," the cities of the Outer Ones remain forever dark, for
"the sun shines there no brighter than a star" (CF 2.518).

   Though brief, Lovecraft's description of Yuggoth plays a critical role in the story, for it links "The Whisperer in Darkness" to
his other stories and with New York, the prototype of the alien
and nightmarish cities he depicts. Like a leitmotif, similar descriptions of what Lovecraft calls "Cyclopean cities" (CF 2.26;
3.52, 250, 447) appear throughout his later works and are featured prominently in "The Call of Cthulhu," At the Mountains of
Madness, and "The Shadow out of Time." These "great Cyclopean cities of titan blocks and sky-flung monoliths, all dripping
with green ooze and sinister with latent horror," differ dramati-
cally from the cities of gold and marble that appear in his Dun-

sanian imitations ("The Call of Cthulhu" [*CF* 2.26]). Labeling the former "eldritch cities" and the latter "oneiric cities," Javier Martínez Jiménez contends that both draw inspiration from the urban landscapes of ancient Greece and Rome (29–30), though he misses the temporal connection between the two: not long after he left New York and returned to Providence, Lovecraft stopped writing about the "impossible dream-cities" he associated with Lord Dunsany and replaced them with Cyclopean cities, the eldritch city being, in essence, a dream-city seen in a nightmare (*Annotated Supernatural Horror in Literature* 90).

This abrupt change reflects Lovecraft's shifting view of New York, which he had described in 1922 as an oneiric city, its "Cyclopean outlines . . . a mystical sight in the gold sun of late afternoon; a dream-thing of faint grey," and which he would describe three years later as an eldritch city, its "Cyclopean modern towers and pinnacles" rising "blackly Babylonian under waning moons" (*Letters to Maurice W. Moe* 84; "He" [*CF* 1.506]). Though readers may associate Lovecraft's Cyclopean cities with R'lyeh from "The Call of Cthulhu," its prototype actually appears in "He," which Lovecraft wrote the year before. In that story, the narrator glimpses the future of New York, "a hellish black city of giant stone terraces with impious pyramids flung savagely to the moon, and devil-lights burning from unnumbered windows" (*CF* 1.514–15).

Noting the concept's origins, one could argue that, at some level, all Lovecraft's "hellish black cities" symbolize New York, a conclusion Michel Houellebecq supports, noting that "the idea of a grand, titanic city, in whose foundations crawl repugnant nightmare beings—sprang directly from his New York experience" (103). Going one step further, one could even argue that Lovecraft's alien gods, including the Old Ones, the Deep Ones, and the Great Race, who all hail from Cyclopean cities, represent not just a sense of cosmic alienation, an awareness of humanity's insignificance in time and space, but also a very modern sense of social atomization, a feeling of being "adrift anchorless and all but traditionless in alien oceans." By providing the Outer Ones with such a homeland, Lovecraft clarifies their true nature, depicting them not as denizens of the hills and forests, but as a race of urbanites, and connecting them to a city that, for him, represented the hateful, alienating forces of the modern era.

In chapter 7, when the False Akeley offers Wilmarth the opportunity to journey "through and beyond the space-time continuum" (CF 2.522), he is asking him to choose between these two poles, one symbolized by Vermont, the other by Yuggoth. It is a Faustian bargain. If Wilmarth accepts, he will fulfill Lovecraft's lifelong dream of transcending the "intolerable bondage" of time and space, but he will lose what, in the landscape of Vermont, he has just rediscovered. He will return to the void he occupied in chapters 1 to 5. Completing the work modernity has begun, he will become a machine, a thing of metal and wires, permanently divorced from the landscape that birthed and raised him. The awful victory of what Lovecraft called "the rule of steel and steam" will be complete (CE 2.14). One can understand why Lovecraft, who once described his nature as consisting of three discordant strains, would be so fascinated by this dilemma, for such a choice would have forced his strongest desires into conflict, compelling him to choose between his "Love of the abstract truth and of scientific logick" and his "Love of the ancient and the permanent" (*Letters to Rheinhart Kleiner and Others* 158). In chapter 5, Wilmarth chooses the former, but then he sees the "green and cryptical hills" of Vermont and, for the first time, realizes what such an exchange would cost. It is a price he cannot pay. That night, after hearing the details of Akeley's proposal, Wilmarth is haunted by a very Lovecraftian dream, a dream not of danger or torture or death but of "monstrous landscape-glimpses" (CF 2.531), of a world—to quote *The Dream-Quest of Unknown Kadath*—devoid "of linkage with anything firm in his feelings and memories" (CF 2.156). Like Lovecraft himself, who shortly after completing "The Whisperer in Darkness" would clarify his desires in a letter to Smith, Wilmarth has come to the realization that

> my wish for freedom is not so much a wish to put all terrestrial
> things behind me & plunge forever into abysses beyond light,

matter, & energy. That, indeed, would mean annihilation as a personality rather than liberation. My wish is perhaps best defined as a wish for infinite visioning & voyaging power, yet without loss of the familiar background which gives all things significance. (*Dawnward Spire* 263)

And so Wilmarth, who is offered the chance to "plunge forever into abysses beyond light, matter, & energy" if only he will give up "the familiar background which gives all things significance," chooses the hills of New England over the mysteries of time and space, as do Francis Wayland Thurston and Henry Armitage and Walter Gilman and Robert Blake, who all peer through a door that, in the end, they try desperately to close. In a sense, they retell the story of Lovecraft's great epiphany, his realization that, despite the intellectual stimulation New York provided, he would be "hopelessly soul-starved" if he remained in that Cyclopean city, for his happiness, perhaps even his sanity, depended upon "beauty & mellowness as expressed in quaint town vistas & in the scenery of ancient farming & woodland regions" (*Letters with Donald and Howard Wandrei* 75). It was, I would argue, the pivotal moment in his otherwise quiet and uneventful life.

Because of the passages Lovecraft borrows from "Vermont— A First Impression," readers understand what Wilmarth is being asked to sacrifice and why, like Lovecraft, he cannot do it. Brief though they may be and easy to overlook, these seemingly gratuitous descriptions of Vermont transform "The Whisperer in Darkness," clarifying its themes of nature versus modernity, of tradition versus knowledge, and providing an answer to the difficult questions it poses. In that sense, the story does not simply borrow from "Vermont—A First Impression," but boldly reimagines it, for both works address the same theme, a theme that haunts all Lovecraft's most characteristic fiction: the fear of losing New England.

And yet, like so many of Lovecraft's best and most characteristic stories, "The Whisperer in Darkness" is not a simple allegory of good and evil or of right and wrong. If the Outer Ones represent, at least in part, the threat modernity poses to "the familiar background which gives all things significance" and the painful and disorienting sense of alterity that follows in its train, they also represent its "promises of cosmic revelations" (CF 2.535), which Lovecraft himself, with his lifelong love of science, could just barely resist. As readers, we may sympathize with Wilmarth, but it is by no means clear that he makes the right choice. After all, one cannot flee from modernity as easily as one may escape from the slums of Brooklyn or the hills of Vermont, and in the end Wilmarth, who resolves "never to go back to Vermont," loses New England as well as the "vast *outside*" (CF 2.530). As readers, we can understand why Wilmarth rejects the Outer Ones and their "horrible cylinders and machines," but we also cannot help wondering if, perhaps, the False Akeley is right when he dismisses such fears as "man's eternal tendency to hate and fear and shrink from the *utterly different*" (CF 2.467, 501), nor can we help pondering what price we would pay for the chance to transcend the human experience and fly beyond the farthest star.

Works Cited

Burleson, Donald R. "Humour Beneath Horror: Some Sources for 'The Dunwich Horror' and "The Whisperer in Darkness.'" In Burleson's *Lovecraft: An American Allegory: Selected Essays on H. P. Lovecraft*. New York: Hippocampus Press, 2015. 181–94.

Houellebecq, Michel. *H. P. Lovecraft: Against the World, Against Life*. Tr. Dorna Khazeni. 2005. London: Gollancz, 2008.

Jiménez, Javier Martínez. "The Impact of the Eldritch City: Classical and Alien Urbanism in H. P. Lovecraft's Mythos." *Foundation* No. 131 (2018): 29–42.

Joshi, S. T. *A Subtler Magick: The Writings and Philosophy of H. P. Lovecraft*. Mercer Island, WA: Starmont House, 1996.

Lovecraft, H. P. *The Annotated Supernatural Horror in Literature*. Ed. S. T. Joshi. New York: Hippocampus Press, 2nd ed. 2012.

———. *Letters to E. Hoffmann Price and Richard F. Searight*. Ed. David E. Schultz and S. T. Joshi. New York: Hippocampus Press, 2021.

————. *Letters to Family and Family Friends*. Ed. S. T. Joshi and David E. Schultz. New York: Hippocampus Press, 2020.

————. *Letters to James F. Morton*. Ed. David E. Schultz and S. T. Joshi. New York: Hippocampus Press, 2011.

————. *Letters to Maurice W. Moe and Others*. Ed. David E. Schultz and S. T. Joshi. New York: Hippocampus Press, 2018.

————. *Letters to Rheinhart Kleiner and Others*. Ed. S. T. Joshi and David E. Schultz. New York: Hippocampus Press, 2020.

————. *Letters with Donald and Howard Wandrei and to Emil Petaja*. Ed. S. T. Joshi and David E. Schultz. New York: Hippocampus Press, 2019.

————, and August Derleth. *Essential Solitude: The Letters of H. P. Lovecraft and August Derleth*. Ed. David E. Schultz and S. T. Joshi. New York: Hippocampus Press, 2008. 2 vols.

————, and Clark Ashton Smith. *Dawnward Spire, Lonely Hill: The Letters of H. P. Lovecraft and Clark Ashton Smith*. Ed. David E. Schultz and S. T. Joshi, New York: Hippocampus Press, 2017.

Leiber, Fritz. "'The Whisperer' Re-examined." In *The Book of Fritz Leiber*. New York, DAW Books, 1974. 143–47.

Schweitzer, Darrell. "About 'The Whisperer in Darkness.'" *Lovecraft Studies* No. 32 (Spring 1995): 8–11.

Wheelock, Alan S. "Dark Mountain: H. P. Lovecraft and the 'Vermont Horror.'" *Vermont History* 45 (Fall 1977): 221–27.

H. P. Lovecraft's First Appearance in Print Reconsidered

Brendan Whyte

In last year's issue, Richard Bleiler identified H. P. Lovecraft's first appearance in print, predating by nine months the previously earliest known publication: a letter in the *Providence Sunday Journal* of 3 June 1906, which Lovecraft himself described a decade later as his "debut before the public" (*Letters to Rheinhart Kleiner* 73). The newly discovered letter was published on page 3 of the 6 September 1905 issue of an upstate New York paper, the *Amsterdam Evening Recorder and Daily Democrat,* in relation to a national weather forecasting contest with a $100 prize, instigated by a New York lawyer named Frederick R. Fast.

The entry in the Amsterdam paper reads (square bracketed text mine):

> H. P. Lovecraft, who says he forecasts for Rhode Island, writes to say that he thinks his predictions will reach over into New York and New England.
>
> "It may interest you to know," he writes, "that I have one mercurial thermometer by Spooner, six maximum and minimum thermomemeters [sic] by Casella, one psychometrical apparatus, one rain [gauge], one hair hygrometer and a wind vane." He spells the name of the thermometer a syllable longer than usual to indicate a superior length of column.

While Lovecraft's youthful interest in meteorology, subsequently abandoned for a longer-lasting interest in astronomy, is well known, Bleiler conjectures as to how and why Lovecraft wrote to this paper in particular, and suggests that he may have written to a number of papers, including those in Providence and Boston, but that only the Amsterdam paper chose to run the letter.

Bleiler then discusses the various instruments Lovecraft enumerated, and speculates upon what was meant by "psychometrical apparatus." He draws upon two definitions of psychometry: the first being the purely mechanical measurement of psychological phenomena, such as the minimum duration or separation in time for images to be visually perceived or differentiated; and the second being the spiritualist practice of obtaining information about an object's history or owners through close proximity or contact with it. He suggests that Lovecraft deliberately used the word "psychometrical" to sound scientific and up-to-the-minute, but also as a "youthful jest" to have a dig at what Bleiler claims was Lovecraft's view of weather forecasting: "little more than an exercise in superstition." Bleiler explains away Lovecraft's failure to retain a copy of the letter, or even remember it, as being the result of the "distress to his family" caused by the teen's "deliberate deception."

While grateful to Bleiler for discovering and researching this earliest Lovecraftian appearance in print, I believe he has misinterpreted some of the evidence before him, specifically in relation to the matter of to whom Lovecraft addressed his letter, and the nature of the psychometrical apparatus. Therefore I offer here what I believe are more likely explanations.

Why *the* Amsterdam Evening Recorder?

First, the question of why Lovecraft wrote to so seemingly obscure a paper as the *Amsterdam Evening Recorder*. Lovecraft's letter consists of paragraphs seven and eight of a nine-paragraph column whose first paragraph is telling (italics mine): "Six hundred prophets are at work on the weather, which accounts for its infinite variety. They are sending bulletins to Frederick R. Fast of New York, who has offered $100 for the most successful forecast. *The New York Herald tells the story thus:* [. . .]"

None of the following eight paragraphs are offset, placed in quotation marks, or otherwise signposted as being a direct quotation, so it is impossible to tell where the quotation of the *New York Herald* ends and therefore where—or indeed if—the edito-

rial commentary of the Amsterdam paper recommences. Paragraph seven introduces Lovecraft's letter, and paragraph eight
reproduces the letter, wrapped in a somewhat patronizing edito-
rial commentary. The ninth and final paragraph then quotes Mr.
Fast. I would argue that the first introductory paragraph, and
the layout and content of the remaining eight paragraphs, most
likely indicate that the latter are lifted entirely and directly from
the *New York Herald*. In other words, Lovecraft wrote, not to
the *Amsterdam Evening Recorder*, but to the *New York Herald*.

This also addresses another issue Bleiler raises: unlike the
Amsterdam paper, the *Herald* would have been known to Lovecraft and readily available in Providence. Indeed, it was an insti-
tution: founded in 1835 by Scottish immigrant James Gordon
Bennett (Sr.), by the 1860s the paper had resources, prestige,
and circulation unmatched by any other American paper
(Sandburg 87). From 1867 it was run by Bennett's scandalous
son Gordon Bennet (Jr.), who established a European edition,
the *Paris Herald*, in 1887.[1] The paper was acquired by its rival,
the *New York Tribune*, in 1924, to become the *New York Herald-
Tribune*, which ran until 1966, while the European edition became successively the *Paris Herald-Tribune*, the *International
Herald-Tribune*, the *New York Times Herald-Tribune*, and, since
2016, the *New York Times International Edition*.

It must also be remembered that it was not at all unusual for
regional papers to fill vacant space with stories either copied directly from papers that came into their editors' hands or, more
usually, from wire services, from which they could pick and
choose and then edit at will. This is exactly how Lovecraft's
famed astronomy letter of 16 July 1906, published a month later
in the 25 August issue of the *Scientific American*, came to appear,
in full, but without any reference to the *Scientific American*, in

---

1. Bennett is listed in the 1984 edition of the *Guinness Book of Records* (187)
for the "Greatest faux pas," when, in New York on 1 January 1877, he entered
the drawing room at his prospective father-in-law's Fifth Avenue mansion
while "obviously in wine" and "mistook the fireplace for a plumbing fixture
more usually reserved for another purpose." For more than a century, the term
"Gordon Bennett" has remained a British exclamation of incredulous disbelief.

half a dozen small-town regional Australian newspapers between November 1906 and February 1907 (Whyte 88–90).

Naturally, the proof of this theory would be the existence of Lovecraft's letter in a mid-1905 issue of the *New York Herald*. Unfortunately, from here in Australia I have been unable to locate Lovecraft's letter in online page-scans of issues of the *New York Herald* between late August (when Fast first announced his contest) and 6 September 1905 (when the Amsterdam paper ran its column). But I have also been unable to locate in that paper any mention of Frederick R. Fast himself or of his competition. Perhaps someone in New York can examine the microfilm copies of the *Herald* and its *soi-disant* "evening edition," Bennett's stablemate the *New York Evening Telegram*, and will find it.

Why the Psychometrical Apparatus?

The second question is the meaning of the "psychometrical apparatus" Lovecraft claims in his letter to use for weather forecasting. Bleiler's suggestion that the youthful Lovecraft was deliberately taking the mickey out of his elders and betters seems highly unlikely. Upon reading the list of instruments in Lovecraft's letter—thermometers, hygrometer, rain gauge, and wind vane—one can see that he had the means to measure temperature, humidity, precipitation, and wind direction. He could thus easily measure and record the prevailing meteorological conditions and, in periods of relative stability, make short-term predictions; but for more accurate and longer-term forecasts, a barometer is vital for measuring atmospheric pressure and, more importantly, *changes* in pressure. A decrease in pressure indicates an incoming low-pressure system, stronger winds, and increased chance of rain; conversely, an increase in pressure indicates increasing atmospheric stability, light winds, and clear skies.

The mercury barometer is generally accepted to have been invented by Evangelista Torricelli, a student of Galileo, in 1643. The aneroid barometer, which uses a collapsible/expandable metal cell or diaphragm instead of liquid, was invented in 1844 and, being much more portable than liquid barometers, was of great benefit to mariners for timely weather prediction and to

land explorers for altimetry. It would beggar belief that Lovecraft, living in a port city, would not have used a barometer of
some type in his weather observations and predictions. Some
twenty months earlier, in the issue for 24 January 1904 of his
own juvenile publication, the *Scientific Gazette*, Lovecraft discussed his "climatological station," noting that "the storm glass
is very accurate." A storm glass, also known as a Fitzroy storm
barometer, after Admiral Robert Fitzroy, who promoted the instrument in the 1860s, was believed to predict weather changes
based on the degree of crystallization of a special liquid within a
sealed glass tube. Yet the storm glass, or any other type of barometer, is missing from Lovecraft's list of instruments in the
newly discovered 1905 letter. Or is it? I would suggest that "psychometrical apparatus" is either a misreading of Lovecraft's
handwriting or a typesetting error for "hypsometrical apparatus."
Note that the two words differ by a single letter *c*, and that in
cursive handwriting a lower-case *p* is often given an ascender as
well as the inherent descender, which could cause it to confused
with an *h*.

Hypsometry, from the Greek *hypsos* (height), is the measurement of altitude. In the days before GPS and other electronic
measuring devices, barometers, particularly the highly portable
aneroid type, were a simple way for explorers, and subsequently
airmen and hikers, to measure altitude: assuming stable atmospheric conditions, air pressure decreases by about 9 hPa per 100 m
change in elevation.

Once we accept that "psychometrical" is a not inconceivable
error for "hypsometrical," Lovecraft's instrument list becomes fit
for forecasting purposes. His subsequent change of hobby from
meteorology to astronomy can then be simply explained as a
change or development of his interests, as happens to everyone
throughout their lives, and particularly during adolescence.
There is no longer any need to suggest "deliberate deception,"
let alone to invent familial "distress," when a simple erroneous
transcription fits the facts more fully. To give a Sherlockian bent
to Ockham's razor: once we have eliminated the improbable,
whatever remains, however prosaic, must surely be the truth.

Works Cited

Bleiler, Richard. "H. P. Lovecraft's First Appearance in Print." *Lovecraft Annual* No. 14 (2020): 26–36.

Guinness Book of Records: 1994 Edition. Enfield, UK: Guinness Superlatives, 1993.

"Long Distance Predictions: Weather Guessers Willing to Take and Sort of Chances and Trust to Providence." *Amsterdam Evening Recorder and Daily Democrat* (6 September 1905): 3. Available at www.fultonhistory.com.

Lovecraft, H. P. *Letters to Rheinhart Kleiner and Others.* Ed. S. T. Joshi and David E. Schultz. New York: Hippocampus Press, 2020.

Sandburg, Carl. *Storm over the Land: A Profile of the Civil War Taken Mainly from Abraham Lincoln: The War Years.* New York: Harcourt, Brace, 1942.

Whyte, Brendan. "The Thing (Flung Daily) on the Doorstep: Lovecraft in the Antipodean Press, 1803–2007." *Lovecraft Annual* No. 9 (2015): 82–98.

Briefly Noted

An interesting work of Lovecraft scholarship is Cédric Monget's *Lovecraft, l'Arabe, l'horreur*, recently published by La Clef d'Argent. The booklet includes a discussion of Lovecraft's response to Islam, Arabian culture, and other issues relevant to his creation of the *Necronomicon* by the mad Arab Abdul Alhazred. This same publisher has issued a book entitled *Lovecraft: Sous le signe du chat* (Lovecraft: Under the sign of the cat) by Boris Maynadier.

New England Fallen

H. P. Lovecraft

[The following poem appears as a handwritten manuscript written on the back flyleaf of Lovecraft's copy of Daniel Wait Howe's *The Puritan Republic of the Massachusetts Bay in New England* (Indianapolis: Bowen-Merrill Co., 1899; *LL* 472). It seems to be an alternate (or, perhaps, early) version of a poem of the same title written in August 1912 (see *AT* 385–88).—ED.]

Observe the ruin caus'd by adverse fate;
New-England's fallen from its high estate.
Ancestral ground, where, as a child, I play'd,
Hath now to foreign peasants been betray'd.
In vain I seek a noble *English* face,
But stand an outcast, sever'd from my race.
What is this region, fill'd with foreign clowns,
Where fith corrupts, and vice maintains the towns?
Why do I thus around my birthplace roam
A man without a country or a home?
Why must I now, 'mid swarthy aliens, plod,
A stranger, mourning on my native sod?
Where is *New England*, that our fathers built?
Is it this land, this home of sin and guilt?
Atlantis, saith the tale, beneath the waves
Convey'd its people to forgotten graves.
Over our land a wave still worse hath pour'd,
No flood of water, but a foreign horde,
And though the soil above the ocean lies,
It fast decays before the blinded eyes
Of our rash selves, who recklessly ignore

The alien swarms that flock upon our shore.
The *British* yeoman made *New-England* great,
And where he leaves, he leaves it to foul fate.
No baser tribe can fill his honour'd place
And with like virtues Old *New-England* grace.

H.P.L. 1912

A Bridge through Chaos: The Miltonic in "Dagon" and Lovecraft's Greater Cthulhu Mythos

Christopher Cuccia

Introduction

The early stories of H. P. Lovecraft are recognized as backward-looking tales, i.e., emulations of other writers admired by Lovecraft, namely Edgar Allan Poe and Lord Dunsany. Lovecraft's early short story "Dagon" (1917), however, is highlighted as a forward-looking tale—that is, to Lovecraft's so-called Cthulhu Mythos, which "Dagon" very much anticipates with its terror-stricken narrator who has gone mad from the sublime sight of a gigantic sea-beast momentarily emerging from the abyss—a kind of microcosmic Cthulhu—and revealing that man does not hold sole dominion over the Earth, and that another, ancient, monstrous race of creatures may one day rise from the depths to reclaim what was once theirs. Yet this forward-looking tale containing the germ of the greater Cthulhu Mythos also looks backward—further back than either Dunsany or Poe. In "Dagon," Lovecraft looks back to the seventeenth-century poet John Milton, explicitly evoking the terrifying cosmos envisioned in Milton's masterwork, *Paradise Lost* (1667; 1674). The weight of Lovecraft's stark references to Milton and *Paradise Lost* in this crucial early tale foreshadowing the very Cthulhu Mythos demonstrates that the Miltonic looms large over Lovecraft's oeuvre.

The Appeal of Milton to Lovecraft

Milton with *Paradise Lost* aspired to "justify the ways of God to men" (1.26) by retelling in epic form the tale of how Adam and Eve lost Paradise, as it were. So iconic was Milton's magnum opus that *Paradise Lost* forever redefined its age-old characters and events, not least its enigmatic fallen archangel Satan and his reign in Hell. "Milton's is the last convincing full-length portrait of the traditional lord of evil," notes Jeffrey Burton Russell, author of a five-volume study of the Devil in history and literature, and indeed Milton "made the traditional story of the fall of angels and humanity into a scenario so coherent and compelling that it became the standard account for all succeeding generations" (127, 95). This is no exaggeration; even the titanic skeptic Voltaire would assert that Milton "force[s] the Reader to say, 'If God, if the Angels, if Satan would speak, I believe they would speak as they do in *Milton*'" (249). In eighteenth-century England, the idolized Milton was set alongside Shakespeare as a twin pillar of British culture, *Paradise Lost* fabulously celebrated as England's great national epic, a cultural treasure that could boast more than one hundred editions published throughout the 1700s. Britons with any pretensions to being cultured took part in the cult of Milton, and the Anglophilic Lovecraft, spiritually misplaced eighteenth-century gentleman that he was, was not prepared to be an exception. "The later seventeenth century has a different mood, or set of moods, and bridges the gulf to modernity," Lovecraft observed in his "Suggestions for a Reading Guide," noting, "Here Milton dominates. Read all of *Paradise Lost* for unforgettable and inimitable grandeur of concepts, imagery, and language" (CE 2.187). Lovecraft's writings illustrate that Milton's *Paradise Lost* was clearly "unforgettable" to him, and while he maintained that the literary treasures stored within it were "inimitable," he often appears to aspire to the Miltonic "mood" in his own works.

There was much in Milton for Lovecraft to appreciate and admire, not least Milton's preoccupation with the cosmic. *Paradise Lost* contains many fine passages describing the magnificence of the cosmos (e.g., 2.1034ff.; 3.416–612), and a substantial portion of the discussion between Adam and the archangel Raphael is given over to astronomy (8.15–168), a subject near and dear to Lovecraft's heart. Milton not only coined the term "space" as we use it today—as in "outer space" (see for example *PL* 1.650)—but also speculated that other life forms may perhaps populate its "other Worlds" (see *PL* 3.560–71). It is not at all difficult to picture Lovecraft's imagination warming to cosmic innovations as bold as Milton's, even though the learned Lovecraft would have scoffed at Raphael's instruction to inquisitive Adam:

> Heav'n is for thee too high
> To know what passes there; be lowly wise:
> Think only what concerns thee and thy being;
> Dream not of other Worlds, what Creatures there
> Live, in what state, condition or degree,
> Contended that thus far hath been reveal'd
> Not of Earth only but of highest Heav'n. (8.172–78)

This admonition, though spoken by a heavenly being in the context of *Paradise Lost*, is representative of the willful ignorance Lovecraft found abhorrent in the religions of the Earth:

> You are forgetting a human impulse which, despite its restriction to a relatively small number of men, has all through history proved itself as real and as vital as hunger—as potent as thirst or greed. I need not say that I refer to that simplest yet most exalted attribute of our species—the acute, persistent, unquenchable craving TO KNOW. (HPL to Maurice W. Moe, 15 May 1918; *Letters to Maurice W. Moe* 69)

Yet Adam's questioning of the significance of his earthly home in the midst of the immensity of space—"this Earth a spot, a grain, / An Atom, with the Firmament compar'd" (8.17–18)—would surely have spoken to Lovecraft, who echoes these sentiments, albeit more misanthropically, in his own atheist ruminations on the absurd notion of God as

> a potent and purposeful consciousness which deals individually and directly with the miserable denizens of a wretched little fly-

speck on the back door of a microscopic universe, and which singles this putrid excrescence out as the one spot whereto to send an onlie-begotten Son, whose mission is to redeem those accursed flyspeck-inhabiting lice which we call human beings— bah!! Pardon the "bah!" I feel several "bahs!", but out of courtesy I only say one. But it is all so very childish. I cannot help taking exception to a philosophy which would force this rubbish down my throat. 'What have I against religion?' That is what I have against it! (*Letters to Maurice W. Moe* 71)

Lovecraft is even more misanthropic than Milton's Satan, who, looking on Adam and Eve, reveals that he finds them "Little inferior; whom my thoughts pursue / With wonder, and could love, so lively shines / In them Divine resemblance" (4.362–64), and who in the midst of Eden cries, "O Earth, how like to Heav'n, if not preferr'd / More justly" (9.99–100). Before the Fall, at least; by the conclusion of *Paradise Lost*, Milton's cosmos, and man's place within it, is much closer to the bleakness of Lovecraft's vision.

Would Lovecraft's avowed atheism—what he had against religion—be reason enough for him to recoil from the Puritan poet Milton? Certainly not. One can imagine Lovecraft thinking along the lines of the great Romantic atheist Percy Bysshe Shelley: "I know that Milton believed Xtianity; but I do not forget that Virgil believed ancient mythology" (Shelley to William Godwin, 24 February 1812; *Letters* 1.260). "We are deceived by names," observed Lovecraft's contemporary Sir Walter Raleigh in his book *Milton*, reasoning that the "same dull convention that calls the *Paradise Lost* a religious poem might call [Michelangelo's] Christian statues," and thus maintaining that "*Paradise Lost* is not the less an eternal monument because it is a monument to dead ideas" (88). *Paradise Lost*'s essential "dead idea" is Milton's asserted aim to "assert Eternal Providence, / And justify the ways of God to men" (1.25–26), and such a cosmos, wherein human beings, though existing in a fallen world, still have "Providence [as] thir guide" (12.647), may at first glance certainly seem incongruent with the Lovecraftian cosmos' fundamental indifference to man. Preeminent Lovecraft scholar S. T.

Joshi, in his introduction to *Against Religion: The Atheist Writings of H. P. Lovecraft*, explains that

> in Lovecraft's universe, humanity is indeed alone in the cosmos; and whereas the object of most religions is, in John Milton's words, to "justify the ways of God to men," Lovecraft's "anti-mythology," as it has been appropriately called, establishes that human beings can appeal to no higher power when faced with threats to our fleeting sinecure on this earth. A moment ago, in cosmic terms, we did not exist; a moment hence, the universe shall have forgotten that we did exist. (xxv)

Yet then again, as we shall see, the cosmos of Milton's *Paradise Lost* is more Lovecraftian than one might suspect, so much so that the twentieth-century atheist Milton critic William Empson would argue in his book *Milton's God* that "the reason why the poem is so good is that it makes God so bad" (13).

Whether or not one agrees with Empson's atheistic or indeed anti-theistic reading of Milton, *Paradise Lost* is surely anything but a work of orthodox Christianity, filled as it is with the kind of otherworldly weirdness to be found in the writings of Lovecraft. Empson felt that *Paradise Lost* has some "tiresomely absurd" and even "unusually stupid Science Fiction" (54), and while the absurdity or stupidity may be disputed, *Paradise Lost* is indeed famously full of sci-fi-style peculiarities. Milton, for instance, goes well out of his way to explain the complexities of angelic anatomy and physiology, including digestion (5.404–13) and even sexual intercourse (8.620–29). Empson understandably found "the biology of the angels too hard to get clear" (59), as Milton's "Spirits when they please / Can either Sex assume, or both" (1.423–24), for instance, and the fallen spirits are seen to alter their dimensions drastically—from "Giant Angels" (7.605) to "less than smallest Dwarfs" (1.779). *Paradise Lost*'s great shapeshifter is of course Satan, who adopts various animal forms (4.194–96, 395–408, 799–800) well before he possesses the body of the infamous Eden serpent (9.187ff.), and even transforms himself into an angel of light (3.613ff.; 10.325–31). Satan is also a perverse creator of sorts, for his daughter Sin explains that she was born Athena-like from his own haughty head (2.749–58)—Sin being the personification of Satan's own "proud imaginations" (2.10)—and the fruit of their incestuous embrace (Satan saw in Sin his own "perfect image" [2.764]) was Death, Satan's "Son and Grandchild both" (10.384), who, having torn from Sin's womb and deforming her lower half into a serpentine monstrosity, proceeded to rape his mother, producing monstrous "Hell Hounds" that gnaw at her bowels (2.757–802). (Not even Lovecraft's Whateley family could compete with "the Race / Of Satan" [10.385–86] imagined by Milton.)

There was plentiful weirdness in *Paradise Lost* for Lovecraft to appreciate, and as we will see, one can identify a certain element of Miltonian science fiction in the Cthulhu Mythos. In any event, there is no need to speculate on Lovecraft's admiration for Milton, for we have his own words, which insist upon the poet's genius: "As for Milton—I don't see how you . . . can argue away the distinctive charm of a large part of his work. He has the power of evoking unlimited images for persons of active imagination, & no amount of academic theory can explain that away" (*Letters to J. Vernon Shea* 124).

Miltonic Chaos in "Dagon"

Lovecraft co-opts Milton's "power of evoking unlimited images for persons of active imagination" most unambiguously in "Dagon," wherein we find his earliest, most explicit, and most significant reference to Milton. While the story's very reference to "the ancient Philistine legend of Dagon, the Fish-God" (CF 1.58) may itself nod to Milton's mention of this deity early on in *Paradise Lost* (1.457–66) in the catalog of false gods worshipped by human beings (1.364–521), that is nothing in comparison to the stark Miltonic reference made by Lovecraft's maddened, doomed narrator as he recounts his days-long trek across the island—or rather the "portion of the ocean floor [which] must have been thrown to the surface" (2)—upon which he had washed:

> [. . .] I think my horror was greater when I gained the summit of the mound and looked down the other side into an immeasura-

ble pit or canyon, whose black recesses the moon had not yet
soared high enough to illumine. I felt myself on the edge of the
world; peering over the rim into a fathomless chaos of eternal
night. Through my terror ran curious reminiscences of "Paradise
Lost", and of Satan's hideous climb through the unfashioned
realms of darkness. (CF 1.55)

This passage reveals much about Lovecraft. For one thing, his
narrator's comparison of his struggle to "Satan's hideous climb
through the unfashioned realms of darkness" in *Paradise Lost*
(2.890ff.) is not only a reference to John Milton but to Gustave
Doré, which is to say, Doré's illustration of this scene in his set
of fifty engravings for an 1866 edition of *Paradise Lost,* a version
of which the Lovecraft family owned (inspiring one of Lovecraft's creatures, incidentally): "I began having nightmares of
the most hideous description, peopled with things which I called
'night-gaunts' . . . I used to draw them after waking (perhaps the
idea of these figures came from an edition de luxe of *Paradise
Lost* with illustrations by Doré, which I discovered one day in
the east parlour)" (*Letters to Rheinhart Kleiner* 66). And of course
Doré is himself mentioned in "Dagon," in the narrator's description of "the Cyclopean monolith" soon to be embraced by the
creature from the sea: "It was the pictorial carving [. . .] that did
most to hold me spellbound. Plainly visible across the interven-
ing water on account of their enormous size, were an array of
bas-reliefs whose subjects would have excited the envy of a Doré" (CF 1.56). The narrator in "Dagon" appears to have "curious reminiscences" more of Doré's craggy Chaos, which pictures
Satan essentially mountaineering through a rocky region, as opposed to Milton's Chaos, an ever-shifting void of clashing conditions—true elemental chaos. Milton's challenging image of
Satan struggling "through the shock / Of fighting Elements"
(2.1014–15) was more ably rendered in the painting of *Satan
Bursts from Chaos* (1794–96), and even the earlier sketch of *Satan Departing from the Court of Chaos* (1781–82), by Henry Fuseli, the British Romantic art world's most ardent Milton devotee,

and another artist Lovecraft admired.[1]

While Lovecraft's passage in "Dagon" referencing *Paradise Lost* calls to mind Doré's illustration of Milton's Chaos on account of the rocky terrain the narrator traverses, Lovecraft's emphasis on "a fathomless chaos of eternal night" and "the unfashioned realms of darkness" does conjure up the terrifying image of the realm of Chaos in Book 2 of *Paradise Lost*, as seen by Satan, Sin, and Death from the opened Gates of Hell:

---

1. For HPL's assessment of Fuseli, see "Pickman's Model": "Any magazine-cover hack can splash paint around wildly and call it a nightmare or a Witches' Sabbath or a portrait of the devil, but only a great painter can make such a thing really scare or ring true. That's because only a real artist knows the actual anatomy of the terrible or the physiology of fear—the exact sort of lines and proportions that connect up with latent instincts or hereditary memories of fright, and the proper colour contrasts and lighting effects to stir the dormant sense of strangeness. I don't have to tell you why a Fuseli really brings a shiver while a cheap ghost-story frontispiece merely makes us laugh" (CF 2.57–8). Fuseli painted various of the subjects HPL mentions in the above passage: *The Nightmare* (1781) was the Gothic triumph with which Fuseli made his name in Georgian London, and it was a picture the artist repeatedly returned to throughout his career (e.g., c. 1790–91, 1810); "a Witches' Sabbath" made for the subject of many of Fuseli's paintings, not least his various *Macbeth* paintings, such as *The Three Witches* (c. 1782), *Macbeth, Banquo and the Witches* (c. 1793–94), and *Macbeth Consulting the Vision of the Armed Head* (1793), or his Milton Gallery painting of *The Night-Hag Visiting Lapland Witches* (1796). As for "portrait[s] of the devil," Fuseli was so wont to paint these—Milton's Satan was represented no fewer than thirteen times in the twenty-seven-painting *Paradise Lost* cycle in Fuseli's Milton Gallery of 1799 (fourteen times among its thirty paintings when the gallery reopened in 1800)—that he acquired the Satanic sobriquet "Painter in ordinary to the Devil," which Fuseli prided himself on. See Cunningham 2.305: "With quiet beauty and serene grace he knew not well how to begin; the hurrying measures, the crowding epithets, and startling imagery of the northern poetry suited the intoxicated fancy of Fuseli. Such was his love of terrific subjects, that he was known among his brethren by the name of *Painter in ordinary to the Devil*, and he smiled when some one officiously told him of this, and said, 'Aye! he has sat to me many times.' Once, at Johnson the bookseller's table, one of the guests said, 'Mr. Fuseli, I have purchased a picture of your's [*sic*]. . . . I don't know what the *devil* it is.'—'Perhaps it is the devil,' replied Fuseli, 'I have often painted him.'"

> Before thir eyes in sudden view appear
> The secrets of the hoary deep, a dark
> Illimitable Ocean without bound,
> Without dimension, where length, breadth, and highth,
> And time and place are lost; where eldest *Night*
> And *Chaos,* Ancestors of Nature, hold
> Eternal Anarchy, amidst the noise
> Of endless wars, and by confusion stand.
> For hot, cold, moist, and dry, four Champions fierce
> Strive here for Maistry, and to Battle bring
> Thir embryon Atoms . . . (2.890–900)

Milton's description of Chaos reads like a passage that could have been written by Lovecraft, and its sheer terror is emphasized by Satan's reaction to it. The Satan of *Paradise Lost* is famously a figure of "dauntless courage, and considerate Pride" (1.603), exhibited not least in the scene immediately preceding the description of Chaos quoted above, when Satan first sights Sin and Death, the dread guardians of the Gates of Hell. Milton paints a terrifying—and proto-Lovecraftian—picture of Death:

>   The other shape,
> If shape it might be call'd that shape had none
> Distinguishable in member, joint, or limb,
> Or substance might be call'd that shadow seem'd,
> For each seem'd either; black it stood as Night,
> Fierce as ten Furies, terrible as Hell,
> And shook a dreadful Dart; what seem'd his head
> The likeness of a Kingly Crown had on. (2.666–73)

This passage embodied the sublime of terror for Edmund Burke, who in his celebrated treatise on the sublime, *A Philosophical Enquiry into the Origin of our Ideas of the Sublime and Beautiful* (1757)—*the* eighteenth-century text on the sublime—singled Milton's description of Death out as an essential example, for "all is dark, uncertain, confused, terrible, and sublime to the last degree" (55). Yet Burke insisted that more sublime still— indeed, the quintessential example of the sublime—was Milton's darkened but still-radiant Satan outshining the reassembled rebel hosts of Hell he towers over (1.589–600). "We do not any where meet a more sublime description than this justly celebrated one of Milton," Burke declares, "wherein he gives the portrait of Satan with a dignity so suitable to the subject" (57), and indeed Milton appears to emphasize the sublime terror of Death so as to reemphasize the sublime heroism of Satan: "Th' undaunted Fiend what this might be admir'd [i.e., wondered at] / Admir'd, not fear'd; God and his Son except, / Created thing naught valu'd he nor shunn'd" (2.677–79). Even when Death and Satan nearly come to cataclysmic blows, and "the grisly terror . . . in shape, / So speaking and so threat'ning, grew tenfold / More dreadful and deform," his would-be opponent remains unfazed, for "Incens't with indignation *Satan* stood / Unterrifi'd, and like a Comet burn'd" (2.704–8). Sin of course intervenes between the two "mighty Combatants" (2.719), and "the Portress of Hell Gate" (2.746) is persuaded by Satan to unlock the infernal gateway for him, at which point this very same dauntless Satan, who was fearless in the face of Death himself, stares out into the realm of Chaos and cannot help but hesitate:

> Into this wild Abyss the wary fiend
> Stood on the brink of Hell and look'd a while,
> Pondering his Voyage: for no narrow frith
> He had to cross. Nor was his ear less peal'd
> With noises loud and ruinous (to compare
> Great things with small) than when *Bellona* storms,
> With all her battering Engines bent to rase
> Some Capital City; or less than if this frame
> Of Heav'n were falling, and these Elements
> In mutiny had from her Axle torn
> The steadfast Earth. (2.917–27)

This is the terrifying cosmography Lovecraft invokes in the "Dagon" passage on *Paradise Lost*. As Satan "Stood on the brink of Hell" looking "Into this wild Abyss" (2.917–18), Lovecraft's narrator "felt [him]self on the edge of the world; peering over the rim into a fathomless chaos of eternal night" (CF 1.55). Lovecraft's invocation of Milton's Chaos adds tremendous power to the oppressive atmosphere of his own tale.

Why does Lovecraft have "curious reminiscences of 'Paradise Lost', and of Satan's hideous climb through the unfashioned realms of darkness" run through the mind of his hapless narrator in this story? Is it to paint a more heroic picture of him? The narrator does, after all, "set out boldly for an unknown goal" (CF 1.54), or at least initially; he ultimately goes suicidally mad from the sight of the sea-beast that rises from the waves to embrace the monolith, which is a far cry indeed from Milton's supremely heroic Satan. While he may be "wary" when he first encounters Chaos, Satan ultimately beards the "wild Abyss" (2.917), and despite the depths of despair into which Satan sinks in the no less than five Shakespearean soliloquies Milton grants him throughout his sorrowful sojourn in Eden (4.32–113, 358–92, 505–35; 9.99–178, 473–93), Satan can never be said to be mad. Lovecraft was of course more concerned with setting and atmosphere over character, and so his narrator likens himself to Satan struggling through Chaos not to compare himself to the complex fallen archangel who journeys "Undaunted to meet there whatever power / Or Spirit of the nethermost Abyss / Might in that noise reside" (2.955–57), but to liken his surroundings to Milton's "dark unbottom'd infinite Abyss" (2.405)—so as to capture the dreadful, mind-shattering gloomth of Milton's Chaos.

The realm of Chaos is arguably chief among *Paradise Lost*'s profound Miltonic idiosyncrasies. While many readers have found most peculiar Milton's sublime and even sympathetic Satan, this curious portrait was not wholly unprecedented[2] and is certainly not unexplainable, hence the hundreds of years of crit-

---

2. It has been observed that *Paradise Lost*'s epic hero Satan is a descendant of the various Lucifers of Renaissance epic (see Revard 198). These various proto-Miltonic Satans are catalogued in Kirkconnell. As it turns out, even the magnificent Hell of which Milton's Satan asserts himself as the "new Possessor" (1.252)—namely the infernal palace of "Pandæmonium, the high Capitol / Of Satan and his Peers" (1.756–57), described as a marvelous sight far outshining all great structures erected throughout human history (1.710–30)—was not entirely unique, as Erasmo di Valvasone's *L'Angeleida* (1590) too had spoken of the fallen angels building a "lofty town" in Hell (Kirkconnell 86).

ical debate over the Miltonic Satan's hero status, stretching from the seventeenth century to the present day.[3] The realm of Chaos through which Satan must travel is far more curious—and, from a Judeo-Christian perspective, far more troubling, as Chaos would seem to destabilize the meticulous structure of Milton's cosmos, watched over by an omnipotent God.

Milton was quite imaginative in picturing a cosmos occupied by beings other than the Almighty and His subordinate spirits. The fallen angels, for instance, discover that they are not alone in their newly created Hell, which is filled with monstrous native denizens (also illustrated by Doré, incidentally):

> A Universe of death, which God by curse
> Created evil, for evil only good,
> Where all life dies, death lives, and Nature breeds,
> Perverse, all monstrous, all prodigious things,
> Abominable, inutterable, and worse
> Than Fables yet have feign'd, or fear conceiv'd,
> *Gorgons* and *Hydras*, and *Chimeras* dire. (2.622–28)

Yet even these infernal abominations pale in comparison to the entities with which Milton populates Chaos. In *Paradise Lost*, the realm of Chaos provides the raw materials for Milton's Creator God to mold Creation: "th' Almighty Maker them ordain[s] / His dark materials to create more Worlds" (2.915–16).[4] That is curious enough, but Milton's imagination ventured even further, populating the realm of Chaos with actual entities, not least the eponymous emperor of this realm, "the Anarch old" (2.988) Chaos himself, who sits with other personifications beside him:

---

3. The complexities of this critical debate are beyond this essay's remit, but for a most thorough exploration of the topic, see Steadman. In regard to the Satan-as-hero reading of *Paradise Lost* that reached its apex in the so-called "Romantic Satanism" movement, see also Schock.

4. "His dark materials" (*PL* 2.916) is of course the line from which Philip Pullman derived the title for his award-winning trilogy of fantasy novels, *His Dark Materials* (1995–2000), described by the author as "*Paradise Lost* for teenagers in three volumes," thus demonstrating once again the extent to which Milton speaks to the science fiction genre. See Burt 48.

> with him Enthron'd
> Sat Sable-vested *Night*, eldest of things,
> The Consort of his Reign; and by them stood
> *Orcus* and *Ades*, and the dreaded name
> Of *Demogorgon; Rumor* next and *Chance*,
> And *Tumult* and *Confusion* all imbroil'd,
> And *Discord* with a thousand various mouths. (2.961–67)

Both Chaos and its "Anarch" are most peculiar Miltonic innovations, but Milton's imagination ventured even further still by suggesting that Chaos and his court exist beyond God's authority. *Paradise Lost*'s cosmos is most curious because while Milton insists that "one Almighty is" (5.469), with regard to the realm of Chaos he establishes that here "*Chaos* Umpire sits" and "high Arbiter / *Chance* governs all" (2.907, 909–10), which, as Jarod K. Anderson notes, upsets the moral schema of Milton's epic:

> The fact that Milton creates a universe in which dwell sentient beings that are not created by God[,] precede the rule of God, and/or are opposed to the will of God, greatly influences the moral structure of the poem. Given that there are entities in *Paradise Lost* which are essentially outside of God's system, God becomes *a* ruler, *a* creator, not *the* ruler, *the* creator. Ancient night is the eldest of things, not simply the eldest creation of God. The realm of Chaos is infinite. God's created system of existence, an affront to Chaos, is seemingly finite. Milton could certainly have chosen to leave these concepts as pure abstraction; yet he chose to give them voice, give them agency. (198)

Milton indeed does give Chaos "voice" and "agency," for Chaos complains to Satan that all God has created has encroached upon his domain:

> I upon my Frontiers here
> Keep residence; if all I can will serve,
> That little which is left so to defend,
> Encroach on still through our intestine broils,
> Weak'ning the Sceptre of old *Night*: first Hell
> Your dungeon stretching far and wide beneath;
> Now lately Heaven and Earth, another World

Hung o'er my Realm, link'd in a golden Chain
To that side Heav'n from whence your Legions fell . . .
                                        (2.998–1006)

Satan vows that in exchange for directions to the material cosmos, where the Fall will be carried out, he will "once more / Erect the Standard there of *ancient Night;* / Yours be th' advantage all, mine the revenge" (2.985–87). Chaos directs Satan's course, stating, "go and speed; / Havoc and spoil and ruin are my gain" (2.1008–9), but of course Chaos will lose even more of his dark domain, for Sin and Death, empowered by Satan's successful orchestration of the Fall, leave the Gates of Hell and construct a triumphal bridge through Chaos to our cosmos (10.229–414), which invites the indignity of the Anarch:

Th' other way *Satan* went down
The Causey to Hell Gate; on either side
Disparted *Chaos* over-built exclaim'd,
And with rebounding surge the bars assail'd,
That scorn'd his indignation . . . (10.414–18)

Leading Lovecraft scholar Robert H. Waugh maintains that Lovecraft did not read Milton's *Paradise Lost* as the so-called "Romantic Satanists" did—with Milton, unconsciously or otherwise, on the side of Satan, so to speak—simply because, in short, "Lovecraft was not of the party of Satan but of the party of Chaos" (16). There would appear much for "the party of Chaos" to appreciate in the final Books of *Paradise Lost,* for vexed though Chaos may be over his loss of territories held from time immemorial, chaos does descend upon Milton's cosmos after the Fall. When Eve eats the forbidden fruit, Milton explains that "Earth felt the wound, and Nature from her seat / Sighing through all her Works gave signs of woe, / That all was lost" (9.782–84), and when Adam follows suit, "Earth trembl'd from her entrails, as again / In pangs, and Nature gave a second groan" (9.1000–1001). When Sin and Death have "made one Realm / Hell and this World, one Realm, one Continent / Of easy thorough-fare" (10.391–93), all Hell breaks loose (Milton's coinage; see *PL* 4.918), with the cosmos itself suffering under the influence of Sin and Death as they make their way to Earth: "they with speed / Thir course through thickest Constellations held / Spreading thir bane; the blasted Stars lookt wan" (10.410–12). More interesting is that not all this malign influence comes from Hell; the Almighty orders the angels to adjust elements of Creation to make it more inhospitable to Man (10.648–714).

So grim is Adam and Eve's state by the end of *Paradise Lost* that many readers were not all convinced by the uplifting note Milton sought to conclude on:

> They looking back, all th' Eastern side beheld
> Of Paradise, so late thir happy seat,
> Wav'd over by that flaming Brand, the Gate
> With dreadful Faces throng'd and fiery Arms:
> Some natural tears they dropp'd, but wip'd them soon;
> The World was all before them, where to choose
> Thir place of rest, and Providence thir guide:
> They hand in hand with wand'ring steps and slow,
> Through *Eden* took thir solitary way. (12.641–49)

This closing passage of *Paradise Lost* was among those subjected to scrutiny by the eminent eighteenth-century scholar Richard Bentley. Among the "corrections" in his notorious 1732 edition of *Paradise Lost* were the poem's final two lines, which he felt were too bleak—surely not what Milton intended—and subsequently altered to, "THEN *hand in hand with* SOCIAL *steps their way* / *Through* Eden *took*, WITH HEAV'NLY COMFORT CHEER'D" (399). Bentley's edition of *Paradise Lost*, which revised and rewrote substantial portions of the text—under the presumption that Milton's epic, which was of course dictated by a blind man, was filled with errors attributable to Milton's amanuensis, editor, and printer (and sometimes even Milton himself)—was of course fated for infamy, but Bentley was not alone in finding the conclusion to *Paradise Lost* rather bleak. Preeminent Milton illustrators such as Fuseli and Doré—or, indeed, John Martin, another artist Lovecraft profoundly admired as "a Milton among painters" (*Letters to Maurice W. Moe* 527)—

pictured the expulsion of Milton's Adam and Eve from Paradise as an incredibly bleak scene, with their Earth and their hopes blasted, and no hint of any "paradise within," as Adam was promised, certainly not "happier far" (12.587).

Miltonic Pandemonium in "Dagon"

By the end of *Paradise Lost*, the Miltonic cosmos can be said to be frightfully close to the Lovecraftian cosmos in its profound inhospitality and even hostility to Man. Lovecraft, in fact, draws his own cosmos a bit closer to Milton's in one final *Paradise Lost* reference in "Dagon":

> I cannot think of the deep sea without shuddering at the name-less things that may at this very moment be crawling and floun-dering on its slimy bed, worshipping their ancient stone idols and carving their own detestable likenesses on submarine obe-lisks of water-soaked granite. I dream of a day when they may rise above the billows to drag down in their reeking talons the remnants of puny, war-exhausted mankind—of a day when the land shall sink, and the dark ocean floor shall ascend amidst universal pandemonium. (CF 1.58)

"Pandemonium" is Milton's coinage—his name for the infernal palace of *Paradise Lost*'s devils: "Pandæmonium, the high Capitol / Of Satan and his Peers" (1.756–57). "Pandæmonium" means "place of all the demons"—a literal demonization of the classical Pantheon ("place of all the gods"), for to Milton's Puritan mind the pagan world had "Devils to adore for Deities" (1.373). The alien entities wrongly worshipped as deities in Lovecraft's my-thos are akin to Milton's devils in this respect. While the "uni-versal pandemonium" line in "Dagon" could be a general reference—"pandemonium" as utter chaos, quite contrary to the impressive organization found in Milton's Pandæmonium—the mention of "the remnants of puny, war-exhausted mankind" by Lovecraft's narrator certainly conjures up *Paradise Lost*'s Pan-dæmonium, wherein Milton emphasizes that the fraternal fallen angels put antagonistic fallen men to shame:

> O shame to men! Devil with Devil damn'd
> Firm concord holds, men only disagree
> Of Creatures rational, though under hope
> Of heavenly Grace; and God proclaiming peace,
> Yet live in hatred, enmity, and strife
> Among themselves, and levy cruel wars,
> Wasting the Earth, each other to destroy:
> As if (which might induce us to accord)
> Man had not hellish foes anow besides,
> That day and night for his destruction wait. (2.496–505)

Lovecraft's narrator could have voiced the very same lament at the conclusion of "Dagon." What's more, his fear for the fate of "puny . . . mankind" cannot help but call to mind Beëlzebub imagining within the council of devils in Pandæmonium "To waste his [God's] whole Creation, or possess / All as our own, and drive as we were driven, / The puny habitants" (2.365–67).

Much like the Lovecraftian entities, Milton's fallen spirits are "ancient" (2.394)—existing from a time when "this World was not, and Chaos wild / Reign'd where these Heav'ns now roll, where Earth now rests / Upon her Centre pois'd" (5.577–79)—and they look on man "In the Purlieus of Heav'n, and therein plac't / A race of upstart Creatures, to supply / Perhaps our vacant room" (2.833–35). What's more, unlike in Dante, say, Milton's Hell does not reside within the bowels of the Earth; Hell exists in another dimension, hence Satan's journey through the realm of Chaos and across the cosmos to reach Earth. The interdimensional entities of Lovecraft's Cthulhu Mythos are closer to Milton's devils than one might suspect, and we are certainly made to remember the latter when the narrator in "Dagon" is at one point "gazing into the Stygian deeps where no light had yet penetrated" (CF 1.55), for Milton's devils emerge from "the Stygian flood" (1.239) of a Hell producing "from those flames / No light, but rather darkness visible" (1.62–63).

Interestingly enough, as the Lovecraftian sea-creatures imagined in "Dagon" are "nameless things" (CF 1.58), Milton's fallen angels too are deprived of names: "of thir Names in heav'nly Records now / Be no memorial, blotted out and ras'd / By thir

Rebellion, from the Books of Life" (1.361–63). Much like the assorted creatures of Lovecraft's Cthulhu Mythos, who both possess names unknowable to man and are misinterpreted by human beings as deities, Milton's nameless fallen angels "among the Sons of *Eve* / Got them new Names," for they would eventually be "known to men by various Names, / And various Idols through the Heathen World" (1.364–65, 374–75). Satan's second-in-command, for instance, will be "Long after known in *Palestine*, and nam'd / *Beëlzebub*" (1.80–81), but we never know his native angelic name. Nor do we even know Satan's; when introduced in Hell at the start of *Paradise Lost*, Milton refers to him as "th' Arch-Enemy, / And thence in Heav'n call'd Satan" (1.81–82), *Satan* being Hebrew for "adversary"—or, indeed, "Arch-Enemy"—but Milton provides no definitive moniker by which Satan was known before his fall from Heaven. Tradition holds that it was *Lucifer*—Latin for "light-bearer," a reference to Venus, the Morning Star heralding the light of the rising Sun— and while Milton does invoke this resplendent name at three separate points in *Paradise Lost* (5.760–62; 7.131–33; 10.424–26), he seems to indicate that *Lucifer* is only a means for man to understand what the Devil was before his fall. Just as the unfallen Satan's "count'nance" was "as the Morning Star that guides / The starry flock" (5.708–9), when describing "The Palace of great *Lucifer*," Milton stresses, "so call / That Structure in the Dialect of men / Interpreted" (5.760–62). Milton says something similar when describing Hell's "City and proud seat / Of *Lucifer*, so by allusion call'd, / Of that bright Star to *Satan* paragon'd" (10.424–26). In his cautionary tale to Adam, Raphael remarks, "*Satan*, so call him now, his former name / Is heard no more in Heav'n" (5.658–59), and the instructive archangel never reveals what that "former name" was, just as the Lovecraftian creatures' names are unknowable, unpronounceable even—only to be "in the dialect of men *interpreted*."

There are, of course, fundamental differences between Milton's devils and Lovecraft's creatures. In *Paradise Lost*, the fallen angels are exceedingly angelic still, despite their diminished glory bearing "Godlike shapes and forms / Excelling human, Princely Dignities" (1.358–59), and none are as princely and godlike as Satan himself—Milton's great "Arch-Angel ruin'd," whose "excess / Of Glory" is merely "obscur'd" (1.593–94). This is a far cry from the "detestable likenesses" and "reeking talons" of the creatures in "Dagon," or indeed the larger Cthulhu Mythos. Yet then again, Milton's devils have elements of the monstrous, not least "monstrous size" (1.197). This line derives from a famous passage in Book 1 of *Paradise Lost*, which paints a picture of Satan's massive form (1.194–210), and Milton compares Satan not only to the Titans of Hesiod's Titanomachy but also to the biblical "Sea-beast / *Leviathan*" (1.200–201), which a sea captain may mistake for an island at his own peril (1.203–8). This seems quite in the spirit of a Lovecraftian creature; "the thing" that emerges from the depths in "Dagon" is "Vast, Polyphemus-like, and . . . like a stupendous monster of nightmares . . . gigantic"— like Satan, as large as a whale, according to the aquatic hieroglyphs on the monolith, whereon "one of the creatures was shewn in the act of killing a whale represented as but little larger than himself" (CF 1.57). Even more notable is the devils' horrific, if long-delayed metamorphosis scene toward the end of *Paradise Lost* (10.504–84). Hard on the heels of the Devil's dazzling reappearance in Pandæmonium, the omnipotent will of Milton's omnipresent God sees Satan transformed into "A monstrous Serpent on his Belly prone" at the conclusion of his exultant speech, his rebel brethren suffering the same ignominy, "all **transform'd** / Alike, to Serpents all as accessories / To his bold Riot" (10.514, 519–21)—and, as such, once more to be misinterpreted as central figures in the creation myths of the pagan world (10.578–84). Satan still retains his preeminence among them, albeit now signified by preeminent monstrousness:

> but still greatest hee the midst,
> Now Dragon grown, larger than whom the Sun
> Ingender'd in the *Pythian* Vale on slime,
> Huge *Python*, and his Power no less he seem'd
> Above the rest still to retain . . . (10.528–32)

Milton, ever merciful to his Satan, ultimately restores the writhing rebel angels—"thir lost shape, permitted, they resum'd" (10.574)—and informs the reader that the devils' transformation is only temporary—merely an "annual humbling certain number'd days, / To dash thir pride, and joy for Man seduc't" (10.576–77). All the same, the reader now knows that from time to time Satan and his infernal hosts would fit right in with the cast of Lovecraftian creatures, with "detestable likenesses" and "reeking talons"—"and other features less pleasant to recall" (CF 1.58, 57).

Miltonic Implications for Lovecraft's Greater Cthulhu Mythos

Lovecraft's short story "Dagon" contains the very kernel of the Cthulhu Mythos (an "Esoteric Order of Dagon" even emerges in Lovecraft's later story "The Shadow over Innsmouth" [1931]), and thus the loaded Miltonic references in "Dagon" demonstrate that the spirit of Milton loomed large over Lovecraft's body of work. *Paradise Lost*, rife as Milton's epic poem is with cosmic horror, was a fine source for Lovecraft to draw from. Milton's cosmos presents a truly terrifying vision, encapsulated in the realm of Chaos, that clearly informed in various ways Lovecraft's own, which is profoundly inhospitable to man.

Lovecraft would go on to reference Milton in various of his other stories.[5] In "A Reminiscence of Dr. Samuel Johnson" (1917), the eponymous man of letters derisively remarks of a commonplace observation made by the narrator, "what all the Town is sensible of, is no great Discovery for a *Grub-Street* Critick to make. You might as well say, you have a strong Suspicion that *Milton* wrote *Paradise Lost!*"" (CF 1.61). "Poetry and the Gods" (1920) makes mention of "the chaos-exploring Milton" (CF 4.24), whose early poem *Il Penseroso* (1645) is partially

---

5. For these various references to Milton in the writings of H. P. Lovecraft outside of "Dagon," as well as the various academic articles on Miltonic aspects of Lovecraft's Cthulhu Mythos, I am indebted to S. T. Joshi, who encouraged the composition of this essay.

recited (ll. 85–92, 97–100), and the poet appears in "The Whisperer in Darkness" (1930) in the form of "a bust of Milton"—or,
indeed, a "ghostly bust of Milton" (CF 2.482, 521)—on Akeley's
bookcase.[6] Somewhat closer to the spirit of Lovecraft's invocation of Milton in "Dagon" is "The Unnamable" (1923), wherein
the character Carter remarks, "from the tomb came such a sti-
fled uproar of gasping and whirring that my fancy peopled the
rayless gloom with Miltonic legions of the misshapen damned"
(CF 1.404).

Milton, and Miltonic concepts, are indirectly but no less ef-
fectively referenced in "The Colour out of Space" (1927),
wherein Lovecraft repeatedly mentions "the blasted heath," and
in one of these instances adds, "It was as if the poet had coined
the phrase from having seen this one particular region" (CF
2.369). It is of course debated whether "the poet" in question is
either Milton or Shakespeare, for the Bard first employed the
phrase in *Macbeth* (1606) as a description of the location where
Macbeth and Banquo encounter the three witches or weïrd sis-
ters (1.iii.79). While this may plausibly be Lovecraft's referent—
not least because of the mention of "witch legends" and "witch
trials" (CF 2.368, 371)—the case Robert H. Waugh makes for
Lovecraft referencing Milton's employment of the phrase, in his
description of Satan's fellow fallen angels as like a lightning-
scorched forest (1.606–15), is quite compelling:

> A number of details from this passage reappear in Lovecraft's
> story, besides that telling phrase itself: the fall from heaven, the
> indeterminate nature of those fallen (for it is unclear whether
> the entity of the Colour is one or many), the colors, the light-
> ning, the woods on fire, and the possibility that this fall means a
> punishment (whether upon the fallen entity or upon the ground
> upon which it falls is not clear). Clearly there is good reason to
> believe that Milton's lines may have sparked Lovecraft's imagi-
> nation in a number of ways. (18)

If nothing else, Milton's befuddling notion of Hell's "darkness

6. HPL owned such a bust; see *IAP* 568 (sketch of HPL's apartment at 169
Clinton St.).

visible"—"yet from those flames / No light, but rather darkness visible" (1.62–63)—would seem in keeping with a "color out of space," as it were.

Lovecraft makes other oblique Miltonic references elsewhere. In "Cool Air" (1926), for instance, the narrator at one point says of the artificially preserved Dr. Muñoz, "he seemed about to hurl defiance at the death-daemon even as that ancient enemy seized him" (CF 2.17), which seems to nod to the Miltonic Satan's defiance of domineering Death himself, as discussed above, but also to *Paradise Lost*'s earlier scene in Hell of Satan and his reawakened legions "Hurling defiance toward the Vault of Heav'n" (1.669). Lovecraft opens "The Dunwich Horror" (1928) with a Charles Lamb epigraph that begins with a reference to *Paradise Lost*'s "*Gorgons* and *Hydras*, and *Chimeras* dire" (2.628), and not long after the Reverend Abijah Hoadley's "memorable sermon on the close presence of Satan and his imps" includes references to Azazel, Beelzebub, and Belial (CF 2.420), who are the Miltonic Satan's standard-bearer (1.531–39), second-in-command (1.79–81; 2.299–309, 378–80; 5.696–710), and one of his four chief devils (1.490–502; II.108–228), respectively.

There are arguably even subtler references to Milton in Lovecraft still. Thomas Quale goes as far as to liken the regenerative and/or shapeshifting abilities of Cthulhu in "The Call of Cthulhu" (1926) and the shoggoths in *At the Mountains of Madness* (1931) to the fundamental incorporeality of Milton's angels (24):

> so soft
> And uncompounded is thir Essence pure,
> Not ti'd or manacl'd with joint or limb,
> Nor founded on the brittle strength of bones,
> Like cumbrous flesh; but in what shape they choose
> Dilated or condens't, bright or obscure,
> Can execute thir aery purposes,
> And works of love or enmity fulfill. (1.424–31)

Quale could have just as fittingly referenced Milton's image of Satan recovering from the archangel Michael shearing his right

Christopher Cuccia

side at the climax of their dramatic battle on the first day of *Paradise Lost*'s three-day War in Heaven:

> Yet soon he heal'd; for Spirits that live throughout
> Vital in every part, not as frail man
> In Entrails, Heart or Head, Liver or Reins,
> Cannot but by annihilating die;
> Nor in thir liquid texture mortal wound
> Receive, no more than can the fluid Air:
> All Heart they live, all Head, all Eye, all Ear,
> All Intellect, all Sense, and as they please,
> They Limb themselves, and color, shape or size
> Assume, as likes them best, condense or rare. (6.344–53)

Quale also identifies other Miltonic echoes in the tales of Lovecraft, arguing (26–27) for the many-eyed shoggoths being anticipated in the convoy of Milton's "Chariot of Paternal Deity" (6.750)—the supernatural vehicle in which the Son of God, the Almighty's "Second Omnipotence" (6.684), effortlessly routs the rebel hosts from Heaven (6.824–77)—described by Milton as "four Cherubic shapes, four Faces each / Had wondrous, as with Stars thir bodies all / And Wings were set with Eyes, with Eyes the Wheels" (6.753–55). This reading is not as much of a stretch as one might imagine, for divinity can take on most terrifying appearances in *Paradise Lost*. The fallen angel Mammon explains in Book 2 that "Heav'n's all-ruling Sire" often "with the Majesty of darkness round / Covers his Throne; from whence deep thunders roar / Must'ring thir rage, and Heav'n resembles Hell" (2.264, 266–68), a rather devilish conception of Milton's Deity, but one later confirmed by the unfallen angel Raphael (6.56–59). The distinction between the divine and the diabolical is similarly blurred in the Cthulhu Mythos. S. T. Joshi explains that certain "commentators have believed that Lovecraft's 'evil' gods ... are themselves representative of the evils of religious belief, since they embody the viciousness that many of the actual gods invented by human beings, not excluding the Christian god, appear to display," even if this intriguing interpretation falls short by virtue of the plain fact that "Lovecraft's 'gods' are not 'evil' in any meaningful sense," being "as much 'beyond good and evil' . . . as we ourselves would be from an ant's perspective" (*Against Religion* xxiii).

The many fine nods to the Miltonic in later Lovecraft tales, from overt references to the poet himself to covert appropriations of his weirder concepts, ultimately pale in comparison to the stark references to Milton's *Paradise Lost*, and the conjuring up of the Miltonic mood, in Lovecraft's early story "Dagon." It is worth reviewing once more his comments on his early exposure to the Doré-illustrated *Paradise Lost*: "I began having nightmares of the most hideous description, peopled with things which I called 'night-gaunts,'" Lovecraft explained in a letter to Kleiner in November of 1916—less than a year prior to his composition of "Dagon"—and Lovecraft goes on to speculate, "perhaps the idea of these figures came from an edition de luxe of 'Paradise Lost' with illustrations by Doré, which I discovered one day in the east parlour" (*Letters to Rheinhart Kleiner* 66). Lovecraft does not unequivocally state that the idea for his night-gaunt creatures came from the Doré-illustrated *Paradise Lost*, only that they *perhaps* came from it—a much more significant confession, as it turns out, for it implies his awareness of Miltonic inspirations within him perhaps unbeknownst to him. Therein lies the Miltonic implications for Lovecraft's greater Cthulhu Mythos.

Just as Lovecraft shed the skin of a Poe or Dunsany imitator, laying claim to his own unique writing style, Lovecraft's evolution as a writer saw him move beyond the need to invoke Milton's cosmos, the outré author creating his own complex cosmology and mythology. Yet the centrality of Milton's own cosmic innovations, particularly Chaos, to "Dagon"—the first truly *Lovecraftian* tale—demonstrates that the Cthulhu Mythos is very much rooted in the Miltonic cosmos and its unsettling implications.

Works Cited

Anderson, Jarod K. "The Decentralization of Morality in *Paradise Lost*." Rocky Mountain Review 64, No. 2 (Fall 2010): 198–204.

Burke, Edmund. *A Philosophical Enquiry into the Origin of our Ideas of the Sublime and Beautiful*. Ed. Adam Phillips. 1990. New York: Oxford University Press, 2008.

Burt, Stephen. "'Fighting Since Time Began': Milton and Satan in Philip Pullman's *His Dark Materials*." In Laura Lunger Knoppers and Gregory M. Colón Semenza, ed. *Milton in Popular Culture*. New York: Palgrave Macmillan, 2006. 47–57.

Cunningham, Allan. *The Lives of the Most Eminent British Painters, Sculptors, and Architects*. London: John Murray, 1830–33. 6 vols.

Empson, William. *Milton's God*. Norfolk, CT: New Directions, 1961.

Joshi, S. T. *A Subtler Magick: The Writings and Philosophy of H. P. Lovecraft*. 1996. Gillette, NJ: Wildside Press, 1999.

Kirkconnell, Watson. *The Celestial Cycle: The Theme of Paradise Lost in World Literature with Translations of the Major Analogues*. Toronto: University of Toronto Press, 1952.

Lovecraft, H. P. *Against Religion: The Atheist Writings of H. P. Lovecraft*. Ed. S. T. Joshi. New York: Sporting Gentlemen, 2010.

———. *Letters to J. Vernon Shea, Carl F. Strauch, and Lee McBride White*. Ed. S. T. Joshi and David E. Schultz. New York: Hippocampus Press, 2016.

———. *Letters to Maurice W. Moe and Others*. Ed. David E. Schultz and S. T. Joshi. New York: Hippocampus Press, 2018.

———. *Letters to Rheinhart Kleiner and Others*. Ed. S. T. Joshi and David E. Schultz. New York: Hippocampus Press, 2020.

Milton, John. *Complete Poems and Major Prose*. Ed. Merritt Y. Hughes. 1957. Indianapolis: Hackett Publishing Co., 2003.

———. *Milton's Paradise Lost: A New Edition*. Ed. Richard Bentley. London: Jacob Tonson, 1732.

Quale, Thomas. "The Blind Idiot God: Miltonic Echoes in the Cthulhu Mythos." *Crypt of Cthulhu* No. 49 (Lammas 1987): 24–28.

Raleigh, Sir Walter. *Milton*. 1900. London: Edward Arnold, 1915.

Revard, Stella Purce. *The War in Heaven: Paradise Lost and the Tradition of Satan's Rebellion*. Ithaca, NY: Cornell University Press, 1980.

Russell, Jeffrey Burton. *Mephistopheles: The Devil in the Modern World*. 1986. Ithaca, NY: Cornell University Press, 1990.

Schock, Peter A. *Romantic Satanism: Myth and the Historical Moment in Blake, Shelley, and Byron*. New York: Palgrave Macmillan, 2003.

Shelley, Percy Bysshe. *The Letters of Percy Bysshe Shelley*. Ed. Frederick L. Jones. Oxford: Clarendon Press, 1964. 2 vols.

Steadman, John M. "The Idea of Satan as the Hero of *Paradise Lost*." *Proceedings of the American Philosophical Society* 120, No. 4 [Symposium on John Milton] (13 August 1976): 253–94.

Voltaire (François-Marie Arouet). "Milton." From *An Essay upon the Civil Wars of France . . . and also upon the Epick Poetry of the European Nations From Homer to Milton*. 1727. In John T. Shawcross, ed. *Milton: The Critical Heritage*. New York: Barnes & Noble, 1970. 248–56.

Waugh, Robert H. "The Blasted Heath in 'The Colour out of Space.'" In Waugh's *A Monster of Voices: Speaking for H. P. Lovecraft*. New York: Hippocampus Press, 2011. 15–37.

The Church That Inspired "The Horror at Red Hook" and the Fall of the House of Suydam

Marc Beherec

"The Horror at Red Hook" illustrates what happens (in Lovecraft's understanding) when a learned and intelligent white American goes backward on the path of evolution. The story is deeply tied to a sense of place, and one of its important settings is a tumbledown, Gothic-style stone church used as a dance hall on Wednesdays and used by a group of Nestorian Christians of impure faith. One particular Red Hook church has long been misidentified as the source of Lovecraft's inspiration. Several other Brooklyn churches may have provided the local color that suffuses the story. But the most important church to inspire "The Horror at Red Hook," St. George's Syrian Catholic Church, was not in Red Hook at all. In Lovecraft's time the church was housed in a tenement and commercial building constructed by Ryneer Suydam and renovated in Gothic style. Now deconsecrated, the building still stands at 103 Washington Street in Manhattan's Lower West Side.

Rereading "The Horror at Red Hook" with St. George's history in mind allows for a reinterpretation of the story. The story is a parallel tale to Edgar Allan Poe's "The Fall of the House of Usher" and Lovecraft's earlier tale "The Street." Lovecraft's Suydam rejects his own ancestry. He accepts alien ways and learns an awful lore. As the story's epigraph states, he turns back upon the path of evolution; that is, he reverses evolution's course and returns to a more primitive state. He gives his ancestral land to a foreign horde, and in so doing not only condemns himself but also infects the very bricks that surrounded him. Suydam's pact with an alien people brings the destruction of an entire city block, which collapses like the House of Usher, taking with it the house of Suydam. It is not his ancestral abode (although Lovecraft makes clear that is infected too), but tenement houses that collapse in the story. This church and tenements are based on the very real tenement-turned-church built by Ryneer Suydam and the neighborhood that surrounded it, Manhattan's Syrian quarter.

The Two Churches of "The Horror at Red Hook"

Two churches play prominent roles in "The Horror at Red Hook," and Lovecraft uses them as foils against each other. Both church buildings first appear in section III. The first to be introduced is "the steepled and ivy-clad Reformed Church with its iron-railed yard of Netherlandish gravestones" (CF 1.486). The church and the cemetery made a profound impression on Lovecraft when he first visited what he called "the principal antiquity of this section" (FFF 76) in September 1922. "[S]ome benign fate has preserved the ancient village church, whose ivy-twined belfry & spire still dominate the local skyline ... As I viewed this village churchyard in the autumn twilight, the city seemed to fade from sight, & give place to the Netherland town of long ago. In fancy I saw the cottages of the simple Dutchmen, their small-paned windows lighted one by one as evening stole over the harvest-fields" (From the Pest Zone 124n49). Lovecraft went so far as to chip a fragment from a gravestone as an evocative souvenir, and his theft served to inspire "The Hound" (FFF 77). The church and churchyard were located less than half a mile and directly down Flatbush Avenue south of Sonia Greene's apartment at 259 Parkside Avenue; Lovecraft would have passed it frequently.

The Dutch Reformed Church was founded in 1654 as the first church in today's Brooklyn. It served most of Flatbush's early residents including the Suydam family, and many Suydams are interred in the churchyard. The extant church building, the third on the site, was completed in 1798. When the foundations were dug, numerous human remains were uncovered and reinterred. In the words of family historian Rev. J. Howard Suydam, "Whenever, therefore, we enter the old but beautiful Dutch church building at Flatbush, we doubtless tread the earth which covers the bones and the dust of our common ancestor, who came to New Amsterdam in 1663, and departed this life at Flatbush in 1701" (24). The Dutch Reformed Church was the scene of one of the happiest events in the story, the marriage of Robert Suydam and Cornelia Gerritsen. It is one of "the occasional graceful churches" that make up "the relics of this former happiness" that existed when New York was exclusively an Anglo-Dutch settlement (CF 1.484).

The Reformed Church's sinister twin first appears at the end of section III. This church was "a tumbledown stone church" that "reared its Gothic buttresses near the vilest part of the waterfront" (CF 1.488). "It was nominally Catholic; but priests throughout Brooklyn denied the place all standing and authenticity," and the rituals practiced there were those of "some remnant of Nestorian Christianity tinctured with the Shamanism of Thibet" (CF 1.488–89). The interior was decorated with "crudely painted panels" (CF 1.492) and Greek inscriptions. Beneath the church, a crypt held "a vast arched chapel with wooden benches and a strangely figured altar" and a "croaking organ" (CF 1.503). This church also has its parallels in the real world.

The Federalist-style church and the happy event that took place there contrasts markedly with the Gothic pile and the "creatures" (CF 1.488) who conducted dark rituals therein. The Reformed Church is physically removed from the waterfront, standing more than two miles from, and 50 feet in elevation above, the sea. Federalist architecture is the colonial variant of the Georgian architecture Lovecraft so loved. By contrast, Lovecraft hated the Victorian neo-Gothic, including "those new-Gothic-Romanesque-Byzantine unnamabilities that leer here and there in N.Y." (SL 1.314). The Federalist Dutch Reformed Church represents the old, colonial, and clean church with its decorous ceremony, in contrast to the decadent Gothic church, with its dances and its strange, foreign, and bloody rituals.

The Sacred Hearts of Jesus and Mary and
St. Charles' Chapel

One church building is widely accepted as the inspiration for Lovecraft's dance hall church, but it is one of the few churches of Red Hook that clearly did not contribute to the story. The Yuletide 1984 issue of *Crypt of Cthulhu* includes a photograph of a derelict church. The caption reads, "This may be the church mentioned by Lovecraft in 'The Horror at Red Hook' as the headquarters for Robert Suydam's cult. It is located in Red Hook and was once used as a dance hall, as mentioned in the story. (Located by Marc A. Cerasini and Charles Hoffman. Photographed by Steven Mariconda.)" (Price, "Humor at Red Hook" 9). This publication was followed three years later by a letter by Cerasini, in which he identified the church as "formerly St. Steven's parish church" and announced that the building had been razed after a partial collapse (55). He gave no other explanations or evidence for the identification.

I untangled the history of the church in Mariconda's photograph with the help of Sacred Hearts and St. Stephen's parish historian, John L. Heyer II. Heyer provided not only his own knowledge and perspective but also news clippings and photographs. The church in the photograph was the first church building of Sacred Hearts of Jesus and Mary parish. The parish was established in 1882, as the first parish in the Diocese of Brooklyn specifically created to minister to Italian immigrants. The building in the photo was constructed in 1885 and stood on President Street between Van Brunt and Columbia Streets (Diocese of Brooklyn 62).

The parish soon outgrew the building, and a new church was constructed about 1900. The parish's name transferred to the new building. The old building was retained and served the parish school, St. Charles' School, and renamed St. Charles' Chapel. The building was called St. Charles' in Lovecraft's time. In 1941 the new building was demolished to construct what is now the Brooklyn-Queens Expressway (BQE); Sacred Hearts of Jesus and Mary parish merged with nearby St. Stephen's parish.

St. Charles' Chapel was used until 1976. According to Heyer, in 1987 "a city planning project undermined the foundation of the church and all of the buildings on the surrounding three blocks" (personal communication). The New York City Department of Buildings claimed the building was constructed with weak wooden columns and trusses (Abraham). Whatever the ultimate cause, the building collapsed during a heavy rain between 4 and 5 A.M. on Monday, July 27, 1987. The former church property is now Mother Cabrini Park.

Most fans have only seen Mariconda's photograph of a spooky-looking derelict St. Charles', either in *Fungi from Yuggoth* or in various reproductions (e.g., *More Annotated H. P. Lovecraft* 137). But in Lovecraft's time there was nothing tumbledown about the well-maintained building (Figure 1). Unlike Lovecraft's church, St. Charles' was constructed of brick, not stone. The façade, with its crow-stepped gable and large central arched window, was Flemish rather than Gothic in design. It had no buttresses, and, as Heyer notes, "at the time that he was writing the church was completely attached to the row houses on either side of it. Therefore even if it had buttresses no one would have been able to see them" (personal communication). Finally, the church was built on an old landfill with a high water table, facts that contributed to the building's collapse and made a basement impossible. Nothing about the church's construction resembles Lovecraft's descriptions of his fictional church

The most convincing evidence that St. Charles' Chapel was the model for the church in "The Horror at Red Hook" is the claim that it doubled as a dance hall. Asked for evidence in 2019, Cerasini stated, "the Italians who I lived around all told me about the dances held there in the '20s and '30s" (personal communication). But Cerasini's informants were probably talking about a different church. Heyer notes that not only was the St. Charles' Chapel not used for dancing, it would have been physically impossible to use the building as a dance hall: "the church had permanent wooden benches filling the entire space, therefore making it impossible for any kind of dancing to occur, especially since there was also no basement space for such a thing" (personal communication). A photograph of the church's interior shows just that: heavy pews occupy the entire interior.

Figure 1: Two views circa 1931 of St. Charles Chapel (formerly Sacred Hearts of Jesus and Mary Church). (John Heyer II and St. Stephen and Sacred Hearts of Jesus and Mary.)

Gothic Dance Hall Churches of Red Hook

Gothic architecture was common among Red Hook churches near the waterfront, and the custom of building basement social halls in which dances were hosted was also common. Heyer identifies four Gothic churches in Red Hook that resemble the church in "The Horror at Red Hook" in that they are located near the Red Hook waterfront, are Gothic in design, and offered dances.

One still stands at 110 Wolcott Street, between Van Brunt and Conover Streets. This church is now abandoned, and Heyer identifies it as formerly Lutheran. Constructed between 1885 and 1898, it served as Christ Protestant Episcopal Chapel. It was later the Church of the Holy Child Jesus (Blanck).

Another is the nineteenth-century structure built to house the Church of the Pilgrims, which stood at the corner of Warren and Hicks Streets. When the parish was first founded, the church belonged to St. Peter's Catholic Church, and Sacred Hearts of Jesus and Mary met in the building. By the 1920s this building was deconsecrated and used as a gym for the parish school; it could have hosted dances. It has since been demolished.

Heyer, who is familiar with "The Horror at Red Hook," suggests his own candidate for the church that inspired Lovecraft: St. Stephen's Parish Church (Figure 2). Constructed in 1873 at what was then the corner of Hicks and Summit Streets, it still stands today at 125 Summit Street, overlooking the BQE. Today the neighborhood is known as Carroll Gardens, but before the BQE was built it was part of Red Hook. The building is constructed of brick in an imposing Gothic style. In Lovecraft's time the church was predominantly Irish (Heyer, personal communication).

Heyer points out that St. Stephen's is a much stronger candidate than St. Charles' Chapel:

It is Gothic in design, the buttresses along the sides of the building are very visible and stand out as do the windows which look down into basement. The parish was known for having dances and many people credit their marriages on those dances from the 1920s through the Korean War. The Church would also have been said to be in Red Hook at that time although now in Carroll Gardens since there was no such thing as Carroll Gardens until the 1960s and the BQE highway was not yet built separating Red Hook from the rest of "South Brooklyn." (Heyer, personal communication)

Perhaps the best candidate is Visitation of the Blessed Virgin Mary Catholic Church, which still stands at 98 Richards Street, less than a quarter-mile from the Red Hook waterfront. Visitation was founded by Irish, Italian, and German immigrants in 1854, although the current building dates to 1896. The buttressed Gothic building, like the church in "The Horror at Red Hook," was built of stone, in this case dark Manhattan schist. Like Lovecraft's church it has a pipe organ, a Reuben Midmer & Sons electro-pneumatic organ installed in 1917—but the organ is kept in the choir loft, not in some hidden crypt (DeSalles Media Group 2019). According to Heyer, it has a basement social hall where the parish held dances. As early as 1920, Lovecraft jotted a note in his commonplace book that prefigured "The Horror at Red Hook": "Hideous cracked discord of bass musick from (ruin'd) organ in (abandon'd) abbey or cathedral" (quoted in *From the Pest Zone* 15). It is easy to imagine Lovecraft passing by Visitation Church on one of his nocturnal walks, hearing the powerful organ and Latin chants emerging from inside, and fantasizing about the foreign ceremonies practiced therein.

Figure 2: St. Stephen's Church, before the construction of the BQE and the merger with Sacred Hearts. (John Heyer II and St. Stephen and Sacred Hearts of Jesus and Mary.)

Figure 3: Visitation of the Blessed Virgin Mary from Visitation Place, ca. 1931. (Photo by Percy Loomis Sperr, © Milstein Division, New York Public Library.)

Any, and perhaps all, of these churches may have inspired Lovecraft. He took offence to the immigrants who used these churches, not only practicing foreign rites but even *dancing* in the stygian depths of their basement social halls. But these were not the people Lovecraft described as the villains of Red Hook. These were German, Irish, and Italian immigrants and their descendants, not Arabs and Kurds. The church that inspired Lovecraft catered to a different immigrant community, in a different part of the metropolis.

Nestorians, Assyrians, Antiochians, and Catholics

Explaining the rites the cult practiced at Red Hook, Lovecraft writes, "Suydam, when questioned, said that he thought the ritual was some remnant of Nestorian Christianity" (CF 1.488–89). He refers to a family of eastern Christian Churches. Some have ties to the Roman Catholic Church, others to the Orthodox Churches, and still others are independent and seen as heterodox or heretical by other Christians. In Lovecraft's time the nomenclature of each of these churches' names was unsettled, and even churchmen were confused about their natures.

The church that can most justifiably be called "Nestorian" calls itself today the Holy Catholic Apostolic Assyrian Church of the East. It fissured from other Christian churches in the fifth century amidst disagreements over the nature of Jesus' divinity and personhood. They were called Nestorians by their adversaries, who claimed they followed the teachings of the monk Nestorius rather than those of Christ. The so-called "Nestorians" were regarded as heretics by Orthodox and Roman Catholics alike. Today the Church of the East rejects the name Nestorian, in part because it does not subscribe to more extreme doctrines attributed to Nestorius. At one time the Church of the East extended throughout the Mongol Empire into Tibet. By the nineteenth century its dominion and influence had shrunk, and church members were found primarily in Kurdistan and the Plain of Nineveh. The patriarchate was established at Mosul, in what is today northern Iraq.

Lovecraft probably read of the Church of the East in both

antiquarian writings and newspapers. It was common for Western antiquarians to visit the leaders of the Assyrian Churches and the Yezidis while conducting missionary or archaeological work in the region. Sir Austen Henry Layard, the excavator of Nineveh, visited both the Nestorians and the Yezidis, and the full title of his popular book is *Nineveh and Its Remains: With an Account of a Visit to the Chaldean Christians of Kurdistan, and the Yezidis, or Devil-Worshippers; and an Enquiry into the Manners and Arts of the Ancient Assyrians.* Lovecraft, whose many descriptions of ancient reliefs resemble the archaeological remains of the Assyrian capital, may have perused Layard's book.

Lovecraft would have also read of the church's persecutions in the newspapers of the 1910s and 1920s. Two patriarchs were killed and a thirteen-year-old member of the traditional patriarchal family took the throne ("Shimun, Assyrian Church Head, Slain"; "New Assyrian Patriarch"). The Nestorians' plight and their unusual customs were common topics of feature stories.

Another church with common roots is the Chaldean Catholic Church. It consists of a faction of the Assyrian Church of the East that broke away and joined the Roman Catholic Church in 1552 (Liesel). In the 1920s they were led by Patriarch Mar Yousef VI Emmanuel II Thomas, who was also based in Mosul.

But there were few members of either of these churches in New York in the 1920s. Of those few Assyrians who immigrated at the time, most settled in Massachusetts and Chicago. The first Church of the East building to be constructed in modern times outside the Middle East was St. Mary's Assyrian Apostolic Church, which was built in 1927 in Worcester, Massachusetts (Donabed and Donabed 77). Most Chaldean Catholics who came to the United States at the time settled in the suburbs of Detroit (Sengstock 3–4). In New York City, as Philip M. Kayal and Joseph M. Kayal note in *The Syrian-Lebanese in America*, "Actually, most [immigrant Arabs] are Semitic Christians from Mount Lebanon, which at the time of the migration was part of the modern Syrian nation" (26–27). These immigrants belonged to other churches with historical and religious ties to the East, and who often used the same nomenclature to describe themselves.

The Orthodox cousin of the Assyrian Churches is the Antiochian Orthodox Church. Syrian Antiochian Church members began coming to the United States due to instability in the Ottoman Empire in the last quarter of the nineteenth century. By the time Lovecraft lived in New York, the Antiochian Orthodox there answered directly to the Greek Orthodox Patriarch of Antioch, who lived in Damascus (Gabriel; Michalopulos and Ham 44–47). But in New York City, the Antiochian Orthodox were still a minority among Arab Christians.

Most Syrian immigrants belonged to one of two churches, both of them in communion with the Roman Catholic Church. The Syriac Maronite Church of Antioch has its base in present-day Lebanon and is named after St. Maron, a monastic leader of the fourth and fifth centuries, and elected its first Patriarch of Antioch and All the East in 685. Maronites found assimilation easy because of their close ties with French missionaries. William Peter Blatty, author of *The Exorcist,* whose great-uncle was a Maronite archbishop, was descended from Maronite Christian immigrants in New York (Blatty). Blatty's family is just one example of a Maronite family that successfully assimilated into the mainstream of American Catholicism and American society.

Most important for understanding Lovecraft's story, the Melkite Greek Catholic Church understands itself to have always been in communion with Rome, although historically it was more closely allied with the Antiochian Orthodox Church. In 1924 the Melkites followed their own Patriarch of Antioch, Demetrius I Qadi, who was based in Damascus. Both Maronites and Melkites practiced their own services and rites in the United States, but in Lovecraft's time they answered to the local Roman Catholic bishop.

This confusion in identity and nomenclature was baffling even to religious authorities. Most of these churches follow a Patriarch of Antioch, and they can all legitimately call themselves Catholic, Antiochian, and Assyrian. Only the Church of the East and the Chaldeans had historic ties to the Nestorian movement, but both would reject being labeled "Nestorian." As late as 1986, in a pamphlet published for Catholic priests, Bish-

op J. Francis Stafford admitted, "We have also become aware
that on the occasion of . . . contacts, Catholic priests are often
unsure of just whom they are dealing with. . . . What do these
Churches profess? he asks himself. Do they have bishops? validly
ordained priests? the sacraments? What are their origins? Who
are their hierarchical leaders?" (1). Even clergymen found the
situation confusing.

The situation was all the more confusing to civil authorities.
Members of the different and often competing religious bodies
sometimes used this confusion as a weapon against one another.
In 1911, Father Thomas H. Fayad, a Melkite priest, complained
to the Scranton police that Deacon John Yohana was collecting
funds without the permission of the local bishop. Yohana was
apprehended and forced to disgorge $945.20, much of it sewn
into the lining of his clothes, before it was determined that he
actually belonged to the Church of the East, and therefore did
not answer to the Catholic bishop ("Assyrian Missionary"). Another Assyrian, John Danoo, was arrested in Mooretown, New
Jersey, in 1922 and accused of collecting $4,000 while posing as
a "Nestorian priest" and fraudulently presenting himself as a
representative of Near East Relief ("Hold 'Rev.' Danoo"). It is
unclear from the available press reports whether Danoo was a
legitimate priest of any jurisdiction.

We must read Lovecraft's description in this ecclesiastical
context. "It was nominally Catholic; but priests throughout
Brooklyn denied the place all standing and authenticity, and po-
licemen agreed with them" (CF 1.488). Technically, all priests
of the Maronite, Melkite, and Chaldean Churches are Catholic,
and in Lovecraft's time they fell under the jurisdiction of the local Catholic bishop. But their Roman Catholic brethren might
not even know if they are legitimate Catholics. Lovecraft knew
St. George's called itself Assyrian, and from that he deduced
that it was Nestorian, and the mistake is embedded in the story.

Lovecraft among the Arabs

Red Hook itself was never an Arabic enclave, but there were
many Arabs who were closer to Lovecraft's home. The center of

the Arabic population in Brooklyn is along Atlantic Avenue in the Borough Hall neighborhood, which was settled by Arabs moving across the Brooklyn Bridge from Manhattan's Little Syria. In 1924, they completed the first stage of construction of Virgin Mary Melkite Church on the corner of Court and Amity Streets (Melkite Exarchate 82–83).

"The Horror at Red Hook" was based not so much on Red Hook as on the "herds of evil-looking foreigners that one sees everywhere in New York" (*Dawnward Spire* 83). Lovecraft conceptualized the story taking place in "a slum district of Brooklyn, betwixt Clinton St. & the waterfront" (*FFF* 331), a large area that includes not only Red Hook but also Carroll Gardens, Cobble Hill, and Brooklyn Heights. In another letter, he claims that his apartment at 169 Clinton Street, in Brooklyn Heights, was located "at the edge of Red Hook" (*MWM* 440). "The Spanish, Syrian, and Arabic slums approach it, but are still a comfortable distance away," Lovecraft's friend George Kirk wrote of the apartment on February 2, 1924 (Kirk 77). Lovecraft wrote that he based the cultists upon the youth gangs he saw on Court Street and around Borough Hall (*From the Pest Zone* 15–16).

Some Arabs were actually *in* Lovecraft's home. By October 1925 at least one Syrian, an importer named Alexander Messayeh, lived in the boarding house below Lovecraft (*FFF* 454). In November 1925, Lovecraft wrote of "my neighbor Abdul Firouz ben Hussein Ali—or whoever he is. In the morning I hear him strangely chanting—& wouldn't wonder if he is saying his prayers to Allah in Arabic. I wonder if he wears a turban?" (*FFF* 480). He informed another correspondent:

> once a *Syrian* had the room next to mine and played eldritch and whining monotones on a strange bagpipe which made me dream ghoulish and incredible things of crypts under Bagdad and limitless corridors of Eblis beneath the moon-cursed ruins of Istakhar. I never *saw* this man, and my privilege to imagine him in any shape I chose lent glamour to his weird pneumatic cacophonies. In my vision he always wore a turban and a long robe of pale figured silk, and had a right eye plucked out . . . be-

cause it had looked upon something in a tomb at night which
no eye may look upon and live. (MWM 440)

Lovecraft believed these people "belong for the most part to the
Orthodox Greek Church" (MWM 440). He otherwise had only
a very dim idea of who these people were.

But Lovecraft also had Lower Manhattan's Little Syria in
mind as he wrote. There is no doubt he was aware of and visited
Little Syria. Writing to Zealia Bishop, Lovecraft extolled his favorite New York guidebook. "To pick up the general traditional
colour of the whole town, the best guide book I know of is the
tiny free brown leather volume distributed by the Bowman hotels
. . . It is called 'The Sidewalks of New York'" (*The Spirit of Revision*
96). The Little Leather Library's *Sidewalks of New York* urged its
readers following its colonial walking tours of New York to "go
through the foreign colony of Washington Street" (36):

> If you do go down Washington, you will find, south of Alba-
> ny Street a quaint little Syrian colony, quiet and peace loving,
> with stores flaunting lovely oriental laces and embroideries, and
> tantalizing Turkish candies. In the restaurants you hear only
> their ancient language, and see few others besides these olive-
> skinned, straight-nosed, handsome orientals. The menus are in
> Syrian and you dine on stuffed grape leaves, unleavened bread,
> and skillfully disguised lamb with okra.
>
> On the last block of Washington Street, before you reach the
> open park, is a little mixed Mohammedan colony, Arabian and
> Turk, with a sprinkling of Greeks. Here is the greatest mingling
> of nationalities in the city. At the corner of Morris Street, of a
> summer's night, one can imagine oneself in Bagdad! (*The Side-
> walks of New York* 36)

As early as 1922 Lovecraft documented his explorations of
lower Manhattan in his letters to his family and friends. "These
lost lanes of an elder city have for me the utmost fascination,
and I am constantly on the lookout for new ones," he explained
(FFF 165). The "southern tip of Manhattan" (Long 163) was a
frequent stomping ground of the Kalem Club, where Lovecraft
and his friends would wander, "stopping occasionally to admire

one of the very old houses which still could be found scattered throughout the financial district in the 1920s" (Long 76).

Lovecraft probably never ate the "skillfully disguised lamb with okra," and clearly did not see these people as "handsome orientals." He never took the opportunity to get to know much about these people as individuals or to learn about their culture first-hand. But his distorted understanding of the Eastern Christian religious groups to which many of these new immigrants belonged inspired him. The parallels between "The Horror at Red Hook" and the history of St. George's Syrian Catholic Church are so close that it is improbable that Lovecraft did not know the church's history and incorporate it into "The Horror at Red Hook."

Ryneer Suydam, Saint George's Syrian Catholic Church, and Little Syria

The history of 103 Washington Street has been extensively documented by Michael D. Caratzas of the Research Department of the New York Landmarks Preservation Commission. The following discussion relies on Caratzas's work except where otherwise noted.

Ryneer Suydam was a partner in Ryneer & John Suydam, which maintained a pier on Manhattan's waterfront (Barrett 2.265). In 1799, Suydam purchased the property on which he later constructed 103 Washington Street. The land was new riverside property, part of landfill on Manhattan's western shore. Sometime between 1802 and 1819 Suydam built a three-story peaked-roofed building in Federal style as a commercial building and tenement. Suydam lived in Manhattan, but by 1810 he, his family, and his slaves relocated to Brooklyn. At the time of his death in 1833, Suydam lived in "a venerable Dutch edifice" (Stiles 1.132), near the intersection of today's Hicks and West Baltic Streets in Cobble Hill, near the waterfront. The house stood on a farm of at least ten acres "on the southeasterly side of Red Hook Road" outside the village of Brooklyn ("To Speculators"). The house was demolished in the middle nineteenth century (Stiles 1.132). Suydam also owned property in Red Hook proper (Stiles 1.145).

103 Washington Street was sold to settle Suydam's estate in 1835 and thereafter served as a lodging house for sailors and German and Irish immigrants. Two floors were added in 1869. The peaked Federal style roof was flattened, marking the first major alteration (Lovecraft might say degradation) from the Federal ideal. In the 1870 census, more than 300 seamen and a dozen couples and small families listed 103 Washington Street as their home. The land west of Washington was gradually built up, pushing the waterfront farther and farther from 103 Washington.

In the late 1850s the building served as a "German dance house." This was not the sort of benign venue as existed in the church basements in Red Hook, where young couples could meet and get to know one another under the watchful eye of parish leaders. Rather, women were employed to dance with male visitors. The dances were often used as cover for, and as a prelude to, prostitution.

Over the course of the late nineteenth century, the building was the scene of various desperate crimes. In 1852 Mary Weigal, a German who came to America following the man who impregnated her, drowned her infant in a sink ("New-York City"). In 1857, Johanna Finn attacked her husband with a hatchet in the building, but was released by the police, who determined "she gave her husband no more than he deserved" ("Police Intelligence"). In 1859, Johana Vent and Catherine Riddle, "inmates of the dance-house No. 103 Washington-street," fought over an indigo bag. The fight escalated until Vent stabbed Riddle with a butcher knife, seriously injuring her ("City Intelligence"). In 1897, during a fight between the two sailors, John Boyson shot Gottfried Tietze and then himself. Both men died ("Sailor Tietze"). The crimes were of the sort that were only occasionally reported in the *New York Times* and then only in single-paragraph summaries. It was scarcely news fit to print.

In the 1890s the entire neighborhood began to change. Immigrants arrived from the increasingly unstable Ottoman Empire, and later from the collapsing Austro-Hungarian and Russian Empires. Syrians came in increasing numbers from 1890 until first World War I, and shortly after the war federal law drastically diminished legal immigration. In 1890, the first year for which Syrian immigrants were specifically documented, 1,126 individuals immigrated. As conditions deteriorated in their homeland, immigration increased to a peak of 9,210 in 1913. After dropping during the Great War, immigration numbers rose again into the low thousands beginning in 1920. But the Quota Limit Act of 1921 and the Immigration Act of 1924 brought Syrian immigration nearly to a halt. In 1924, the year Lovecraft wrote "The Horror at Red Hook," just 1,595 individuals immigrated legally from Syria to the United States. "That a mere 10,000 immigrants a year could inspire such paranoid reactions among Americans indicates the general anti-immigrant climate prevalent in the country at the time" (Kayal and Kayal 74).

103 Washington Street next served as a tenement for the new immigrant groups, with shops on the ground floor. George Forzly & Co., which was both a bank and a dry goods store serving mostly Syrians, operated on the ground floor in the 1890s. The owner was jailed and for larceny when the firm collapsed in 1899 ("Syrian Banker Surrenders"). The building had one Syrian resident during the census of 1900. By 1920 most of 103 Washington was occupied predominantly by central Europeans, but two-thirds of 105 Washington next door were Syrians or their American-born children. Washington Street was then known as Little Syria.

Will Irwin described the scene in 1927:

> Viewed from Battery Park . . . the beginnings of Greenwich Street and Washington Street resemble the profile of a mountain valley. To the left towers like a red Alpine crag the Whitehall Building. To the right shoots up the main range. Washington Street is the valley between; and a venerable three-story building begins it. By virtue of a stepped roof, quarter-circle windows on the seaward side, and leaded dormers, this building looks colonial. Old maps, however, prove that its site was water before the thirties of the last century. Beyond, run

rows of square old-fashioned tenements, their fronts embel-
lished with the futurist designs of fire-escapes. Two generations
ago, before the era of sky-scrapers, the first Syrian families settled in these buildings. As is the way of foreign colonies, the later arrivals gathered under the wing of their more sophisticated
countrymen. ... Eventually Syrian wholesale and retail commerce in goods of the Near East absorbed four blocks along
Washington Street together with the tributary alleys. (31)

Romanian-American writer Konrad Bercovici wrote in 1924
that "a descent upon the Syrian quarters is like a dream travel. It
is as if some undreamed-of means of transportation had suddenly
been realized, and we could at will, in a few minutes, land across
the seas into some remote, outlying district of Damascus ... the
city that has remained as ancient as it was two thousand years
ago" (24–25). But he, like Lovecraft, felt the people were a negative influence on the buildings themselves. He imagined these
people, who were city-dwellers in Syria, to be desert nomads:

> How people do transform the quarter they live in to suit their
> national temperament and habits! These houses had all originally
> been occupied by good Dutch burghers a hundred years ago. It is
> not only age that has told on the houses, but also a different atti-
> tude of the inhabitants toward them. The Dutch looked upon
> these places as homes, as permanent habitations for themselves
> and the future generations. They Syrian quite unconsciously con-
> siders every abode as a temporary housing-tent. (30)

Nearby, Manhattan still had an active waterfront used by
tramp vessels. "Skirt the waterfront again, pass the Brooklyn fer-
ry; and you come to a broad, double wharf where snub-nosed
canal-boats, four deep, wallow in the oily harbor-swells" (Irwin
36). "Symbolically, [the Syrians'] homes were conveniently located near the piers—the center of trade for the city and country" (Kayal and Kayal 86).

In 1899 the nation's first Melkite parish was formed on the
Lower West Side, led by Lebanese missionary Father Abraham
Backewate. In 1920, parishioner George E. Bardwil, an importer
of linens and fine embroideries, purchased the building at 103

Washington Street (Melkite Exarchate 85). The church was named for Bardwil's patron saint, St. George. Lovecraft would have known George as the patron saint of England. But according to tradition, St. George was from Lydda, today's Lod, in Palestine. In both the east and the west, St. George is a soldier-saint known for slaying a dragon.

The Melkites of Little Syria sought to integrate into American society. They adopted some Western liturgical practices and chose to model their church building along Western lines. Brooklyn architect W. B. Wills created a Gothic structure within the bottom two stories of the building. He installed a large pointed-arch Gothic doorway and two flanking, smaller pointed-arch doorways. He installed a large central circular window, probably holding a rose window—another signature Gothic feature—in the second story. This renovation was complete by 1921 and survived until 1929: this is how Lovecraft would have seen the church (Figure 4).

Lovecraft probably read newspaper accounts of the consecration of the renovated building. On 28 February 1921, a photo appeared widely in United States newspapers under the headline "Consecrate Assyrian Church." Elaborately robed Melkite priests stand outside the building holding censers. Men wearing western suits and thick, curled Turkish mustaches stand nearby. The caption reads, "FATHER BECKWATE [sic] and this group of priests yesterday consecrated what was called the first Assyrian Church in the United States. It is St. George's, at 103 Washington street" ("Consecrate Assyrian Church"). Whether this was the first Assyrian church depended on how one counts. As we have seen, the first building constructed by the Assyrian Church of the East in the United States was constructed in Worcester in 1927. St. Joseph Maronite Church was established in the Lower West Side in 1891, and opened a dedicated church building at 57 Washington Street in 1916 (Dunlap; Small et al.). But St. George's was the first dedicated Melkite church building in the United States.

Figure 4: St. George's Church in 1929, shortly before the exterior was renovated. Note the pointed arched doorways and round window, common features of Gothic architecture. (Photo by Percy Loomis Sperr, © Milstein Division, New York Public Library.)

Entering the church, Lovecraft would have seen icons of saints and angels painted in traditional Byzantine fashion. He would encounter an icon of the church's patron saint, St. George, in the entry porch or narthex of the church, and additional icons in the nave of the church. A wall of icons known as an iconostasis divided the altar from the congregation. An undated photograph shows an iconostasis holding four nearly life-size, full-body paintings on linen mounted on wooden panels of Christ and three saints (Melkite Exarchate 86).

Eastern iconography is deliberately *anagoric;* that is, Byzantine-style icons are unnatural, spiritualized depictions of their subjects, "pointing to a reality beyond the physical, lifting those who see it to a higher level of thought, feeling and consciousness" (Cavarnos 36–37). The saintly figures are shown with deliberately distorted features. Heads are unnaturally large. Facial expressions are somber. Eyes are enlarged, the better to see the beatific vision. Noses are elongated to smell the odor of sanctity. Fingers are elongated, adding to the indication of the saints' heightened senses. Bodies are schematized to indicate their new, divinized nature. Unearthly colors are used to indicate the heavenly setting. Icons are meant not to be realistic, but rather spiritual aids to meditation.

To Lovecraft, who grew up in the aniconic American Protestant tradition, St. George's icons may have appeared to be "crudely painted panels he did not like—panels which depicted sacred faces with peculiarly worldly and sardonic expressions" (CF 1.492). Lovecraft might have taken exception to seeing England's patron saint depicted not as a medieval knight, but rather as a Byzantine soldier. He would have seen inscriptions in Greek and Arabic. He would have seen "foreigners in figured robes, mitres, and other inexplicable devices" (CF 1.497).

Bercovici described the churches of Little Syria in 1924:

> There are two red-brick churches, one the St. George and the other the St. Joseph, belonging to the Ecclesia Maronita Catholica. Within these churches at all hours devotees can be found kneeling and prostrating themselves, very much in Moslem manner, before the candy-white decorative altars. The decorations and pictures and images, of the crudest kind, and in the

loudest color, make one think of the beginnings of Christianity some two thousand years ago, when the Copts buried their prayer-houses deep in the ground. (31)

Here, in the "heart of the town in Dutch and early British days" (MWM 91), just around the corner from historic Trinity Church, a house built by Ryneer Suydam was consecrated the temple of a foreign sect. It was transformed from a Georgian tenement to a neo-Gothic church. It at one time served as a "dance hall" that doubled as a brothel. The church was more than just "nominally Catholic," but it would be understandable if the "priests throughout Brooklyn denied the place all standing and authenticity" (CF 1.488). The predominantly Irish, French, and German Catholic priests were as likely to be ignorant of who the Melkites were as most of their parishioners, and may have even believed they were Nestorians. The church was decorated with "painted panels" (CF 1.492) that appeared strange to the Western eye, where "foreigners in figured robes, mitres, and other inexplicable devices" (CF 1.497) performed strange rites. This was the church that Lovecraft transported to Red Hook.

The Fall of the House of Suydam

The moral of "The Horror at Red Hook" is expressed in the epigraph, that "man may sometimes return on the track of evolution" (CF 1.480); that is, humanity may go backward to a more primitive state. Lovecraft took the line from Arthur Machen's "The Red Hand," in which amateur sleuths seek cavemen in the streets of London, only to find a Stone Age murder. Lovecraft had treated devolution extensively less than two years earlier in "The Rats in the Walls," wherein Delapore devolves so far that he speaks dead languages. Suydam, the assimilated scion of a Dutch family, turns back on the track of evolution in a different way, becoming the leader of a barbaric cult.

The horror that struck Red Hook impacted not only the people but also the architecture. In this respect the tale resembles Lovecraft's 1919 short story "The Street" and Edgar Allan Poe's "The Fall of the House of Usher." A parallel reading of the three tales alongside the history of Little Syria reveals the core of "The Horror at Red Hook" to be a racist examination of physical decay resulting when an intelligent person retraces the path of evolution.

All the Suydams in America are descended from a single ancestor, Hendrick Rycken, who came to New Amsterdam in 1663. For unknown reasons, around 1710 the entire Rycken family abandoned that name and adopted the name Suydam, meaning South of the Dam. About the turn of the twentieth century J. Howard Suydam estimated that 1,000 people had borne the name Suydam (37–38).

Lovecraft probably first learned of the family in Washington Irving's *The Knickerbocker History of New York*, which he acquired in September 1924 (*LL* #493; *FFF* 160). The earliest Suydams were not refined Anglo-Dutch. Irving explains, "As to the Suydams, they were thrown upon the Long Island coast, and may still be found in those parts" (1.177). At the time of the skirmishes over New Amsterdam between the English and the Dutch, these Dutch were a still-unassimilated, dangerous "tribe of warriors who came from the neighborhood of Hell-gate. These were commanded by the Suy Dams and the Van Dams, incontinent hard swearers, as their names betoken; they were terrible looking fellows, clad in broad-skirted gaberdines, of that curious colored cloth called thunder and lightning, and bore as a standard three devil's darning-needles, *volant*, in a flame-colored field" (Irving 2.183).

By Lovecraft's time the Suydams had refined, assimilated with the Nordic stock, and developed into prominent New Yorkers. In Lovecraft's view, "gradual intermarriage . . . has today completely fused the Dutch & English colonists into one native stock—a stock, alas, now menaced in its turn by the appalling tidal wave of modern inferior immigration" (*Letters from New York* 28). By 1924 there were seven Suydams had listed in the *Social Register* (*New Annotated H. P. Lovecraft* 256–57n20; 266n39). The Suydams emerged out of darkness and chaos to become part of New York's established native stock, and the name stood as a symbol of a New York Lovecraft feared would be eroded away by hordes of invading immigrants.

As Lovecraft saw it, the evil influence of Red Hook and the vice it encouraged led to the degeneration of his beloved Nordic stock. They devolved to the extent that they were indistinguishable from the immigrants he detested. Lovecraft wrote that he "would have been blind if I had not noted the coarse degeneracy of the physiognomies—a kind of pervasive local decadence and brazen insolence peculiar to the region, and so characteristic that it nearly overrode the marks of race and gave a sinister quality in common to every sort of gang from Nordic to Oriental." The result was a "hideous element of putrescent homogeneity . . . wearing down the line of demarcation between the various national colonies." The disturbing effects of degeneration went beyond the neighborhood's human inhabitants, affecting even the built environment. The "various architectural areas—which latter differ all the way between the rumbling mansions of vanished aristocracy and the dingy frame tenements of autochthonous slumdom" shared this same "putrescent homogeneity" (*From the Pest Zone* 16). The vice and rot that degraded the Nordic inhabitants of Red Hook extended even to Lovecraft's beloved colonial architecture.

Lovecraft witnessed this mutual decay of house and inhabitant in his boarding house at 169 Clinton Street. He observed that initially he did not notice the degeneration. "My guess is that its decay had just set in, owing to the spread of the Syrian fringe . . . beyond Atlantic Avenue" (*MWM* 439), he decided. He blamed the changing neighborhood for his landlady's transformation from the daughter of an Anglican vicar to a shrewish and neglectful yet miserly woman. In Lovecraft's estimation, her attitude must have declined with the demographic change. "I think her decadence must have been a gradual one . . . she must have stopped asking references when the sinking of the neighbourhood made the house harder and harder to fill with people of the right sort" (*MWM* 439). He came to view even the building itself as a conscious and malicious entity.

> I conceived the idea that the great brownstone house was a malignly sentient thing—a dead, vampire creature which sucked some-

thing out of those within it and implanted in them the seeds of some horrible and immaterial psychic growth. . . . Something unwholesome—something furtive—something vast lying subterrenely in obnoxious slumber—that was the soul of 169 Clinton St. at the edge of Red Hook, and in my great northwest corner room "The Horror at Red Hook" was written. (MWM 441)

Lovecraft believed that the arrival of Syrians led both to decadence in the Anglo population and to the onset of some malevolent force into the built environment.

"The Street" was written in response to a specific event in Boston years before Lovecraft relocated to New York, but it resembles "The Horror at Red Hook" both in the source of its menace and in its denouement. It was written in response to the Boston police strike of 1919, during which the Massachusetts National Guard was mobilized (IAP 341). Lovecraft saw the fragile nature of civilization revealed in the event, which he somehow linked to the Western fight against bolshevism imported by new immigrants.

"The Street" opens with a description of the settlement of The Street by white colonists. It is obviously Boston, which similarly began as a small cluster of homes near a spring near Beacon Hill (Shurtleff 1.25). After the settlers exterminate the Native American population, something Lovecraft calls the soul of the place descends on The Street. Neither increasing urbanization nor the passing of generations displaces the soul of The Street, because "The blood and soul of the people were as the blood and soul of their ancestors who had fashioned The Street" (CF 1.115).

The arrival of new immigrants brings decay. "Then came days of evil, when many who had known The Street of old knew it no more; and many knew it, who had not known it before" (CF 1.116). Just as in Red Hook, "New kinds of faces appeared in The Street; swarthy, sinister faces with furtive eyes and odd features, whose owners spoke unfamiliar words and placed signs in known and unknown characters upon most of the musty houses" (CF 1.116). "War and revolution were raging across the seas; a dynasty had collapsed, and its degenerate subjects were flocking with dubious intent to the Western Land. Many of these took lodgings in the battered houses that had once known the songs of birds and the scent of roses" (CF 1.116–17). Although Lovecraft is clearly describing the arrival of Russians after the Bolshevik revolution, his words could almost as easily be inserted into "The Horror at Red Hook" to describe Syrians fleeing the slow collapse of the Ottoman Empire.

At the climax of "The Street," these new immigrants are finally poised to attack the Westerners. on the Fourth of July. But on the eve of the great destruction, the soul of The Street strikes back.

> It was, indeed, an exceedingly singular happening; though after all a simple one. For without warning, in one of the small hours beyond midnight, all the ravages of the years and the storms and the worms came to a tremendous climax; and after the crash there was nothing left standing in The Street save two ancient chimneys and part of a stout brick wall. Nor did anything that had been alive come alive from the ruins. (CF 1.120)

Lovecraft indicates that the block was somehow destroyed by the soul of the place. One is reminded of *Myths and Legends of Our Own Land*, wherein Charles Skinner describes a personified "spirit of New England," a figure who appears in antiquated clothing at critical times in the land's history, including the Battles of Lexington and Bunker Hill. "And it is told that whenever any foreign foe or domestic oppressor shall dare the temper of the people, in the van of the resisting army shall be found this champion" (1.282). Skinner's book had a well-documented influence on Lovecraft and notably provided the germ around which he constructed "The Shunned House" just nine months before "The Horror at Red Hook" (*From the Pest Zone* 108–9n16). But Lovecraft's soul of the place is not anthropomorphic. After the collapse, two witnesses observe ghostly traces hovering over The Street: one sees the manifestation of a tree-lined street of dignified houses, and the other smells long-vanished rose gardens. The conclusion of "The Street" prefigures Lovecraft's reverie at the Dutch Reformed Church described above.

The neighborhood on Parker Place faces an end similar to that of the decayed neighborhood of "The Street." After Suydam's reanimated corpse pushes Lilith's throne into the "undreamable gulfs of lower Tartarus" (CF 1.502), the force holding together both Suydam's body and the building surrounding it is undone. Body and building disintegrate. Suydam is reduced to "a muddy blotch of corruption" (CF 1.502) while "three old houses in Parker Place doubtless long rotten with decay in its most insidious form, collapsed without visible cause" (CF 1.502) "amidst a thunderous crash which seemed to blot out all the evil universe" (CF 1.502). Consequently the story's hero, Thomas F. Malone, develops "a horror of houses and blocks and cities leprous and cancerous with evil dragged from elder worlds" (CF 1.482).

The climax of "The Horror at Red Hook" evokes several of Poe's tales. One is "A Descent into Maelstrom." The Lovecraft's invocation of the well of Democritus is an allusion to the epigraph of Poe's story. He quotes Joseph Glanville: "The Ways of God in Nature, as in Providence, are not as *our* ways, nor are the models that we frame in any way commensurate to the vastness, profundity, and unsearchableness of His works, *which have a depth in them greater than the well of Democritus*" (341). Lovecraft applies the quotation not to Providence but to blasphemy: "Age-old horror is a hydra with a thousand heads, and the cults of darkness are rooted in blasphemies deeper than the well of Democritus" (CF 1.504). Both Poe and Lovecraft apply the analogy to a physical watery depth. For Poe it is the great Maelström, a whirlpool east of Norway so deep that some fishermen believe it penetrates clear through the earth. For Lovecraft it is the "well too deep for dredging" (CF 1.503) beneath the house of Suydam.

The well of Democritus also appears in Poe's "Ligeia." Poe associates the well with Ligeia's abnormal eyes, but equally with the occult mysteries with which Ligeia is associated. Robert M. Price has detailed Lovecraft's debt to "Ligeia," particularly in "The Thing on the Doorstep," in which, like Ligeia, a brilliant woman of mysterious past and occult achievements survives by snatching a body through an exchange of souls ("Lovecraft and 'Ligeia'"). The impact of Poe's story is also evident in "The Horror at Red Hook." In "Ligeia," the soul of the narrator's first wife claims the body of his second. In "The Horror at Red Hook," Lilith claims the life of Suydam's earthly wife, while Suydam is raised from the dead. Suydam is wedded to Lilith in the strange ceremony underground: "Lilith, Great Lilith, behold the Bridegroom!" the worshippers chant when Suydam's body is offered up (CF 1.501). Poe's narrator asks, "Where were the souls of the haughty family of the bride, when, through thirst of gold, they permitted to pass the threshold of an apartment so bedecked, a maiden and a daughter so beloved?" (228). We are left to wonder the same about Miss Cornelia Gerritsen's parents, who allowed their daughter to become betrothed to the strange man from Flatbush.

"Ligeia" was linked in Lovecraft's mind with "The Fall of the House of Usher." In "Supernatural Horror in Literature," which Lovecraft began just months after writing "The Horror at Red Hook," Lovecraft offers the two stories as Poe's "very summits of artistry" (CE 2.103). He explains, "both of these tales owe their supreme magic to the cunning development which appears in the selection and collocation of every least incident" (CE 2.103). The plots of "Ligeia," "The Fall of the House of Usher," "The Thing on the Doorstep," and "The Horror at Red Hook" are all moved by the shocking actions of a reanimated (or at the very least prematurely entombed) corpse. The sheer will Suydam displays in his final, tendon-ripping push to banish Lilith, like Ligeia's rising, is evidence of Glanville's statement quoted in the Poe's epigraph: "For God is but a great will pervading all things by nature of its intentness. Man doth not yield him to the angels, nor unto death utterly, save only through the weakness of his feeble will" (222).

The climaxes of "The Street" and "The Horror at Red Hook" mirror Poe's "The Fall of the House of Usher." Poe describes the fate of a house and a man, Roderick Usher, who are so intertwined that the name Usher "seemed to include, in the minds of the peasantry who used it, both the family and the family mansion" (264). As the house decays, so does the man; or, perhaps, as the man decays, so does the house. The house is mysteriously associated with a tarn above which it was built, in the depths of which the house is reflected. As Poe's narrator explains:

I had so worked upon my imagination as really to believe that about the whole mansion and domain there hung an atmosphere peculiar to themselves and their immediate vicinity—an atmosphere which had no affinity with the air of heaven, but which had reeked up from the decayed trees, and the gray wall, and the silent tarn—a pestilent and mystic vapor, dull, sluggish, faintly discernible, and leaden-hued. (264)

Throughout the story Usher's sanity deteriorates. He becomes fascinated with occult books describing "the old African Satyrs and Aegipans"—two of the supernatural entities Malone encounters beneath Red Hook—and with "the manual of a forgotten church—the *Vigiliae Mortuorum*" (271), the Vigil of the Dead, a name reminiscent of Lovecraft's *Necronomicon*. He produces a painting of a tunnel beneath the house of Usher that reminds one of the smugglers' tunnels beneath Lovecraft's Red Hook. Poe's narrator describes it as follows:

A small picture presented the interior of an immensely long and rectangular vault or tunnel, with low walls, smooth, white, and without interruption or device. Certain accessory points of the design served well to convey the idea that this excavation lay at an exceeding depth below the surface of the earth. No outlet was observed in any portion of its vast extent, and no torch or other artificial source of light was discernible; yet a flood of intense rays rolled throughout, and bathed the whole in a ghastly and inappropriate splendor. (268)

Ultimately, Usher grapples with the corpse of his sister, while the corpse of Suydam escapes from its female pursuer, Lilith. As Roderick Usher dies, the house of Usher collapses. Poe's narrator barely escapes and stands by as "there was a long tumultuous shouting sound like the voice of a thousand waters—and the deep and dark tarn at my feet closed sullenly and silently over the fragments of the 'HOUSE OF USHER'" (277). As Lovecraft summarizes it, the story "hints shudderingly of obscure life in inorganic things, and displays an abnormally linked trinity of entities at the end of a long and isolated family history—a brother, his twin sister, and their incredibly ancient house all sharing a single soul and meeting one common dissolution at the same moment" (CE 2.103). Similarly, the tenements in "The Street" collapse due to some *genius loci* that takes offense at the un-American character of the new inhabitants. And in "The Horror at Red Hook," Suydam's corpse pushes the throne of Lilith into the well, somehow banishing the alien spirit that has taken up residence in the place and breaking whatever spell held both together not only Suydam's inanimate body but also the entire decayed neighborhood. The buildings on Parker Place collapse into the canals and the deep well beneath "the house of Robert Suydam" (CF 1.502), although it is clear this is his basement apartment, not his ancestral manse. The church did not collapse. But while Lovecraft tells us, "The dance-hall church is now mostly a dance-hall" (CF 1.505), he implies that the contagion has spread to its physical structure, "and the cancer lurks secure and spreading where furtiveness hides in rows of decaying brick" (CF 1.505). Disintegration seems imminent.

St. George's Church After Lovecraft

What happened on Washington Street was the opposite of what Lovecraft feared. The new immigrants took over a decrepit neighborhood and revitalized it; they did not seize a living place and breed its decay. "The homes along Washington Street had grown dingy and dilapidated by the time the Syrians inherited them. But the Arab community, once in possession of this area, turned it into a thriving Oriental trading mart that made the neighborhood internationally famous" (Kayal and Kayal 86). The neighborhood was different, but it did not become some homogenous slum.

Suydam's house was renovated again in 1929. Architect Harvey Farris Cassab, sheathed the façade of Suydam's building with terra cotta panels designed to look like stone. Whatever vestiges of the original Federal design that may have still been visible from the street were hidden by the new façade, which mimics a white marble Gothic church. Above the door, a polychrome bas relief shows St. George as a medieval European knight on horseback spearing a dragon. The building is very different from the brick façade Lovecraft saw in the early 1920s, which concealed the mysteries of the Eastern sect.

Figure 5: 103 Washington Street in 2011, now sheathed in terra cotta tiles. (Photo by Tom Miller, *Daytonian in Manhattan*.)

Figure 6: St. George Triumphant over the main door of the former St. George's Syrian Catholic Church. (Photo by Tom Miller, *Daytonian in Manhattan*.)

But if the United States has a *genius loci*, it is the all-consuming spirit of progress. Already in the 1920s rising real estate prices around the Financial District drove many of Little Syria's inhabitants to leave Manhattan and settle in Brooklyn. In

1940, St. Joseph's Maronite Church and many of the homes in the Lower West Side were demolished for the Battery Tunnel, the BQE's northern terminus, just as Sacred Hearts had been in Brooklyn (Rizek et al.). In 1970, more homes were destroyed north of 103 Washington Street to build the World Trade Center.

As the residential district disappeared and the Syrian population moved on, St. George's was increasingly a place where Roman Catholic office workers attended weekday services. In 1957, the Melkites formally turned the church over to the Archdiocese for use as a Latin Rite Roman Catholic Church (Melkite Exarchate 86). The Melkites briefly regained use of the church in the 1970s, but by 1982 the church was no longer used as a church and was deconsecrated and sold.

In 2009 the City of New York Landmarks Preservation Commission declared the former St. George's Syrian Catholic Church a New York City Landmark, as "Lower Manhattan's most vivid reminder of the vanished ethnic community once known as the Syrian Quarter, and of the time when Washington Street was the Main Street of Syrian America" (Caratzas 1). Today the house that Suydam built is the home of St. George Tavern.

Conclusion

During his time in New York Lovecraft met regularly with the diverse group who made up the Kalem Club. Samuel Loveman, like Sonia Greene, was Jewish. James F. Morton was the former president of the Boston Theosophical Society who converted to Baha'ísm. He was also an anarchist who spoke out against anti-semitism and racism in lectures and writings such as *The Curse of Race Prejudice*. Discussions in Kalem meetings were eclectic. In one meeting, the men spoke frankly about sex, with a variety of viewpoints expressed. According to George Kirk, "One was a homo, one an avowed fetishist, one quite nothing where sex is concerned" (28). Lovecraft's personal friends included a variety of ethnic backgrounds and personal outlooks. But while Lovecraft could respect individuals, multiculturalism was too much for him.

If Lovecraft had taken the time to get to know the local Syrians, he might have documented their various cultural traits and history. If, like Bercovici, he made an effort to meet Syrian literary men, he might have encountered Khalil Gibran, who published *The Prophet* while living in New York in 1923. He might even have been invited to Arabia, as William B. Seabrook was at about the same time—and like Seabrook might have gone there and returned to publish accounts of Yezidis, Bedouin raiders, and Muslim mystics, as Seabrook did in *Adventures in Arabia* (1927). But if he had done these things then he would not have been Lovecraft, and he would not have written what he wrote. Lovecraft's horror, which derived from a fear of the other and a horror of decay, grew out of his "impressionistic observation and overheard fragments linked together by the thread of fancy" (*From the Pest Zone* 16). His writings shed light on himself, not on the communities that surrounded him.

Lovecraft retained a rigidly hierarchical and racist understanding of humanity in general. He did not simply view white people as good and advanced and dark-skinned people as backward. Instead, as he explains in a letter, he believed there are gradations of human beings, with his own ethnicity naturally being the best. There are inferior Semites, and then there are "Superior Semites" who "can be assimilated *one by one* by the dominant Aryan" (*FFF* 535). Whites, similarly, were graduated. In Lovecraft's view, "low-grade Southern Italians & Portuguese, & the clamorous plague of French-Canadians" (*FFF* 536) were lesser whites, the sheer numbers of whom flooding into New England made them unassimilable. Similarly, Suydam was of Dutch stock was therefore lesser than that of the English. Through his own deliberate actions, he went backward to become something less than a civilized Anglo-Dutchman of the twentieth century.

Lovecraft used St. George's Syrian Catholic Church an example of the dual decay of built environment and populace. An alien race transformed Suydam's Federalist house into a Gothic temple for Eastern rites. The story's church and Parker Place were converted by a degraded Suydam into "teeming rookeries" (*CF* 1.488) whose inhabitants corrupted the very bricks around them. The dancehall church provided a stark contrast to the more civilized Dutch Reform Church. The ultimate horror of "The Horror at Red Hook" is that a learned man of old stock Dutch descent could destroy himself and the soul of a part of New York by bringing in aliens with promises of "rulerships in a strange land" (CF 1.490).

Works Cited

Abraham, Jennifer. "Gardens, Hill Faithful Salvage Church Relics." *Brooklyn Paper Publications.* 8–14 August 1987. Unpaginated news clipping courtesy of John Heyer II and St. Stephen and Sacred Hearts of Jesus and Mary.

"Assyrian Missionary Loaded Down with Money." *Binghamton* [NY] *Press* (27 January 1911): 9.

Barrett, Walter. *The Old Merchants of New York City.* New York: M. Doolady, 1870. 2 vols.

Bercovici, Konrad. *Around the World in New York.* New York: Century Co., 1924.

Blanck, Maggie Land. *Red Hook Churches and Other Institutions.* www.maggieblanck.com/BrooklynRedHook/Churches.html 2015. Accessed 31 December 2020.

Blatty, William Peter. *I'll Tell Them I Remember You.* New York: W. W. Norton, 1973.

Caratzas, Michael D. (Former) St. George's Syrian Catholic Church. Document prepared for City of New York Landmarks Preservation Commission. s-media.nyc.gov/agencies/lpc/lp/2167.pdf 2009. Accessed 1 January 2021.

Cavarnos, Constantine. *Orthodox Iconography.* Belmont, MA: Institute for Byzantine and Modern Greek Studies, 1977.

Cerasini, Marc A. "'Dancehall' Church Razed." *Crypt of Cthulhu* No. 52 (Yuletide 1987): 55.

———. Personal communication to Marc A. Beherec. 10 August 2019.

"City Intelligence: A Female Fight in a German Dance-House." *New York Times* (11 January 1859): 5.

"Consecrate Assyiran Church." *Daily News* (New York) (28 February 1921): 10.

DeSalles Media Group. Visitation of the Blessed Virgin Mary:

Parish History. visitationbvm-brooklyn.org/parish-history/. Accessed 8 February 2021.

Diocese of Brooklyn. *Diocese of Immigrants: The Brooklyn Catholic Experience, 1853–2003.* Strasbourg: Editions du Signe, 2004.

Donabed, Sargon, and Ninos Donabed. *Assyrians of Eastern Massachusetts: Images of America.* Charleston, SC: Arcadia Publishing, 2006.

Dunlap, David W. *From Abyssinian to Zion: A Guide to Manhattan's Houses of Worship.* New York: Columbia University Press, 2004.

Gabriel, Archpriest Anthony. *The Ancient Church on New Shores.* San Bernardino, CA: St. Willibrord's Press, 1996.

Heyer, John L., II. Email to Marc A. Beherec, 12 August 2019.

———. "Parish History." *Sacred Hearts and St. Stephen.* sacredhearts-ststephen.com/parish-info/parish-history/ Accessed 14 February 2021.

"Hold 'Rev.' Danoo as Relief Grafter." *New York Times* (5 March 1922): 6.

Irving, Washington. *Knickerbocker's History of New York.* New York: G. P. Putnam's Sons, 1894. 2 vols.

Irwin, Will. *Highlights of Manhattan.* New York: Century Co., 1927.

Kayal, Philip M., and Joseph M. Kayal. *The Syrian-Lebanese in America: A Study in Religion and Assimilation.* Boston: Twayne, 1975.

Kirk, George. "The Kalem Letters of George Kirk." In Maria Kirk Hart and S. T. Joshi, ed. *Lovecraft's New York Circle: The Kalem Club, 1924–1927.* New York: Hippocampus Press, 2006. 19–116.

Liesel, Rev. Nikolas. *The Eucharistic Liturgies of the Eastern Churches.* Collegeville, MN: Liturgical Press, 1963.

Long, Frank Belknap. *Howard Phillips Lovecraft: Dreamer on the Night Side.* Sauk City, WI: Arkham House, 1975.

Lovecraft, H. P. *From the Pest Zone: The New York Stories.* Ed. S. T. Joshi and David E. Schultz. New York: Hippocampus Press, 2003.

———. *Letters to Family and Family Friends.* Ed. S. T. Joshi and David E. Schultz. New York: Hippocampus Press, 2020. [Abbreviated in the text as *FFF*.]

———. *Letters to Maurice W. Moe and Others*. Ed. David E. Schultz and S. T. Joshi. New York: Hippocampus Press, 2017. [Abbreviated in the text as *MWM*.]

———. *More Annotated H. P. Lovecraft*. Ed. S. T. Joshi and Peter Cannon. New York: Dell, 1999.

———. *The New Annotated H. P. Lovecraft: Beyond Arkham*. Ed. Leslie S. Klinger. New York: Liveright, 2019.

———. *The Spirit of Revision: Lovecraft's Letters to Zealia Brown Reed Bishop*. Ed. Sean Branney and Andrew Leman. Glendale, CA: H. P. Lovecraft Historical Society, 2015.

———, and Clark Ashton Smith. *Dawnward Spire, Lonely Hill: Letters of H. P. Lovecraft and Clark Ashton Smith*. Ed. David E. Schultz and S. T. Joshi. New York: Hippocampus Press, 2018.

Melkite Exarchate. *Melkites in America: A Directory and Informative Handbook*. n.p.: The Melkite Exarchate, 1971.

Michalopulos, George C., and Herb Ham. *The American Orthodox Church: A History of Its Beginnings*. Salisbury, MA: Regina Orthodox Press, 2003.

Middleton, Edgar C. "Lady Shimum Wins London's Admiration as a Crusader Pleading for Assyrians." *Sun and New York Herald* (25 April 1920): 7.

Miller, Tom. "A Terra Cotta Gem at No. 103 Washington Street." *Daytonian in Manhattan*. 21 October 2011. daytoninmanhattan.blogspot.com/2011/10/terra-cotta-gem-at-no-103-washington.html Accessed 14 February 2021.

"New Assyrian Patriarch." *The Times* (London) (26 May 1920): 11.

"New-York City: Murder of an Infant by Its Mother." *New York Times* (10 June 1852): 1.

O'Mahony, Anthony. "Syriac Christianity in the Modern Middle East." In Michael Angold, ed. *The Cambridge History of Christianity: Eastern Christianity*. Cambridge: Cambridge University Press, 2006. 511–35.

Poe, Edgar Allan. *The Complete Tales and Poems of Edgar Allan Poe*. New York: Barnes & Noble Books, 1992.

"Police Intelligence." *New York Times* (13 May 1857): 2.

Price, Robert M. "The Humor at Red Hook." *Crypt of Cthulhu* No. 28 (Yuletide, 1984): 6–9.

———. "Lovecraft and 'Ligeia.'" *Lovecraft Studies* No. 31 (Fall 1994): 15–17.

Rizek, Barbara, Martin Rizek, and Joanne Medvecky. *Images of America: The Financial District's Lost Neighborhood, 1900–1970.* Charleston, SC: Arcadia Publishing, 2004.

"Sailor Tietze Dies of His Wounds." *New York Times* (17 October 1897): 15.

Seabrook, W. B. *Adventures in Arabia.* New York: Harcourt, Brace, 1927.

Sengstock, Mary C. *Chaldeans in Michigan.* East Lansing, MI: Michigan State University Press, 2005.

"Shimun, Assyrian Church Head, Slain." *Sun* (New York) (15 April 1918): 7.

Shurtleff, Nathaniel G. *A Topographical and Historical Description of Boston.* Boston: Published by Order of the Common Council, 1891. 2 vols.

Sidewalks of New York. New York: Little Leather Library Corp., 1923.

Skinner, Charles M. *Myths and Legends of Our Own Land.* Philadelphia: J. B. Lippincott Company, 1896. 2 vols.

Small, Evelyn Karam, Randa Gemayel Hakim, and Joseph John Soma. *History of the Maronite Catholic Church in the United States, Volume I: The Clergy.* Brooklyn: Eparchy of Saint Maron of Brooklyn, 2014.

Stafford, Most Rev. J. Francis. "Introduction." In Robert F. Taft, S.J., ed. *The Oriental Orthodox Churches in the United States.* Washington, D.C.: Secretariat, Bishops' Committee for Ecumenical and Interreligious Affairs, National Conference of Catholic Bishops, 1986. 1–2.

Stiles, Henry Reed, ed. *History and Commercial and Industrial Record of the County of Kings and the City of Brooklyn, N.Y., from 1683 to 1884.* New York: W. W. Munsell & Co., 1884. 2 vols.

Suydam, J. Howard. *Hendrick Rycken, the Progenitor of the Suydam Family in America: A Monograph.* New York: Knickerbocker Press, 1898.

"Syrian Banker Surrenders." *New York Times* (1 June 1899): 14.

"To Speculators." *New York Evening Post* (22 October 1835): 3.

A Portrait of Charles Dexter Ward as a Haunted Young Man

James Goho

H. P. Lovecraft wrote *The Case of Charles Dexter Ward* in a burst of creativity from late January to 1 March 1927 (Joshi, "Afterword" 225). The novel was never published while Lovecraft lived. Indeed, he disparaged the novel, but many artists despair about their works. It appeared in an abridged form in the May and July 1941 issues of *Weird Tales* and was first collected in the Arkham House edition of *Beyond the Wall of Sleep* (1943). The novel is a suspenseful, supernatural mystery thriller that merges historical people and actual geographic locations with fictional characters and incidents into a troubling narrative of the young Charles Dexter Ward losing his quest for identity through a transgenerational haunting.

Here I will explore the Gothic notion of dark family secrets, ancestral haunting, and transgenerational disturbance in the novel. And I will briefly explore some sources of Lovecraft's novel in the American Gothic. But the major focus of this essay is to explore the character of Charles Dexter Ward through the notion of the "phantom," as theorized by Nicolas Abraham and Maria Torok. The concept of the phantom helps us understand the driving compulsion of Ward to unearth knowledge of the past. Abraham and Torok suggest that terrible experiences of an ancestor can be transmitted to their children and beyond. Such experiences begin a transgenerational haunting. The ancestral phantom troubles later generations. These generations are in distress, but they do not know the cause of their distress. Abraham argues that a shameful secret can be unconsciously inherited from a previous generation. And this comes to be expressed in disorders of behavior and language. Bringing such phantoms to awareness is challenging because such "phantoms inhabiting our minds do so without our knowledge" (Abraham, "The Phantom of Hamlet" 188). These phantoms secretly hide encrypted in the unconscious. The crypt lodged in one's (for example, Ward's) unconscious belongs to and is the abode of a preceding generation. As I understand it, the "crypt" is an unconscious, psychic space that barricades unspeakable experiences, memories, or secrets from consciousness (Schwab 185).

The notion of the phantom suggests that Ward's unconscious mind harbors deep, unspeakable secrets, which remain hidden to him during his pursuit of knowledge until he calls up his long-dead ancestor, Joseph Curwen, and directly experiences the horror of Curwen's violence and atrocities. Abraham says that what is "phantomized" is "unspeakable in words" ("The Phantom of Hamlet" 189), which describes the terrible activities of Curwen in the underground catacombs and vaults at his Pawtuxet Village farm in the eighteenth century. Abraham and Torok claim the phantom returns to haunt its host and may cause "phobias, madness, and obsessions. Its effects can persist through several generations and determine the fate of an entire family line" ("The Lost Object-Me" 140). If we think of Joseph Curwen as a "phantom," we can understand how he causes Ward's obsessive-compulsive behavior, which ultimately leads to the end of the Curwen lineage.

American Supernatural Horror Works Related to The Case of Charles Dexter Ward

S. T. Joshi identifies similarities and differences between Lovecraft's novel and Walter de la Mare's novel of 1910, *The Return* ("Afterword" 228). Joshi notes that de la Mare's novel involves actual psychic possession, while Lovecraft's does not. In the novel, Nicholas Sabathier possesses Arthur Lawford to the extent of changing Lawford's physical appearance. Perhaps de la Mare suggests that one's self-identity is fragile and uncertain, and it may be disrupted by unknown supernatural forces. In

Lovecraft's novel, Joseph Curwen, as the phantom, works to dis-order and redirect the young Ward's search for self-identity.

Lovecraft's novel also reprises themes in early American Goth-ic tales. Charles Brockden Brown's *Wieland; or, The Transfor-mation* (1798) and his other novels established the American Gothic. Alan Axelrod states that Brown "has long haunted American literature as a ghostly presence" (xiii). And he may be doing that in Lovecraft's novel. *Wieland* is a novel about the tran-sition of family horror from generation to generation. The elder Wieland was a religious zealot. He was mysteriously consumed by fire. His presence ominously pervades the novel. But the spark for Gothic contagion arises from the arrival of Francis Carwin (a name close to Curwen), who may have manipulated the minds of the elder Wieland's son Theodore and daughter Clara to become haunted. They hear voices whispering to them. They re-enact, sometimes in distorted ways, past events in their family's history, with an unknowing sense of a family secret. The secret seems to be: why did their maternal grandfather hear voices and fling him-self off a cliff; what had he done? Clara repeats his standing on an abyss, but she does not leap. In Lovecraft's novel, Charles Dexter Ward re-enacts the activities of his ancestor, Joseph Curwen.

Wieland depicts a case of transgenerational haunting through the return of a family's repressed secret to subsequent genera-tions. Their ancestral house is not safe. It becomes a haunted place, ringing with disembodied voices. Clara broods "darkness suited the color of my thoughts" (147), while plagued by intan-gible voices. She "is tormented by phantoms" (69). Theodore Wieland is pictured at first as an upstanding family man. But, as if inheriting his father's religious mania, he is transformed by "voices" into a killer who slaughters his wife and children and their ward, Louisa Conway, believing he has been divinely commanded. His house becomes a scene of death. He also breaks out of jail three times and tries to kill Clara. But Theo-dore ends up killing himself as if killing an other who has taken over his body. *Wieland* is a novel about a phantom haunting a family, where the secrets of ancestors infect their progeny. Love-craft comments favorably on the novel in "Supernatural Horror in Literature," although Joshi points out that Lovecraft admitted he never read the entire book (*SHL* 108n19).

Edgar Allan Poe's "The Fall of the House of Usher" (1839) centers on a haunted family, a haunted house, and a vengeful figure arising from a crypt. Roderick Usher unwittingly entombs his sister Madeline alive in a crypt in the underground vaults of his ancestral home. These vaults are a "region of horror" and "in remote feudal times" were used "for the worst purposes of a donjon-keep"[1] (410). Madelaine is a phantom in the house. A house that shares with Roderick and Madelaine "a single soul," as Lovecraft concluded (*SHL* 59). Madelaine returns as the living/dead revenant to fall upon Roderick, triggering the house to collapse. The three die as one. It is the end of the Usher lineage, as the Curwen lineage ends in *The Case of Charles Dexter Ward*.

Another closely related story is Poe's "Ligeia" (1838). The unnamed narrator becomes enraptured by Ligeia's nearly supernatural, raven-hair beauty. He marries her and finds that she is learned in many things: mathematical, scientific, and metaphysical. She sickens. After prolonged anguish and struggle, Ligeia asks for her poem "The Conqueror Worm" to be read; she dies. Later, the narrator marries the fair-haired Lady Rowena Trevanion, of Tremaine. Soon after the marriage, Rowena dies. While the unnamed narrator keeps vigil by her body, she thrashes to revive and he attempts to aid her. After the "greater part of the fearful night had worn away" the body stirs again (329). She rises from the bed, which chills the narrator to stone. But as the shroud falls from her head, he sees raven hair and the dark eyes of Ligeia, who imposes her "physical appearance" (Lovecraft, *SHL* 59) on the reanimated body of Rowena. Does Ligeia's metaphysical knowledge power her appropriation of Rowena's body?

Nathaniel Hawthorne's *The House of the Seven Gables* (1851) also exhibits the theme of the inheritance of ancestral guilt and how it manifests itself in succeeding generations. Indeed, the narrator of the book says "the ghost of a dead progenitor—

---

1. Dr. Willett finds "mediaeval instruments of torture" (CF 2.155) in the hidden underground of Ward's Pawtuxet bungalow. It is an underground akin to the dungeons of a Gothic castle.

perhaps as a portion of his own punishment—is often doomed to become the Evil Genius of his family" (17). In Hawthorne's novel, the family inhabits a haunted space, the house of the seven gables, where generations seem to inherit the horror and guilt of an ancestor. That inheritance of a family phantom arises from Colonel Pyncheon's false accusation of witchcraft on Matthew Maule, the owner of property on which Pyncheon desired to build his grand house. The "wizard Maule" (17) is hanged but curses Pyncheon before he dies. Akin to Lovecraft, Hawthorne grounded his novel in a realistic setting, namely, the town of Salem, Massachusetts, of the late 1840s and early 1850s. The novel is also set in real history, the Salem witch mania of 1692, the year Curwen fled from Salem to Providence, Rhode Island.

The "Phantom" in The Case of Charles Dexter Ward

A small issue in the discussion of *The Case of Charles Dexter Ward* centers on the idea of the type of "possession" over the young Ward by his notorious ancestor, Joseph Curwen (see Joshi, "Afterword" 232, and *The Weird Tale* 211–12).[2] The young Ward calls up (that is, reanimates) his great-great-great-grandfather Joseph Curwen (buried in 1771) as a physical entity from the "essential Saltes of humane Dust" (CF 2.232–33) contained in his coffin. But Ward is unable to put Curwen down. Ward suffers the deadly consequence of that failure. At the end of the novel, Dr. Willett (the Ward family doctor and friend) uses a counter occult formula to end Curwen's existence permanently. Willett leaves Curwen a "cloud of fine bluish-grey dust" (CF 2.217) on the floor of his (not Ward's) room in the private hospital where he had been confined.

But Ward's calling up of Curwen occurs after years of study, research, and travel. What impelled Ward to undertake such a lengthy and difficult search for his heritage and such a deep study of the arcane, deadly occult knowledge that Curwen pos-

---

2. Barton L. St. Armand states that the young Ward is possessed by Curwen. I think he means this metaphorically, suggesting that the evil deeds of an ancestor may affect their progeny by altering their identities as they learn more about that evil.

sessed? In Lovecraft's novel, Curwen's hidden and silenced horror ripples through time, infecting a descendant. *The Case of Charles Dexter Ward* expresses how a haunted individual may repeat the silenced horrors of a previous generation.

Ward is haunted in the sense that past events influence present behavior through the action of the "phantom." Abraham argues that "the phantom" represents the return of a family's repressed secret to subsequent generations. It is a secret encrypted (that is, hidden) in the unconscious that passes from a parent's into a child's. The secret in Lovecraft's novel is the person and horrid activities of Curwen. After his death, the entire town of Providence worked to obliterate any record, file, report, and mention of Curwen or any of his activities. But that secret persisted in the Curwen lineage. Abraham argues the phantom's return works hauntingly within the child's mental topography ("Notes on the Phantom" 290). Charles Dexter Ward is a young man—born in 1902—in the novel and appears to be susceptible to such a return because of his youth. The concept of "the phantom" helps to understand and appreciate Lovecraft's imaginative portrayal of the gradual yet increasingly invasive haunting of Ward by his dead ancestor.[3]

This haunting started early since Ward "was an antiquarian from infancy" (CF 2.217). Indeed, his early life belonged to the past. He was a "dweller in the past" (CF 2.273). And over the years his "devotion to ancient things increased" (CF 2.217), while the haunting presence of Curwen grew stronger. Ward enjoyed his adventures in antiquity and he delved deeply into antiquarian and genealogical data. These pursuits fated him in 1918, as a teenager, to discover that his great-great-grandfather Welcome Potter had married an Ann Tillinghast in 1785. Her mother, Mrs. Eliza Tillinghast, was a daughter of Capt. James Tillinghast.[4]

---

3. Jacques Derrida states: "everyone alive knows without learning and without knowledge [. . .] that the dead can often be more powerful than the living" (60). This appears to be true for Joseph Curwen in comparison to Charles Dexter Ward.

4. Tillinghast is an old family name in Rhode Island. A branch of the family suffered through the consumption (and "vampire" craze) scourge of the late 18th and 19th centuries in Rhode Island.

The young Ward goes on to discover that Eliza was the widow of Joseph Curwen when two pages, which had been carefully pasted together, separated during his search of town records, revealing that Eliza had changed her and her daughter's name from Curwen back to her maiden name, Tillinghast. This incident discloses Ward's uncanny ability to find exactly what Curwen wants him to find. Now Ward knows "Curwen's blood" flows within him (CF 2.264). At this point the influence of the phantom increases by "insidious degrees" (CF 2.225) over Ward, but he does not know it. Essentially the phantom is hidden in the unconscious, and its workings are not clear to the person so haunted. Colin Davis says the "*phantom* is the presence of a dead ancestor in the living" (374). That phantom, Curwen, appears to direct the young Ward to whatever is needed for him to continue his search for information and knowledge of his long-dead ancestor.

Next, Ward finds the Eleazar Smith diary recording the spying of Smith and Ezra Weeden (who had been Tillinghast's fiancé until Curwen intervened) on the Curwen Pawtuxet farm in the eighteenth century, where Curwen conduced his necromancy, torturings, and killings. Ward also discovers copies of informative letters, including a letter from Jedediah Orne (who turns out to be Simon Orne, who came back to Salem undercover as his son Jedidiah, to allay suspicions surrounding his advanced age) in the private archives of the Smith family.

After that discovery, Ward's obsession causes him to travel in 1919 to Salem, where he searches for information on Curwen's early activities and any connections he may have had in the town. At the Essex Institute, the Court House, and the Registry of Deeds, Ward unearths an extensive amount of Curwen data, including his association with Edward Hutchinson of Salem-Village and Simon Orne of Salem (Curwen's accomplices in diabolical activities). Much later Ward visits these two long-lived accomplices of Curwen in Europe. In Salem, Ward also finds an unfinished manuscript in Hutchinson's handwriting couched in an undecipherable cipher. Ward also conveniently finds preserved correspondence with cryptic formulae and diagrams and "one extremely mysterious letter in a chirography that the searcher recognised from items in the registry of Deeds as positively Joseph Curwen's" (CF 2.267).

In this letter from Curwen to Orne dated "not much later than 1750 by Ward," Curwen wrote: *"And of ye Seede of Olde shal One be borne who shal looke Backe, tho' know'g not what he seekes"* (CF 2.269). Charles Ward does not know it, but he is that "One." He is the *"one shal bee in yeares to come that shal looke backe and use what Saltes or Stuff for Saltes you shal leaue him"* (CF 2.270), foretelling the activities of Ward. In this letter, Ward also finds a hint to the location of Curwen's house in Providence.

Following this, Ward unsuccessfully studies the Hutchinson cipher. But his research of the Curwen data proves fruitful. It impels him to travel to New London and New York, where he finds the Fenner (owner of the farm adjacent to Curwen Pawtuxet farm) letters with their recounting of the 1771 raid on the Curwen Pawtuxet farm compound. He also finds the Nightingale-Talbot letters in which he learns of the portrait of Joseph Curwen painted on a panel of the Curwen library in his Providence house. After the birth of his daughter Ann in 1765, Curwen sat for that portrait, knowing it would be a key asset to leave his progeny now that he had established a lineage.

The young Ward is excited to learn of the possible existence of a portrait of his ancestor on a panel in the house that Curwen built and occupied in Olney Court in Providence. Not surprisingly, in 1919 Ward finds the precise location of the portrait, but it takes an expert to reveal it. It is a process that Ward assiduously observes. When the portrait is revealed, he sees himself in the portrait, it bears "his own living features," because through "some trick of atavism the physical contours of Joseph Curwen had found precise duplication after a century and a half" (CF 2.273) in the young Ward. The portrait of Curwen leads Ward to more critical information left behind by his great-great-great-grandfather.

Behind that portrait, Charles Ward finds a trove of documents, including one inscribed *"To Him Who Shal Come After, & How He May Gett Beyonde Time & ye Spheres"* (CF 2.275), which is directed to Ward by Curwen, knowing that Ward would find it. Other documents include Curwen's journals and notes, a key to the cipher used in documents and Hutchinson's letter, more letters of Orne and Hutchinson, and a record of Curwen's travels. The young Ward hides these documents from others. This arises from Ward's increasing obsession with Curwen, or perhaps, with the increasing control of his actions by the phantom, Curwen. This set of documents proves essential for Ward to continue his research, which he now conducts in his increasingly off-limits rooms in his parents' grand house. Ward hides his activities, copying Curwen's clandestine research and experimentation.

Charles Ward's father has the panel bearing the Curwen portrait removed from the Olney Court house and installed in Ward's third-floor study in the family house on Prospect Street. There it would preside over Ward's further study and experiments. And there the portrait returns Ward's gaze as if a mirror. The portrait seems to increase its similarity to Ward, but Ward changes, not the portrait. This portrait symbolizes the presence of Curwen as the phantom in the unconscious of the young Ward. Ward's physical changes reflect the increasing power Curwen gains over Ward's identity and actions.

Shortly after he discovers the treasure of Curwen's documents, Ward shifts his studies more and more to the occult and necromancy. He travels to research rare works in the Boston Public Library, the Widener Library at Harvard, and the Zion Research Library in Brookline (CF 2.278). He also travels again to Salem. What he finds there inspires him to set up a chemical laboratory for experimentation.

Ward also searches for Curwen's grave. Of course, he unearths a "fragmentary record of Curwen's burial" (CF 2.279) that had somehow escaped the attempted obliteration of all such records related to Curwen's burial. But the record did not give the name of the graveyard, only that the coffin had been buried "10 ft. S. and 5 ft. W. of Naphthali Field's grave in y^e—" (CF 2.279). This makes Ward's search more challenging, but it is an essential clue that helps Ward eventually find the gravesite.

Lovecraft hints that Curwen knew he would be resurrected

by a progeny. The leader of the raiding party on his Pawtuxet compound, Capt. Whipple, complained that Curwen laughed while he screamed when he was caught and killed: "'Twas as though the damn'd ———— had some'at up his sleeve" (CF 2.264). Of course he did: it would be the young Charles Dexter Ward. Curwen married Eliza Tillinghast to produce offspring who would lead to the birth of the young Ward.

With his parents and Dr. Willett finally worrying about Ward's strange activities and his hiding of the trove of Curwen documents, Ward allows Dr. Willett into his rooms to look at selected sections of the Curwen material that he kept hidden. Willett catches a glimpse of an odd entry in Curwen's diary: "It will drawe One who is to Come, if I can make sure he shal bee, and he shall think on Past thinges and look back thro' all ye yeares, against ye which I must have ready ye Saltes or That to make 'em with" (CF 2.282). This is yet another Curwen note telling of his plans for his progeny. The entry unsettles Dr. Willett, but the portrait scares him more. Willett thinks the portrait of Curwen radiates an aura of terror. And he worries that the painted Curwen eyes evince a "wish, if not an actual tendency, to follow young Charles Ward" (CF 2.282). The portrait draws life from Ward, as Curwen increases his power over the young man.

Subsequently, Ward asks to travel to Europe, but his parents refuse to allow their eighteen-year-old son to do so. But they acquiesce in his refusal to attend college. So Ward begins three years of "intensive occult study and graveyard searching," eschewing anything else, apparently with his parents' blessing (CF 2.283). When he is twenty-one in April 1923, Ward travels to Europe for three years thanks to a bequest from his maternal grandfather (Ward's mother is in the Curwen lineage). Thus, Ward is off to see Curwen's long-lived compatriots in necromancy. For six years Ward studies and experiments in strange, occult matters and travels in Europe to meet with old Curwen associates with seemingly little contact with his parents or any other person. For six years he is solely focused on matters, investigations, and discussions with persons associated with Joseph Curwen. Such an immersion suggests Ward suffers from an ob-

sessive-compulsive behavioral disorder arising from the unconscious influence of his phantom, Curwen.

Upon returning to Providence in May 1926, he recommences
his dangerous experiments in his rooms with a deeper and dead-
lier knowledge of the occult "sciences." Now his rooms resound
with a cacophony of chants, foreign phrases, and other odd
noises, compounded at times by strange aromatic or noxious
fumes. As Abraham and Torok argue, an individual under the
influence of an ancestral phantom re-enacts the actions of that
ancestor. In January 1927, a fearsome rattle resounds from
Ward's rooms; it seems as if the house is struck. And Ward is
triumphant. He cannot wait for the spring thaw. In March,
Charles Ward has the remains of Curwen borne up to his rooms.

Ward now carries out the Curwen necromancy. In April
1927, he calls up Curwen from his essential salts preserved in his
"sealed leaden coffin" (CF 2.262). The odors, sounds, and flash
of light arising from Ward's rooms match those observed at the
old Curwen compound in Pawtuxet. Curwen arrives and upon
his re-fleshing, his portrait on the paneling from Olney Court
crumbles and scatters on the floor of Ward's library as a "fine
bluish-grey dust" (CF 2.296), portending Curwen's ultimate
end. But the portrait's disintegration also signals the end of
Ward, because Curwen is back in the flesh and ready to renew
his terror. The phantom has been released from the crypt in
Ward's unconscious.

Charles Ward's actions arose from the unconscious (to
Ward) voice of Curwen whispering (or directing) from Ward's
unconscious. It is a transgenerational haunting[5] that becomes
real for Ward. He obsessively re-enacts past events in his family's history with an unknowing but gradually increasing aware-

---

5. Another way of explaining transgenerational effects comes from the field of
epigenetics, which is "the study of heritable changes in gene expression that
are not due to changes in the underlying DNA sequence" (Kellermann 34).
The Transgenerational Transmission of Trauma (TTT) refers to the finding
that trauma affecting a first generation may be passed down to other generations. Youseff et al. found an accumulating amount of evidence confirming an
enduring effect of trauma exposure passed to offspring transgenerationally.

ness of a family secret. Ward works to unearth this secret, that is, who and what was Curwen. And after his historical, bibliographic, geographic, and occult researches, Ward repeats the secret actions of his ancestor. Lost in his research, obsessed with gaining knowledge, and driven by the phantom, Ward calls up that which he cannot put down.

Under the direct power of Curwen now, Ward purchases a bungalow in Pawtuxet, which sits on the site of the old Curwen compound, where Curwen practiced his occult "science" and conducted his tortures and mass killings. Beneath the bungalow lies a vast labyrinth of vaults and rooms built by Curwen years in the past as a secure lair for necromancy. Seemingly Curwen and Ward work together at times. Ward continues to change physically, as he experiences directly the barbarous activities of Curwen. He looks "haggard and hunted" (CF 2.300); he continues his "anemic decline" showing an "increasing pallor (CF 2.301) and becomes "more emaciated" (CF 2.303), as Curwen seems to drain him of life. Or perhaps Ward ails because he becomes more aware of the hideousness of Curwen's activities. That is why Ward writes to Dr. Willett telling him to repeat the 1771 raiding party action against his Pawtuxet bungalow. For Ward, it is too late. Curwen kills Ward.

Curwen tries to impersonate Ward, but his archaic language and his failure to be aware of modern things lead Dr. Willett to know that Ward is dead, killed by the ancestor who had inspired Ward's antiquarian, genealogical, and occult "science" studies. That person confined in the private hospital is Joseph Curwen, not Ward, which the psychological and physical medical notes on the first pages of Lovecraft's novel foretell. Dr. Willett turns Curwen to ash in that room. After that, he rescues the thing that was Ward, which Curwen had hidden behind the "ancient overmantel where [his] picture once was" (CF 2.364). After burning the remains, Dr. Willett buries Ward's ashes in his family's plot in the North Burial Ground. Curwen and Ward end in dust and ash, terminating the Curwen family lineage.

Conclusion

Lovecraft's *The Case of Charles Dexter Ward* is a supernatural horror novel about ghostly hauntings by a phantom from a silenced past. An ancestral past that haunts the young Charles Ward and usurps his attempts to shape his identity. An identity deranged by an ancestor hiding in the crypt of Ward's unconscious. An ancestor that the young Ward discovers through his compulsive ancestral studies. An ancestor who is a perpetrator of monstrous crimes. Gabriel Schwab argues that the descendants of perpetrators of violence unconsciously relive the ghostly legacies and secrets of those ancestors. As the posterity of ancestors who suffered trauma re-experience that trauma, so also do the posterity of those who inflicted trauma. Joseph Curwen is such a perpetrator of violence. He is the phantom who haunts Ward as a foreign, but familial, presence hidden in his psyche, in his unconscious.

Lovecraft depicts Ward as an inquisitive young person fascinated with the past and with a passion for an archeology of his family history. But that is dangerous ground. Curwen's activities were largely silenced in the public sphere, but not in Ward's unconscious. Lovecraft depicts part of that chaotic and monstrous unconscious through Dr. Willett's exploration of the horrific vaults, cells, laboratories, and torture chambers of Curwen's underground of horrors below his old Pawtuxet compound and accessible under Ward's Pawtuxet bungalow. That is the horror that infects Ward. From Ward's unconscious, Curwen, as the phantom, takes over Ward's innocent ancestral study. Through gradual revelations and clues Curwen guides Ward to rediscover his occult knowledge, which will lead to Curwen's reanimation.

Lovecraft depicts Ward left on his own to conduct his research until it is too late. Ward's mother's response upon first hearing of her Curwen family connection from the young Ward is simply that "she was not particularly pleased to own an ancestor like Curwen" (CF 2.265). Later she suggests the discovered portrait of Curwen should be burned, but her husband, "a practical man of power and affairs" (CF 2.274) preserves it for his son. His parents allow the young Ward to research and travel extensively on his own with little or no supervision or monitoring. This was true not only when he was open about his researches, but also as he became increasingly more furtive about his activities and discoveries. Schwab suggests that it is almost impossible for an individual to overcome his or her trauma from an ancestral phantom without communal support. One cannot face a powerful perpetrator of violence alone, but that is what happens to Charles Dexter Ward. One cannot face the ghosts of the past without concern, aid, and involvement from others. These come too late for Ward.

Lovecraft describes the young Ward striving to shape his self-identity within a family tradition. He fails at this because of an inheritance he cannot escape—the terrible secrets of an ancestor. Many worked to bury Joseph Curwen's past life and his horrific practices. This attempt at silence fails. Schwab argues that ancestral trauma or violence can never be completely silenced, since its effects continue to work unconsciously through later generations. Indeed, the silence planned to cover up a traumatic or violent history leads to its unconscious transmission.

Through his compulsive ancestral research, Ward eventually discovers what was hidden in his family's history, what was shunned and silenced. This repressed secret comes back as the phantom to haunt Ward, as Abraham and Torok's theory of the phantom predicts. That happens through the transgenerational transmission of violence. One so young and one left on his own to investigate whatever and travel wherever he wants loses his identity to the phantom—Joseph Curwen—the ancestral perpetrator of violence and horror.

In the Curwen lineage, Charles Ward is the descendant who suffers the "interpersonal and transgenerational consequences of silence" and becomes the "unwitting recipient of someone else's secret" (Rand 168–69), that is, Joseph Curwen's history of violence and necromancy. Curwen is the phantom, who "had welled up from some profound subconsciousness to engulf" (CF 2.313) Ward. As Dr. Willett accuses Curwen, "you drew him [Ward] into the past and got him to raise you up from your detestable grave" (CF 2.364–65).

While it is true that the young Ward raises his ancestor from the dead, that happens because, as Dr. Willett says, Curwen compelled Ward to do so. Hiding in Ward's unconscious, Curwen, the phantom, guides the unknowing Ward to re-enact past events. For the young Ward, the repetition and re-enactment of that past brings no solace, because the past eventually engulfs his present with all its unspeakable horrors. Ward is a victim in the novel. In part, he is that young man eager to know the past, especially his past. And he is that haunted young man bred to release an ancestral perpetrator of violence. It is his research, his occult studies, and his actions that permit Curwen to resume his hideous tortures and murders. By doing so, Ward becomes an unwitting abettor in that violent legacy. But as Gabriele Schwab might suggest, Ward suffers a psychic deformation that perpetrators of historical violence will necessarily leave to their progeny. In Lovecraft's novel, the perpetrator is Joseph Curwen, understood as the phantom. Ward's intergenerational, psychic trauma means that not only does he inherit the crime of his ancestral torturer and killer, he also becomes a victim of that ancestor.

Works Cited

Abraham, Nicolas. "Notes on the Phantom: A Complement to Freud's Metapsychology." Tr. Nicholas Rand. *Critical Inquiry* 13 (1987): 289–90.

———. "The Phantom of Hamlet *or* the Sixth Act, *preceded by* the Intermission of 'Truth.'" 1978. In *The Shell and the Kernel, Volume 1*. Ed. and tr. Nicholas Rand. Chicago: University of Chicago Press, 1994. 187–205.

———, and Maria Torok. "'The Lost Object-Me': Notes on Endocryptic Identification." 1975. In *The Shell and the Kernel, Volume 1*. Ed. and tr. Nicholas Rand. Chicago: University of Chicago Press, 1994. 165–71.

Axelrod, Alan. *Charles Brockden Brown: An American Tale*. Austin: University of Texas Press, 1983.

Brown, Charles Brockden. *Wieland; or, The Transformation*. Ed. Philip Barnard and Stephen Shapiro. Indianapolis: Hackett Publishing, 2009.

182 James Goho

Davis, Colin. "Hauntology, Spectres and Phantoms." *French Studies* 59 (2005): 373–79.

de la Mare, Walter. *The Return*. 1910. Doylestown, PA: Wildside Press, n.d.

Derrida, Jacques. *Specters of Marx: The State of the Debt, the Work of Mourning, and the New International*. Tr. Peggy Kamuf. New York: Routledge, 1994.

Hawthorne, Nathaniel. *The House of the Seven Gables*. Ed. Robert S. Levine. New York: W. W. Norton, 2006.

Joshi, S. T. "Afterword." In H. P. Lovecraft. *The Case of Charles Dexter Ward*. Ed. S. T. Joshi. Tampa: University of Tampa Press, 2010. 211–36.

———. *The Weird Tale*. 1990. Holicong, PA: Wildside Press, 2003.

Kellermann, N. P. "Epigenetic Transmission of Holocaust Trauma: Can Nightmares Be Inherited?" *Israel Journal of Psychiatry and Related Sciences* 50 (2013): 33–39.

Lovecraft, H. P. *The Annotated Supernatural Horror in Literature*. Ed. Ed. S. T. Joshi. New York: Hippocampus Press, 2nd ed. 2012. [Abbreviated in the text as *SHL*.]

Poe, Edgar Allan. *Tales and Sketches, Volume 1: 1831–1842*. Ed. Thomas Ollive Mabbott. Cambridge, MA: Harvard University Press, 1978.

Rand, Nicholas. "'Editor's Note' to "Secrets and Posterity: The Theory of the Transgenerational Phantom." In Nicholas Abraham and Maria Torok. *The Shell and the Kernel, Volume 1*. Ed. and tr. Nicholas Rand. Chicago: University of Chicago Press, 1994. 165–70.

St. Armand, Barton L. "Facts in the Case of H. P. Lovecraft." *Rhode Island History* 31, No. 1 (February 1972): 3–19.

Schwab, Gabriele. "Haunting Legacies: Trauma in Children of Perpetrators." *Postcolonial Studies* 7 (2004): 177–95.

Youssef, N. A., et al. "The Effects of Trauma, with or without PTSD, on the Transgenerational DNA Methylation Alterations in Human Offsprings," *Brain Science* 8, No. 5 (2018): 83.

The Reverberation of Echoes: Lovecraft in Twenty-First-Century Cinema

Duncan Norris

It is difficult to image anyone, most especially its author H. P. Lovecraft, considering the omnipresence of his fiction in popular culture almost a century after his first paid publication appeared in print in 1922. It is not merely that Lovecraft continues to be frequently republished and widely read. Although that is itself no small achievement, it is one made truly remarkable by the fact that this publication of his works in collected editions began after his death. Furthermore, in addition to his fictional writings individually there are the collective ideas of cosmic horror and its more specific subset in the artificial mythopoeia of the Cthulhu Mythos, which is so connected to him that its very name has become a descriptor of a type of fiction: Lovecraftian. Festivals are held in celebration of his works, and Lovecraft himself has become a fictional character, often in his own conceptual universe, and with a bewildering amount of metafictional intermingling with his own works. Every possible permutation of consideration with his creations has been mined, sifted, pastiched, copied, emulated, and recrudesced in all manner of media, and his creations have passed into that nebulous realm of cultural osmosis wherein people are familiar with his inventions who not only have not read Lovecraft, but don't even know that he is their creator, or that he exists at all. The dread figure of Cthulhu makes appearances far from his hideous realm in sunken R'lyeh, from the edgy cartoon comedy *South Park* to plushies and Covid-19 masks. The theoretically rare dread tome, the

Necronomicon, is now so ubiquitous that it can be found in the name of a Lovecraftian cookbook, the *Necronomnomnom,* and that of Japanese kawaii metal[1] band Necronomidol, whilst the Facebook group for the H. P. Lovecraft Pie Society has more than 600 members.

The ubiquity of Lovecraft in connection with certain of his ideas and creations led to immediate speculation that the Cloverfield monster from the 2008 movie of the same name was Cthulhu, given no more information that a gigantic size and oceanic emergence. Likewise to the same point, Neasa Hardiman, the writer-director of the 2019 Irish science fiction/horror/thriller *Sea Fever,* was immediately questioned as to her Lovecraftian connections given that the film deals with a monstrous entry from the deep affecting the crew aboard a fishing boat. In fact, the description of the film for its United States East Coast debut at the Brooklyn Horror Film Festival calls it "an unsettling chamber piece that brings to mind similarly doomed settings like the Nostromo and U.S. Outpost #31" (BHF Sea Fever), referencing the very Lovecraftian films of *Alien* (1979) and *The Thing* (1982), respectively. That Hardiman had never read Lovecraft and had simply come up with her ideas independently is immaterial to the bigger picture, which highlights the idea of the now default assumption in science fiction, fantasy, and horror that certain things spring from Lovecraft. The previous two examples are not chosen by happenstance, and it is the purpose of this paper to look at the influence— direct, overt, tangential, and perhaps even occasionally unintended or subconscious—of Lovecraft in recent cinema. This is not, nor is it designed to be, an exhaustive list. Rather it is a more scattershot approach, designed to show the range, curious commonalities, and occasional anomalies of Lovecraft's influence in filmmaking, culminating in a deeper examination of two of the larger budget, more demonstrable Lovecraft adaptations of recent years.

Cold Skin (2017) is typical in a number of ways of many of

---

1. An unholy mixture of heavy metal with J-Pop and the aesthetic of Japanese idol bands.

the main trends in Lovecraftian films in the second decade of the twenty-first century. First, it is a literary adaptation, based upon the relatively short Catalan-language novel *La Pell Freda (Cold Skin)* by anthropologist Albert Sánchez Piñol. As such book-to-film adaptations go, it is reasonably faithful, both in broad outlines of events and overall atmosphere, although the harsher edges of one character are removed and used to sharpen the other, and there is a notable difference in the ending, which in the book takes on a decidedly surrealistic quality. Second, the film is far more thematically and distantly connected to Lovecraft as opposed to being a clear-cut specimen of something set in his conceptual universe or drawing directly upon his creations. Third, questions of its artistic merit being naturally a matter of individual taste, it is neither a commercially successful nor an overly lauded film in a collective consensus as expressed by review aggregator sites such as Rotten Tomatoes. Lovecraft, for all the mainstreaming of many of his ideas and creations into the popular culture, seems be produce a success inversely proportional to the depth of the Lovecraftian ideas on display. Mass appeal, the depths of cosmic horror, and true indifference to the supposed importance of humanity are strongly repelling magnetic poles, and there is frequently the shadow of the outsider and the individual rather than the herd and the populist in those who build around Lovecraft's works and ideas. Curiously, *Cold Skin* was initially in development under a different director and with a script co-written by Alex Garland, writer and director of *Annihilation* (2018), a film that will be examined in due course. The final script for *Cold Skin* was written by Jesús Olmo, who also co-wrote the sequel to the Garland-scripted *28 Days Later* (2002), called *28 Weeks Later* (2007).

Returning to specifics, the plot of the film is rather simple. An unnamed and disaffected young man around the era of the First World War volunteers to be sent to an isolated island weather-monitoring station. He soon discovers that the island suffers nightly incursions from an intelligent, hostile, amphibian race and is forced to ally with the locale's only other resident, a clearly deranged lighthouse keeper who delights in the nightly combat against the creatures. A major source of the hostility of the creatures is the female pseudo-captive of their kind that the lighthouse keeper possesses in a state of degradation and sexual servitude. The soldier manages to communicate with the beings and form a détente, and the film ends with the death of the lighthouse keeper. The soldier takes the dead man's place as the keeper had done before him even as the soldier's own replacement arrives by ship, thus perpetuating the cycle.

As a brief aside it is worth noting that there is a curious trend of lighthouses appearing in many of the films under discussion. Lovecraft makes occasional usage of the lighthouse, especially in his early work "The White Ship," which concerns a lighthouse keeper, yet it is not a notable leitmotif in his work. An argument could be made for the lighthouse as a liminal piece of architecture, delineating the land and the sea and thus symbolic of threshold as well as the obvious connection with dangers. However, this may well be a case of overinterpretation and possible selector bias in the films chosen. The happenstance of coincidence cannot be discarded in the absence of overwhelming evidence.

Lovecraftian is a notoriously difficult designation to define, and is in many ways akin to Supreme Court Justice Potter Stewart's famous pronouncement of what constitutes pornography, where in his ruling he was unable to define it "but I know it when I see it." *Cold Skin* certainly has a very Lovecraftian atmosphere; isolated, brooding with menace and insanity, featuring creatures that are clearly a small fragment of a larger picture we the viewers are not privy to but which are implied in so many ways. The idea of the individual isolated on an island in the midst of the ocean as a result of the Great War is reminiscent of "Dagon," and the images of the monstrous yet intelligent creatures swarming up the sides of the lighthouse recalls to mind the creature worshipping or lamenting at the monolith in the aforementioned tale. Yet even more than "Dagon," the entire film seems to be a negative reflection of "The Shadow over Innsmouth," in which the literal miscegenation in that community is inverted; here a human is the one forcing interbreeding with the creatures from the sea. The horror of such actions, the subtle ideas and fetid undercurrents of the tainted bloodline which runs in numerous of Lovecraft's tales including "Facts concerning the Late Arthur Jermyn and His Family," "The Rats in the Walls," "The Dunwich Horror," and most especially "The Shadow over Innsmouth," are turned in *Cold Skin* from subtext and denouement and reconceptualized as a central piece of the narrative. This is all very Lovecraftian, although far from the discrete version in which Lovecraft chose to present it. Instead, it has a distinct focus on human evils, motivations, and emotional journeys that are rarely emphasized in his work, although it is often present subtextually.

Such re-examining of Lovecraft from alternative angles is a far from uncommon take. Perhaps most famously this is done in the 2018 novel *The Ballard of Black Tom* by Victor LaValle, which deals with the incidents described in the notoriously racist "The Horror at Red Hook" from the view of a different protagonist, a black man named Tommy Tester caught up in the events. In examining *Cold Skin* it is important not to ascribe a Lovecraftian influence merely because it deals with themes Lovecraft made famous, as in the aforementioned *Sea Fever*, or to attempt to fit broad and generic references as specificities. Metatextually the film's Lovecraftian credentials are certainly assured by its screening at the H. P. Lovecraft Film Festival in 2018. Perhaps the final word should be given to director Xavier Gens, who is even more explicit in an interview, stating the obvious: "we have the shadow of Lovecraft over our film" (Kermode).

Holding commonality in themes, although certainly not in tone, is the adult fantasy of *The Shape of Water* from director Guillermo del Toro. Del Toro's homages to, and the influences of Lovecraft on, his work are patent. It is most especially manifest in his two Hellboy films (*Hellboy* and *Hellboy II: The Golden Army* [2004 and 2008, respectively]), but traces are common in all his works. Even this ambiguity of that ever-nebulous term of influence was removed when del Toro guest-directed the extended opening of the television episode *The Simpsons Treehouse of Horror XXIV*, filled with homage and references to his horror loves and influences. Almost all these depictions are from films, but the literary Cthulhu is still given a relatively long few seconds' screen time as a central focus. Indeed, del Toro's (as of this writing) unrealized, and likely never-to-be-realized, adaptation of *At the Mountains of Madness* is considered one of the great "What Ifs" of genre cinema. The script was eventually leaked onto the Internet to decidedly mixed reviews by fans, although in fairness it must be noted that scripts rarely survive intact from the page to the screen, and the validity in judging an unmade film from an unknown version of a leaked script is certainly open to question,[2] even allowing for the setting aside of the inherent moral issues of such. Ultimately, however, this has not discouraged interest in the film. Even a cursory Internet search will bring up a plethora of fan-made posters to lament the lack of its reality; and Richard Stanley, director of *Color out of Space* (2020), has expressed shock and his own disappointment that del Toro hasn't been able to produce the film (Cochrane).

The Shape of Water is, like *Cold Skin,* an inverse of many of the themes of "The Shadow over Innsmouth," the film being concerned primarily with a mute woman falling in love with a captive amphibian humanoid and ultimately securing its escape, which enables them to be together. The main protagonists are all sympathetic outsiders from the mainstream early 1960s society in which they live, and the idea of the outsider is certainly one much associated with Lovecraft. The ending of the film again echoes "The Shadow over Innsmouth," wherein the protagonist plans on rescuing his cousin from captivity in the asylum and going off to join the Deep Ones in the ocean. Yet unlike the potential horror implied by that course of action, the ending of *The Shape of Water* is decidedly and unqualifiedly upbeat. On a superficial examination this is a thin thread upon which to make the link to Lovecraft and there are obviously many other influences, such as a glancing reference made to the creature as having similar origins to the eponymous *Creature from the Black Lagoon* (1954), of which again this film is, very

---

2. There is an old canard in the movie business that a film is made three times: first in the script, second in the filming, third in the edit.

broadly speaking, an inverted version. This seemingly natural connection between Lovecraft and *Creature from the Black Lagoon* has been much observed over the years, with the firmly tongue-in-cheek *A Field Guide to Monsters* (2004) (whose trio of authors includes well-known Lovecraftian C. J. Henderson) noting the Creature's relatives as "most of the residents of Innsmouth," while Caitlín R. Kiernan's contribution to *Weird Shadows over Innsmouth* (2005), "From Cabinet 34, Drawer 6," posits that the actual film derives in part from knowledge about the inhabitants of Lovecraft's most famous accused sea-town. Indeed, with *The Shape of Water* there may be questions of too many influences, as the film was plagued by accusations of plagiarism from both literary and filmic sources.

Notwithstanding the fact that *The Shape of Water* is clearly not designed to be a Lovecraftian adaptation in any traditional sense, there are deeper clues pointing more to the Deep Ones' Y'ha-nthlei than the Creature's Amazon in the narrative. The main character, Elisa Esposito, is an orphan of unknown parentage found by a river, unable to speak, with three curious and symmetrical scars across her throat, and who has a decided affinity combining water with her sexuality. The very opening scene is of her self-pleasuring in a bathtub, and she uses an egg-shaped egg timer to decide her allotment of time to the activity even as she boils her eggs. This motif of eggs, the means of reproduction for amphibians that generally requires laying in water, is repeated through the film. Indeed, it is eggs Elisa offers as enticement to the creature in her early interactions with it. Elisa herself seems related to the creature in some manner, and it is strongly implied that she is a changeling or (and here the expression is used as Lovecraft would have perceived it) of tainted blood who is responding to hereditary genetic impulses. Likewise, the creature is shown to have amazing regenerative and healing abilities and uses them at the end of the film to save Elisa and open her scars as functional gills. The Lovecraftian reader will thus be reminded of the immortality promised to the descendants of those who would share their bloodlines with the Deep Ones.

In a probably deliberate intertextual correlation, the villain

Strickland, who uses biblical references on several occasions in the film, tells the story of Sampson as a model upon which his own self-perceived righteousness is modeled. Notably, Sampson in the biblical account dies in the temple of Dagon, whose Lovecraftian connection to an amphibious being thrice called a god in the film seems rather distinct. Curiously, perhaps the greatest indication of the distant yet present Lovecraftian connection in all del Toro's work is not in *The Shape of Water* itself, nor is it even a spoken acknowledgment; rather, it is a simple observation. Del Toro was clearly wearing a Miskatonic University alumni ring upon his finger when he accepted his Academy Awards for Best Picture and Best Director for the film. By del Toro's own admission this is due to his unrealized *At the Mountains of Madness* project: "This is why I wear this ring, since the project got cancelled. This is the fake ring about a fake university, the one that appears in the book, Miskatonic University, and I'm gonna wear it until I make the movie. They may bury me with it" (Chand).

Annihilation (2018) is another film with a distinct Lovecraftian pedigree, one that is immediately apparent even from a glimpse at the most common advertising poster, seemingly showing a female military task force in a forest surrounded by an unnatural spectrum of light. The film literally concerns itself with an unknown color out of space, which affects reality in a now prohibited area known as the Shimmer, centered around a lighthouse. The Lovecraftian connection is patent. A favorite story of its author, "The Colour out of Space" has proved alluring to both other writers and filmmakers. An homage, "The Distortion out of Space" by Francis Flagg (pseudonym of Henry George Weiss), appeared in *Weird Tales* as early as August 1934, and at least seven commercially available direct film adaptations have been created based on Lovecraft's tale. Richard Stanley, in a backhanded reference to the perception of influence, stated that his isolation from movies of the last decade was beneficial and that "I was kind of grateful that I skipped *Annihilation* for example, going into" his adaptation (Cochrane). All the commercial product resultant from the tale is particularly ironic, as Lovecraft was paid only $25 for it when it was first published in

Amazing Stories in September 1927, and even that meager sum required the sending of three letters to the infamously delinquent editor Hugo Gernsback, earning him from Lovecraft the sobriquet Hugo the Rat.

Annihilation, however, is not an adaptation of Lovecraft's tale but rather of the relatively slim 2014 novel of the same name by Jeff VanderMeer, being the first book of his Southern Reach Trilogy. In addition to Lovecraftian ideas, the central conceit in the book seems initially reminiscent of the seminal 1972 Soviet science fiction novel *Roadside Picnic* by Arkady and Boris Strugatsky, with its forbidden area touched by alien presence known as the Zone, although this connection was categorically denied by the author. Interestingly, the aforementioned Stanley cites the Strugatsky brothers as writers he read as a teen that "adequately prepared me for the 21st century" (Curzon).

The book and movie *Annihilation*, as is common in such adaptations, differ substantially, but both are filled with a sense of dread and the weird that is decidedly at home in the realms of cosmic horror. In the book there is a distinct lack of the common humanizing traits generally found in novels, with characters being known by their professions rather than names. Lovecraftian ideas of alien geometry pervades both the landscape and creatures, the protagonists' image of a subterranean staircase as a Tower, raptors "circling as if in geometric patterns" (90), while the protagonist dreads acknowledging changes happening, for "to try to name it, might be a way of letting it in" (116). The diary entries of her dead husband from a previous expedition, itself a common trope associated with Lovecraft, speak of bushes "becom[ing] sullen" (161), which is strongly reminiscent of the "insolent" bloodroots and blasphemous roses, zinnias, and hollyhocks of Lovecraft's tale, while the diary's description of the Tower (described as far more like a well, as noted earlier), revealed at the end of the book as letting loose "a beam of light shot out into the sky, then abruptly cut off" (166), has a similarity to the climax of "The Colour out of Space" that is contextually highly unlikely to be coincidental. Preeminent Lovecraft scholar S. T. Joshi has also noted many similarities and cited another four direct borrowings in the trilogy from Lovecraft additional to those cited above.

Yet all this notwithstanding, VanderMeer openly claims he is a "not a fan" of Lovecraft and that his trilogy is "the antithesis of what Lovecraft valued" (Bolf)—a curious comment from an author of a work seemingly all about creating a weird atmosphere and whose characters are ciphers enough to be named solely for their profession. To the same point VanderMeer's introduction to the 2006 reprint of Clark Ashton Smith's *Lost Worlds*, originally published by Arkham House, was described by S. E. Lindberg as "short and trite: it covers the first two tales only and is hardly flattering." In fact, VanderMeer claimed in 2018 never to have even read "The Colour out of Space" and was proud of actively lobbying the board for the World Fantasy Award to remove Lovecraft as the trophy image.

The movie *Annihilation* differs substantially from the book, but this paradoxically ties it in back to Lovecraft and betrays the inevitable influence of Andrei Tarkovsky's very loose film adaptation of *Roadside Picnic*, entitled *Stalker* (1979) (Vishnevetsy). *Annihilation*'s director Alex Garland is himself a noted novelist and screenwriter, and in writing the film's script he stated that it was not a slavish recreation of the book, even to the extent that he did not even re-read the novel for clarification of events. Rather, to Garland "it was like an adaptation of the atmosphere" (Vlk) and "an adaptation of the memory of the book" (Guglielmo), both sentiments of which Lovecraft would probably have approved, given his known approach to weird fiction. While it would be incorrect to assert that Garland is in any particular way a creator who is Lovecraftian, his interest in the wider consequences of science, notably artificial intelligence, and his penchant for horror connect him tangentially with Lovecraft's cosmicism and other creations. As noted earlier, Garland wrote the script for *28 Day Later*, which is often cited as reviving the moribund zombie genre,[3] and his infected are certainly coming directly off the mold

3. Arguments occasionally (ahem) rage about *28 Days Later* being classified as a zombie film, as the infected technically are not dead. Garland specifically calls it a "zombie flick" in the CNET interview cited.

of Herbert West's most furious initial creations in "Herbert West—Reanimator," while the script of *Sunshine* (2007) was born after his interest was sparked reading "an article projecting the future of mankind from a physics-based, atheist perspective" (Kermode). *Annihilation*'s structure is told as a survivor interrogation narrative, very much in keeping with Lovecraftian tropes, as is the idea of the expedition investigating its failed forbears. The film for most of its running time manages to generate Garland's stated goal of an atmospheric weirdness. Such events are rare in the higher levels of Hollywood production, where appeal to a broad market tends to dilute the more obscure and inexplicable aspects of productions down to lower common denominators. Significantly, the film ends with a flash of the Shimmer color in the eye of the protagonist, mirroring the undefeated and still active Colour told of in the end of "The Colour out of Space."

Apart from the finished film itself, there are several interesting aspects to the production. First is its budget, estimated to be between approximately $40 and $55 million, depending on sources, making it one of the higher production Lovecraftian films, whose budgets are notorious curtailed. For comparison, *The Shape of Water* was substantially financed at $20 million, while *Color out of Space* discussed below cost approximately $12 million and is considered well funded as many independent features are adjudged. The cast of *Annihilation* incorporates many notable actors, and many specifically from inside very popular genre cinema, including Academy Award winner Natalie Portman (*Star Wars* prequel trilogy), Oscar Isaac (*Star Wars* sequel trilogy), and Tessa Thompson and Benedict Wong, who both appear in various of the Marvel Cinematic Universe films. Both these facts are significant as demonstrative of the ongoing shift of Lovecraft ever further away from the more niche category in which horror writers are often shunted. Equally significant is that the film overall was a box office failure. Anticipated to fail, and indeed failing, to recoup its budget at the cinema, it was as a result sold to streaming service Netflix, only playing in theatres in North America and China. While Lovecraft and his particular outlook, output, and most especially influence continue to spread into the wider culture, it is still alienating enough that genuine success on a large scale is still decidedly elusive for those following in his ever-expanding wake.

This is not to say that Lovecraftian films cannot garner popular success. The billion-dollar grossing *Aquaman* (2018) is assuredly the comic book movie it proclaims to be, being the story of the titular character, son of a lighthouse keeper and the Queen of Atlantis, and his ascent to the throne in order to prevent the underwater kingdoms rising up in war against the land. Tonally it is decidedly un-Lovecraftian, with the exception of the short nightmarish horror of the attack on the protagonist's boat by the creatures of The Trench. Yet it is steeped in Lovecraftian influence and reference. The subject is covered extensively in my article "Lovecraft and *Aquaman:* An Unlikely Mating," but in short the film goes as far as placing Lovecraft's writings on screen and having characters quote his works as dialogue. These divergent streams of creation flowing from the Lovecraftian well, as opposed to more direct adaptations, seem to be in three main branches, although they are not entirely separate.

The first, and least relevant, is the shout-out, homage, or reference without any real attempt to connect to Lovecraft's creations, style, ideas, or cosmic horror. A good example would be the animated children's comedy *Smallfoot* (2018). This film concerns a civilization of Yetis who live on an isolated mountaintop above a cloud layer in the Himalayas and who think humanity is a myth. The protagonist seeking to prove that the smallfoot (humans) are real is named Migo, almost certainly a Lovecraft homage. Yet other than this one link the film is an unapologetically unrealistic musical filled with scatological jokes, pratfalls, and pop-culture-based humor. The second branch is the opposite of this arrogation of superficial aspects, and draws rather upon the atmospheric, weird, and cosmic horror aspects of Lovecraft's work, sometimes entirely omitting any blatant connections with the regular trapping and names associated with the Mythos. Such endeavors often produce worthy works, but they equally tend to have a smaller and distinct following and limited support. Typical of this type of film is *The Endless*

(2017), about two brothers returning to visit the UFO cult they escaped as children. It is a deeply weird, tense, and highly engaging Lovecraftian odyssey yet without any of the commonplace Mythos exposition. Characteristically, it was well reviewed both critically and with general audiences, yet made less than a million dollars at the worldwide box office. The third branch is one that is less tonally related to Lovecraft but draws more broadly upon Lovecraftian tropes (or at least perceptions thereof) and features extensive reference to his works, often with Lovecraftian aspects grafted onto more conventional narratives. Such films as the aforementioned *Aquaman* often have a broader appeal but also more conventional stories, and their Lovecraft connections may not be easily discernible to the average viewer.

With the forgoing being said, *The Lighthouse* (2019) is a film frequently called Lovecraftian in reviews and analysis, but this brings into sharper focus again the perhaps unanswerable question of what makes something Lovecraftian. Filmed entirely in black and white, the movie concerns two men, at least of whom carries a dark secret, who are on an isolated island off the New England coast tending a lighthouse, and it depicts the events that lead to their deaths. Brooding ideas of insanity and indefinable menace drench the film, which is as much about creating a weird atmosphere as it is about telling a narrative. Robert Eggers, the film's director, spoke in interviews about drawing among other things (as summarized by Meagan Navarro) "from H. P. Lovecraft's *Weird Tales* pulp magazines, too, but less in the sense of Elder Things and more fear of the unknown tinged with the supernatural." He even more directly stated:

> There are Lovecraftian influences to this movie, but if this were properly Lovecraftian, when Rob finds Willem's journal, it would have been filled with occult Dagon stuff that would explain that Dafoe is part of a Dagon cult and that there's a slimy god that lives inside the tentacles and so on, you know what I mean? [laughs] That's definitely what we did not want to do. (Schager)

Eggers's previous film, *The Witch: A New England Folktale* (2015), was both widely acclaimed and financially successful, and was set very much in the darker aspects of the colonies of Puritan New England, going as far as to include period dialogue from written records, and this overlap with Lovecraft is obvious. *The Lighthouse* too uses period dialogue, deals with themes of isolation and madness, and includes glimpses of the monstrous and unnatural, with the narrative entirely unreliable not just from the characters' perspective but as presented to the viewer. The edge of surrealism in the entire film, which was nominated for an Academy Award for Best Cinematography, leaves the interpretation of events as being about a genuine Proteus guarding some kind of sacred fire, the madness caused by alcoholism and isolation, or any combination the viewer feels is appropriate. Thus likewise the film is perhaps as Lovecraftian as the viewer chooses.

Wounds (2019) is another relatively low-budget film that was released directly onto streaming services, a paradigm that seems to be a relatively successful dynamic for Lovecraftian films. The streaming business model doesn't require immense initial viewership of individual projects or box office, but rather is driven by a need for new, engaging content to attract new viewers and keep current members actively subscribed. As such, the evergreen horror genre finds a natural place in such an environment. *Bird Box* (2018) is perhaps the most populist example of this trend having a Lovecraftian connection. Like many of the films under discussion, it is derived from a novel of the same name and deals with a nightmarish apocalypse wherein the world is seemingly overrun by entities that drive their viewers to suicide, with its influences from Lovecraft both thematic and in direct imagery (Norris 192–93). *Wounds* is likewise derived from a written text, the novella "The Visible Filth" by Nathan Ballingrud. Significantly, this novella was originally published as an individual artefact but was later assembled in the collection *Wounds: Six Stories from the Border of Hell,* which gathered six standalone and seemingly unrelated stories that when read collectively intersect on various levels with one another and create a far larger world and an original mythology. In many ways the book's contents are upon a superficial reading decidedly at odds with Lovecraft's artificial mythologies and cosmology, dealing as they do with devil worship and the mysteries of hell. Yet Ballingrud is creating a distinct, unfamiliar, and unsettling version of such ideas that has little in common with popular perceptions or previous depictions. This makes for a true atmosphere of cosmic horror and the weird, and it is not coincidental that Jeff VanderMeer and Victor LaValle are two of the three other authors quoted about the book and author on the Amazon purchase link. This weirdness is translated directly to the film, which shifts between different media.

Unlike the other films so far discussed, the narrative and setting of *Wounds* is decidedly, almost resolutely, contemporary and grounded in real-world verisimilitude. Again with the film's creator, Babak Anvari, the figure of the writer-director appears in connection with Lovecraftian adaptations. Anvari is an emergent director of note and had his only other feature film submitted by the United Kingdom as their country's selection for the 89th Academy Award for Best Foreign Language Film. Casting is likewise filled with contemporary actors decidedly seen as having their stars on the ascendant, including Armie Hammer, Dakota Johnson, and Zazie Beetz. The plot concerns a bartender who is drawn into a preternatural nightmare after opening a phone accidentally left behind at his bar by some college students following a fight between other patrons, and which ultimately involves the summoning of a being of a different reality through wounds. The Lovecraftian ideas are in a new shape but are clearly identifiable. The hints of summoning experiments seen on the phone are enough to shade the whole episode with terror yet fail to make explicit what is happening, and this limited parceling out of information and explanation gives the film an edge of constant dread: the idea of the college students as cultists perhaps now possessed, the accidental encounter with the outside of reality that brings madness and destruction along with its knowledge, the rituals for summoning other entities inside a forbidden book entitled *The Translation of Wounds*, which is briefly seen by never exposited upon.

Yet for all its Lovecraftian dread, *Wounds*, like *Annihilation* and *Bird Box*, is heavily invested in the emotions of the characters and their relationships with one another. This trend is a notable, and indeed for commercial purposes probably essential, aspect of Lovecraftian ideas on screen. To illustrate with a negative, one of the acknowledged best films in the Lovecraftian oeuvre, John Carpenter's *The Thing* (1982), was a significant financial flop upon initial release. It is noteworthy that the film contains no romantic subplot, an almost inevitable aspect of most horror films, and in fact no female characters at all, the closest hint being a chess computer with a woman's voice.[4] However, it is not necessarily a case of one aspect or the other. In *Wounds* it is the protagonist's ultimately shallow emotional affect and emptiness that mark him as a candidate for the translating being. Yet in classic Lovecraftian fashion the person who investigates the unknown is brutally punished for his audacity, and to quote the director Anvari, "doesn't really find any redemption in the end, which was done on purpose" (Reilly).

Of all the films under examination, writer-director Huan Vu's *Die Farbe* (*The Colour*) (2010), commonly known as *The Color out of Space* in English-speaking markets, is probably the most faithful to Lovecraft, both as a thematic and direct adaptation. This might not seem immediately apparent, given that the location of events is largely switched from New England to Germany and the inciting incident of the story involves a son's hunt for his missing father, who seems to have gone back to the region he was posted to in Germany shortly after the Second World War. Yet after this change, obviously necessitated by the geographic locale of the filmmakers, the movie unfolds with a remarkable adherence to Lovecraft's original story. The son tracing his missing father replaces the tale's original narrator, and the forensic investigating party at the end of the story are instead GIs, yet almost all the narrative remains true to Lovecraft. Nor it is just in the broad picture, certain key events, and occasional nods to moments in the tale, as with *Color out of Space* (2020), which will be discussed in turn. Indeed, to list all

---

4. For the curious, the voice belonged to actress Adrienne Barbeau, then the spouse of John Carpenter.

the connections in *Die Farbe* would hover between the tedious and redundant; a select sample is highly illustrative. The names of the central characters, for the most part, have recognizable German versions of those from Lovecraft's tale: Armin Pierske for Ammi Pierce; the family being the Gärteners, consisting of Marwin, Samuel, and Thaddäus, for Merwin, Zenas, and Thaddeus from the original; Mrs. Gärtener, generically unnamed in both, while Nahum's name makes the transfer intact. The obvious story beats from tale are of course replicated—the majority of the tale being a narrative told by Armin, the meteor crash, the investigation by scientists, drawing the lightning, the tainting of the fruit, the slow madness of the Gärteners, the final escape of the Colour[5] from the well—with many scenes transferred directly, such as the madness of Nahum calling upon more wood for a fire that is not going from people who are not present. Indeed, in a clever visual call-back a final scene of Armin wrapped in a blanket alone in his home mimics Nahum's own behavior and posture in his penultimate moment. Occasional snippets of dialogue come directly from the source material as well.

But it is not in the larger moments of adaptation that *Die Farbe* shows its true authenticity, but in the smaller. In direct transference from the original tale, mention is made of the upland fruit not being spoiled, the stone shrinking, the idea of the events being thought of as God's punishment, the obvious cause of the foul fruit being from the meteor being stated, the Gärteners listening for something, the unnaturally moving trees, horses shying near the property, the snows melting faster on the Gärtener property, the Colour feeding on the family, its escape via the window when Armin looks in on the confined Mrs. Gärtener. The ostracism of the Gärteners from the village, which notes the strange behavior of the family, is connected with the mention of the children staying home from school. Then there are deeper cuts. Samuel at one point is sharpening an axe to cut down the tainted fruit trees, reflecting Zenas's cutting down the blasphemous vegetation in the story. The end credits

---

5. Despite the title the subtitles use the English rather than the American spelling.

show a tracking shot of water from the contaminated reservoir going into pipes and slowly making its way into the water supply for the town, and the last shot of the film looking down on the lights of the city holds the dark menace and undertones of bad things yet to happen that conclude Lovecraft's tale. But probably the most intriguing adaptation is a small moment of the two children Marwin and Thaddäus playing a game with a coin to determine chores. This reflects a small aspect and humanizing moment of the original story where Merwin suffers especially after "the shutting away of the brother who had been his greatest playmate." Such attention to detail is what makes *Die Farbe* stand out as a genuinely unique adaptation of Lovecraft's work rather than merely a framework to hand another type of story on.

Interestingly, in light of all the foregoing, *Die Farbe* is also one of the least professional films under examination, although this is not meant as a disparagement of its quality, which is excellent; rather, it is that director Vu and co-producer Jan Roth were not professional filmmakers in the more established sense. The twain were friends studying Media and VFX at university, and *Die Farbe* was originally developed as a final examination project, but grew beyond their initial conception. Unlike many other adaptations, the question Vu posed to himself included the seemingly most obvious one that many filmmakers seem not to consider. In the special features on the DVD Vu restated his initial thoughts and queries about making the film, specifically stating: "If you do a Lovecraft film, the question is; how much do you show? . . . Lovecraft leaves a lot of things in his tales open to the reader's imagination." In this balance Vu has succeeded far more than most. As an aspect of metanarrative it is interesting to note the effect the film has for largely being in German, with subtitles. This adds an element of the exotic, possibly even the surreal, that would be absent to a native speaker of German who watched the film, and adds a facet of the literary back into the film that seems oddly appropriate although probably unintentional. The German aspect also gives an alternative perspective than what would likely be made by an American filmmaker; even though much of the film is set immediately before and after the Second World War and Armin is a returned soldier, no mention or imagery of the obvious Nazi connection is made, something that would have added an unnecessarily jarring element to the film.

Perhaps the most conspicuous aspect of the film is that it is shot, in the main, in black and white. Only the Colour is, well, a color, which makes it especially striking contextually. Yet it is not simply as a modern movie in black and white that *Die Farbe* is filmed. A special camera, the DRAKE, was utilized to simulate the feel of old 35mm film, distinctly adding to the feeling of place and time, which is set in the main in the 1930s (Armin's story) and 1970s (Davis's search). While it would be a mischaracterization to state that the look of the film is too heavily influenced by German impressionistic films of the '20s and '30s, there is just enough of that inspiration to make it worthy of adding as a minor note of the film's aesthetic. Ultimately the color chosen for the Colour was, after various testings, a mauve/magenta. The filmmakers felt that "red would have been stronger and more aggressive, but we are more used to it, and pink looks stranger." There is very little of the Colour in the film, which renders its appearance infinitely more effective and menacing. The brief scene with the Colour filling the eyes and mouth of the alive but skull-visaged Frau Gärtener is genuinely horrifying, and probably the highlight of the film from a horror perspective.

In addition to the faithfulness of the adaptation, there is the overall tone and approach. Vu speaks specifically about the scientific attitude to horror he is taking, and as such is following in Lovecraft's own footsteps far more than the common (and understandable) majority who tend to focus on the more famous and unnatural aspects of Lovecraft's work. Vu specifically discusses idea of parasites and the lancet liver fluke, which has a particularly oblique and convoluted incubation and infection cycle. The scientific testing on the meteorite is dwelt upon in some depth in the film, rather than the frequently perfunctory attention it is given in other adaptations. Widmanstätten patterns, which are distinctive symmetrical geometrical structures only found on meteorites, are twice mentioned, while images of

the Colour under examination appear somewhat like a DNA he-
lix. The globular nature and the movements of the Colour have
a distinct resonance with common images of cell division. How
much this is absolutely intentional cannot be determined—the
specific effects were limited by the rendering power available to
the production—but it certainly adds to the weirdness and atmosphere. The final image of the Colour as a congeries of bub-
bles likewise calls to mind Yog-Sothoth and some of the
travelers in other dimensions in "The Dreams in the Witch
House," but again this may be a case of overinterpretation.

There are a number of other Lovecraftian nods in the opening scenes that show a defter hand than many who attempt
such. Indeed, the film would be picked up for distribution by the
H. P. Lovecraft Historical Society (HPLHS), and this seems an
appropriate home for *Die Farbe* given its own penchant for highly faithful adaptations in various media of Lovecraft's work. Vu
is not attempting to hide his Lovecraftian light under a bushel
outside of the film as well as in it; as soon as the film begins, in
the second spoken line, a character introduces himself as Detective Ward. This might seem a little on the nose, as is the protagonist Jonathan Davis being a former student of Miskatonic
University in Arkham, Massachusetts. Davis soon goes seeking
his old mentor in the neo-classical Armitage Memorial Library,
Dr Henry Armitage of course being the head librarian in 1928
who dealt with the Whateley siblings in "The Dunwich Horror."
The librarian is an old man, and we swiftly learn that he is
Danforth, famously the other survivor of the Miskatonic University Expedition to the Antarctic of 1930 in *At the Mountains of
Madness*.

These references, which some might argue are tired, actually
show one of the rarest of things in Lovecraftian pastiche and
reference: further development. Time has moved on, and that
gives the setting a sense of place in Lovecraft Country without
the inherently static rehashing that previous events and stories
can give. Showing a nimbler touch, Danforth, standing in the
library stacks, sees Davis approach and mentions that Davis
must be lost, for there is "nothing in this section for a respecta-

ble scientist." The oblique reference to Miskatonic Library's famed collection of magical lore, never made explicit, adds to the world-building and makes a nod to Lovecraft without becoming cloying or damned into dullness by explicitness. The references to the Limes in Germany and Celtic headstones, functionally unnecessary to the plot, also make a nice connection with Lovecraft's famed antiquarian passions. The film won numerous awards, and leading Lovecraft scholar S. T. Joshi in 2014 called *Die Farbe* "the best Lovecraft film adaptation ever made" (Joshi, *Blog*).

Another movie, of the more traditional smaller budget production that is most commonly the Lovecraftian filmic paradigm, new to streaming service Shudder in July 2020 but shot in 2017, is *The Beach House*. There is nothing of the direct adaptation of Lovecraft's work in the tale, but writer-director Jeffrey A. Brown cited the evergreen "The Colour out of Space" as an influence in his Director's Statement, and was distressed to learn of the then forthcoming Richard Stanley production of that story, which will be discussed below. Nor were such fears unfounded. *The Hollywood Reporter, RogerEbert.com,* and *Screen Queens* all noted the connection with the story in their respective reviews, with the last-named also specifically mentioning *Color out of Space* (2020) as being with *The Beach House* in its own small subgenre of "weird horror." Brown openly acknowledges this as his favorite Lovecraft story, "a pure form of cosmic horror, and in my opinion his scariest tale" (Vaughn).

Unsurprisingly, as is almost ubiquitous in modern Lovecraftian cinema, Brown mentions the influence of John Carpenter, and the twin *Alien* and *Aliens* films. This Lovecraftian influence is strongly resonant in *The Beach House*, which concerns two disparate couples accidentally sharing a house at a largely deserted beachfront town in the off-season who are exposed to unknown chemical and biological forces from the ocean, resulting in horrific infections and mutations. Again the association of Lovecraft with body horror is on full display, and the scene of the character of Emily removing some form of parasitic worm from her horribly infected foot is mentioned again and again in reviews for its gruesome effect on the viewer. Even by the standards of the limited parceling of information one encounters, or perhaps more truly fails to encounter, in Lovecraft, *The Beach House* is sparse with its exposition. There is no direct explanation of what is occurring, or why, aside from general ideas derived from Emily's studies as an astrobiologist and the wider universal ideas of life and our unusual position in it. *The Beach House* is genuine cosmic horror, the uncaring universe a monstrous force that can be neither understood nor fought against.

In a like vein of the smaller, self-created projects is writer-director Gus Holwerda's *Intersect* (2020), available to buy directly on Blu-ray from the creators or to rent or buy via many of the major streaming services. Like the poster for *The Void* (2016), with its praying figure before a glowing triangular portal with emergent tentacles, the marketing image for *Intersect* is instantly evocative of the Lovecraftian. It shows a human figure standing before an illuminated blue doorway that has a nebulous black quality filling its interior while a mirror of the doorway underneath shows a different dimension with some huge tentacloid limbs emergent from it, the relative scale of the two images (the bottom image is roughly twice the size of the upper despite an identical size of doorway) making the threat even more apparent. Such playing to a specific audience is not a single effort, or unacknowledged; the first descriptor used on the back of the Blu-ray case about the film is "Lovecraftian." The plot itself concerns a main trio of students at Miskatonic University who have invented a time travel portal. The narrative actually unfolds in a non-linear fashion, going backwards to show all the stages of the protagonist's work and friendship in a reverse chronology. It is apparent in this flashback narrative that some very alien watchers are observing, and seemingly manipulating, the protagonist toward the creation of the portal. The protagonist is led to believe such beings are benign, yet their obvious air of malignity gives the viewer an entirely different impression, and it eventually becomes clear that they are in fact the vanguard of an invading force, influencing the characters to create their bridgehead. These malefic creatures of time have a certain resonance with Frank Belknap Long's "The Hounds of Tinda-los," one of the earliest stories now seen as part of the Cthulhu Mythos not written by Lovecraft himself, yet *Intersect* is largely an original creation drawing deeper from the science fiction side of the Lovecraftian well, and using some of the more recognized elements associated with fictional time travel, including circular narrative threads and an ambiguous ending. To this quite scientific approach mention must be made of the voice of the computer being celebrated author, scientist, and atheist proselytizer Richard Dawkins. In addition to the coup this represents to the filmmakers, it adds an interesting metatextual element to the story and (ahem) intersects nicely with Lovecraft's own cosmic perceptions.

It is worth digressing a moment to note a place in popular culture from which, until recently, Lovecraft was most certainly absent. Speaking extremely broadly, both *Star Trek* and *Star Wars* have some commonalities with Lovecraft. These franchises, beginning in 1966 and 1977 respectively, have had a long-lasting cultural influence far in excess of both their own contemporary shows and later, similarly themed phenomena. In additional to the original productions still being watched by generations long after their initial release, many subsequent sequels and innumerable ancillary materials are still being produced. Indeed, those originals have had every moment strip-mined for further enlargement to keep up a production of newer yet connected *materiel,* and whose subsequent influence extends far beyond those who have ever seen the shows in question. It is a rare person in the Western world who isn't familiar with the idea popularized by *Star Trek* of warp speed as a synonym for fast (the US government initiative to find a Covid-19 vaccine was called Operation Warp Speed), or who would fail recognize Darth Vader as an iconic symbol of villainy.[6]

Yet there has been a distinct lack of cross-pollination of ei-

---

6. Chris Taylor, author of *How Star Wars Conquered the Universe* (2014), unsuccessfully spent a year trying to find anyone who didn't know about *Star Wars,* hoping to get a truly genuine reaction of someone seeing it for the first time.

ther with Lovecraft. Lovecraft protégé Robert Bloch wrote three episodes of the original series of *Star Trek*. which contain hints of (some extremely undefined) Old Ones. Yet upon examination of the *Star Trek* canon, these Old Ones are not the unknowable alien beings of Lovecraft's work. In *What Are Little Girls Made Of?* the extinct Old Ones who created the androids are clearly just another of the sentient humanoid civilizations that populate the *Star Trek* universe, while the Old Ones mentioned in *Catspaw*, despite being equally ill-defined, are obviously a different type of beings altogether. *Catspaw* in particular, along to a lesser degree with *Wolf in the Fold*, seems very much out of place in the Star Trek universe, with an emphasis that is far more supernatural than science fiction. Both have aspects that clearly involve the symbolic imagery, and hastily redressed workings, of magic, and *Wolf in the Fold* contains that most decidedly unscientific ritual, a séance. It is no surprise to learn they are adaptations of Bloch's already published short stories, "Broomstick Ride" and the famous "Yours Truly, Jack the Ripper" respectively, reworked to be shoehorned into the *Star Trek* milieu. In the associated novels and in other created materials adjunct to both the primary *Star Trek* and *Star Wars* series there are occasional references to Lovecraftian ideas and concepts, or playful homages and shout-outs such as a character wearing Miskatonic University sweatshirt in the tie-in Star Trek novel *How Much for Just the Planet?* But they are very thin given the huge volume of such paraphernalia produced, and such materials are generally considered non-canonical to the filmed versions. Given the very humanocentric view of both shows, and the focus on the characters and their adventures, the lack of connection with Lovecraft and his cosmic horrors and malign indifference to humanity makes sense.

But this natural division has recently begun to change. The spin-off prequel highlighting the adventures and making of the titular character in *Solo: A Star Wars Story* (2018) has a decidedly Lovecraftian detour, at least visually. As the main characters seek to escape in their craft through via the Kessel Run, a notoriously dangerous region of space, they are confronted by a truly

Cyclopean horror that instantly conveys a Lovecraftian sensibility to its design, a beast of malice and tentacle, overlarge head and numerous alien eyes. Of course, huge creatures are not new to the Star Wars universe. *The Empire Strikes Back* (1980) famously has a giant space slug, known in the extended lore as an exogorth, trying to eat the very same ship, and absent other information this could be seen as an homage to that very famous moment. But the Lovecraftian connection is confirmed by the script co-writer Jonathan Kasden on his official Twitter account:

> In the earliest drafts, the Kessel Run was interrupted with a forced pit stop on a spooky Ridley Scott–type planet. On that Nameless Planet, Beckett's crew encounters enormous Lovecraftian monsters that claim one of their number...Later, when working on the sequence with RH [Director Ron Howard], the notion of a Lovecraftian monster returned (as were both huge Lovecraft fans) . . . The name Summa-verminoth [the tentacle monster noted earlier] is another Cthulhu mythos homage to Robert Bloch' s fictional tome, *De Vermis Mysteriis* . . . In the script, the area of Savareen where the refinery is located is identified as the Pnakotic Dunes, another Lovecraft nod.

It is worth noting that the "spooky Ridley Scott–type planet" is a reference to LV-426, the location of the derelict spacecraft holding the eggs that are the genesis of the nightmarish Giger creation in the famously Lovecraftian film *Alien* (1979). Even the capitalized "Nameless Planet" is decidedly a Lovecraftian element, both conceptually and in Lovecraft's references to *Nameless Cults*, borrowed from Robert E. Howard's expansion to the Mythos and Lovecraft's own "lone nameless rock" of the moonbeasts "from which vile howlings reverberate all through the night" (CF 2.173) in *The Dream-Quest of Unknown Kadath*. All these elements in connection with the shout-out to Bloch brings out an interesting factor that will be more fully explored later: the connection and creation of Lovecraft adaptations and influences that no longer come directly from Lovecraft, or that come from cultural perceptions of Lovecraft.

The first season of *Star Trek: Picard* (2020) again illustrates the omnipresence of Lovecraft looming in cosmic horror. The

show, a direct follow-on from the highly successful television re-
launch of the franchise *Star Trek: The Next Generation* (1987–
94), focuses on the now retired Captain Picard of the starship
Enterprise, and has as its central motivations issues arising from
the conflicts between biological and synthetic life. Although obviously a television series, designed for a streaming service, rather than a feature film, each of the first season's ten episodes
does run directly into the following episode and they are intended to be a single long narrative rather than a series of events occurring with the same character on a weekly basis. Likewise, the
reported budget of $8–9 million per episode gives it a production
value more in line with a feature film. Such matters aside, the
important issue for our analysis is that *ST: Picard* culminates in
the final episode, *Et in Arcadia Ego, Part II*, with a higher form of
synthetic life being summoned via a portal to enter our galaxy
and scourge it clean of organic life. The appearance of this om-
nicidal uber-synthetic is instantly Lovecraftian, a mass of writhing, albeit mechanical tentacles. Akiva Goldsman, who in
addition to being a credited creator and producer on the show
was the director and co-writer of the story for the final episode,
gave the following response in an interview, of which the ques-
tioner's own remarks are equally telling:

> *Paste:* Another big moment that felt like a reference was when
> the other synthetic beings begin to invade from the other
> realm—in my notes, I wrote down "techno-Cthulhu." What was
> the thought process behind developing that design?

> *Goldsman:* I think that there is always some version of the lurk-
> ing hulking thing which lives behind the walls of the world, and
> I think that it's hard not to go to Cthulhu . . . It's funny because
> the shapes [of the tentacles] are so organic, so we had to keep
> driving many iterations, because we saw it was still feeling a lit-
> tle too bio-slimy. (Miller)

It is noteworthy that the idea of preventing the cyclical return of tentacled genocidal machines intent on scouring the galaxy free of organic life is the fundamental story underpinning
the hugely successful *Mass Effect* video game series. Again we

see the interaction of Lovecraft from both primary source material and subsequent tributary evolutions flowing back together into the idea of the Lovecraftian, simultaneously altering, broadening, and diluting the concept even as it draws upon its roots. The *Mass Effect* series is noted for the influence of Lovecraft in its framework, and equally criticized at a philosophical level for the abnegation of the deeper terrors inherent in the both the Cthulhu Mythos specifically and cosmic horror in general (ontologicalgeek.com). This is not a specific criticism solely of *Mass Effect*. It is unfortunately a truism of populist video games in general. This diminution of terror is a natural side effect of game mechanics explaining the ineffable and the need for players to be able to win the game, something that is impossible in the framework of true cosmic horror; and while it might be satisfying as fiction, it is decidedly less enticing as a player-controlled game.

It is significant that both *Solo* and *Picard* have been very divisive within both their specific fan communities and with the wider viewing audience. *Solo* is officially the first failure at the box office for the canonical *Star Wars* franchise, while *Picard* was at the time of its release the only *Star Trek: The Next Generation* spinoff to have a rotten rating in the audience score of Rotten Tomatoes. Obviously the minor Lovecraft connections are not responsible for this, but it is interesting to see the addition of Lovecraftian tropes and concepts to arenas in which they do not natively belong coincide with a diminution in these franchises' popularity. Lovecraft's reach has grown so long that it spills into things that are clearly not its domain, often to the detriment of both parties.

No discussion of Lovecraft in television could be complete without mention of the 2020 HBO series that bears his name, *Lovecraft Country*.[7] The term Lovecraft Country originally came into use via the *Call of Cthulhu* role-playing game to describe the

---

7. As anecdotal evidence of its market penetration and the value of Lovecraft's name as recognizable intellectual property, more people spoke or wrote to the author about this series than any other movie or series detailed in this monograph, by a wide margin.

setting of Lovecraft's fictionalization of New England with its
recurrent geography and locales, and was adopted by Matt Ruff
for his 2016 novel. The book is famously seeking to re-address
the racist ideas that influenced some of Lovecraft's writings, and
well as his own actual xenophobia in life, an increasingly popular
postmodern approach on the subject. This is part of a response
to changing cultural times and partly a necessity for reinvigora-
tion of the Mythos after the endless (and frankly often tedious)
output of Lovecraft pastiches that had begun even in Lovecraft's
lifetime. As might be expected, the novel and series differ great-
ly, which itself become a clever point inside the series. When
the main character, Atticus "Tic" Freeman, obtains a book from
the future by his as yet unborn son George that describes the
events occurring in the series but with some significant differences, Tic sums them up as "'Christina is a man, Uncle George
survived Ardham and Dee's a boy named 'Horace,'" these being
major differences between Ruff's book and the series.

The series starts with a fantastical depiction of a trench battle featuring stereotypical flying saucers, Martian war machines
from H. G. Wells's *The War of the Worlds*, a red-skinned humanoid alien beauty in a gold bikini, and Cthulhu itself. However, this is merely a dream sequence, as might be guessed from
the fact that Jackie Robinson appears and splits Cthulhu down
the middle with a baseball bat, and the sleeper awakens with
Edgar Rice Burroughs's *A Princess of Mars* in his lap.[8] For a show
with Lovecraft's name in the title there is almost nothing of his
work, or more importantly his ideas, on screen. After the opening described above, only a few brief mentions of Lovecraft's
name and a copy of the Arkham House edition of *The Outsider
and Others* (1939) are shown in the first episode. This episode
also anachronistically brings up his infamous short poem "On
the Creation of Niggers," written in 1912 and never published as
part of his works until the rise of Lovecraft scholarship brought
it out whence it had rightfully languished forgotten in the
depths of the John Hay Library's Lovecraft Collection archive

---

8. For those who haven't read the book, the titular princess Dejah Thoris is a
beautiful woman with red skin who wears very little clothing.

long after the period setting of the show. This usage actually points to the true nature of the show.

Rather than drawing on Lovecraft's cosmicism and ideas of the unknown and unknowable, *Lovecraft County* focuses almost exclusively on the paradoxically simple and complex ideas of racism, which admittedly does underpin some of the thematic elements of Lovecraft work, albeit in a much transmuted and recrudesced form frequently not textually apparent. As such, the show actually has very little in common with Lovecraft, drawing instead on elements from the wider science fiction, fantasy, and horror genres such as voodoo, ghosts, the Garden of Eden, monsters of folklore such the *Kumiho* (구미호) of Korea, mages acquiring spells, curses, and the like. Outside of vague generalities common to such genres—cults, magical tomes, monsters with tentacles and eyes—there is very little that seems to be drawing in any other than the most superficial way from Lovecraft's writings, or indeed from the Cthulhu Mythos as it developed after his death. References are made to various items connected with Lovecraft, such as the books in the library including those of William Hope Hodgson, Clark Ashton Smith, and Algernon Blackwood, but simply utilizing this model a wag could say the second episode be called *Hodgson Country*, as the mansion the heroes find themselves in is subjected to outside forces and collapses into ruin in the end like *The House on the Borderland* (1908), whose plot is actually described in the episode.

The ubiquitous *Necronomicon* is mentioned in passing but only as a comparison and point of difference to the *Book of Names* in the series, obviously taking inspiration from the idea that *Necronomicon* is often said to translate as *The Book of Dead Names*. A character refers to a monster in the woods jokingly as a shoggoth and then gives a brief but accurate description of one before its manifestation. The actual appearance of the creature of a decidedly stereotypically broad Lovecraftian aspect in a humanoid shape is later shown as birthed from a cow and with infective properties. ScreenRant calls such beings, both accurately and inaccurately, "the vampire-like Shoggoths," and states that they "don't like light" (Harn). This is not to dismiss the creature design by Jerad S. Marantz, which is exquisite, nor the excellent on-screen glimpses of the disturbing monsters. It is just that the visualization is a relatively far distance conceptually from Lovecraft's original protoplasmic nightmares. I have read many and varied accounts trying to shoehorn portrayals in *Lovecraft Country* with Lovecraft's creations, but in almost all instances they are implausibly broad or dubiously vague in their linkages.

Of course, Lovecraft has always been open to wildly differing interpretations. Some of the earliest published usages of the *Necronomicon* other than that by Lovecraft himself[9] were in works by his friends Frank Belknap Long and Clark Ashton Smith, in their stories "The Space-Eaters" (*Weird Tales*, July 1928) and "The Return of the Sorcerer" (*Strange Tales of Mystery and Terror*, September 1931), respectively. In both tales the book is of a decidedly different cast. Long uses it as a quotation for the epigraph, giving it a decidedly Christian slant, while Smith's interpretation of the *Necronomicon*, in its original Arabic, is filled with the names of ghouls and demons and with a formula for exorcism of the dead, paradoxically making it more akin to the often stupefying dull reality of actual grimoires, and it is thus used to combat a murderous revenant. This all seems not to have bothered Lovecraft even slightly, and he waxes at length over the latter tale in a letter to Smith himself after his first reading of it, and goes so far as to offer minor edits to the story, which Smith would incorporate (*DS* 292–93). Likewise, Lovecraft was unfazed by Hugh B. Cave—with whom he did not have such as cordial relationship as he did with Smith—appropriating some of his creations in "The Isle of Dark Magic" in *Weird Tales* for August 1934 (*OFF* 163).

Perhaps the exception to this heavily diluted Lovecraft in *Lovecraft Country* is the character of Hippolyta traveling through numerous dimensions and alternative realities to be all the differ-

---

9. The book was mentioned under its Arabic title in "The Last Test" by Adolphe de Castro in the November 1928 issue of *Weird Tales*, but that tale was of course a Lovecraft revision. Robert E. Howard's "The Children of the Night" in the April–May 1931 *Weird Tales* also mentions the *Necronomicon* but does not much expound upon its contents.

ent versions of herself, including rather cleverly an Amazon queen who is her original namesake. This is decidedly reminiscent of Randolph Carter's travels in "Through the Gates of the Silver Key." Significantly, that story actually co-written with E. Hoffmann Price. Price wanted a sequel to "The Silver Key" so keenly that he essentially forced Lovecraft to collaborate by first writing a version himself that Lovecraft rewrote to become the final tale. Yet in common with the aforementioned "The Isle of Dark Magic," the entire tone of *Lovecraft Country* is concerned with the earthly events and travails of the characters, almost in diametric opposition to Lovecraft's creation of a malignantly indifferent cosmos. As an exploration of racism, the African-American experience and viewpoint on the purportedly halcyon "good old days" of the 1950s, it certainly succeeds in creating an original and unflinching show, with a surprising depth to any number of genre, cultural, and historic connections, such as the photography of Gordon Parks, or Emmett Till's nickname of Bobo. *Lovecraft Country* likewise uses both allegory, fantasy, and unflinching reality to create an often brutally violent and highly confronting horror program. It just isn't a particularly Lovecraftian one.

Most of the foregoing films discussed have been influenced by Lovecraft either notionally, thematically, in certain often minor specifics, or even without any demonstrable specifics but still fitting into the tradition that is generally recognized as Lovecraftian. The final two films under analysis are different in that they draw directly and substantially from Lovecraft's actual works. They are also films designed for, and having achieved, a general theatrical release rather than being created for or picked up by streaming services, or being solely of the lower-budget sort destined by modern forces of economic necessity and marketing to be outside the higher tiers of distribution. Such a release, however, is not the entirety of the story with either film, as will be explored presently.

Underwater (2020) suffered from an unforeseeable confluence of negative events that acted as a detriment to its garnering a larger commercial success, as seems curiously commonplace with many would-be Lovecraft adaptations and homages. *The Void* for example lost a major backer for funding the day before principal photography began, setting in place a series of scrambles and delays by the filmmakers that are rarely beneficial to the often time-sensitive nature of filmmaking. Of course, such issues are endemic inside the arena of modern filmmaking, and yet even allowing for this *Underwater* seems particularly ill-starred.

Unlike numerous Lovecraftian films, these issues with *Underwater* were not in budget, which has been reported between $50 and $80 million. This is quite possibly a record for a truly Lovecraftian film, although such things are difficult to determine, given both the infamous vagaries of Hollywood accounting and determinations of the nebulous ideas of what passes for Lovecraftian. For illustration, *Hellboy* (2004) may have cost more and *Prometheus* (2012) certainly did, but the Lovecraftian connections to the latter are so distorted by other murky layers of the constantly changing mythology of the *Alien*-derived universe, and later arrogations of the ideas from *At the Mountains of Madness* into more general circulation, that they might not be in any way apparent to the average viewer. The distinct Lovecraftian connections of *Hellboy* pale in comparison to the actual appearance of Lovecraft's best-known creation as the major plot driver in *Underwater*. These budgetary comparisons would be a somewhat inane and unbecoming as a way of adjudging art, save that the financial implications of a major Lovecraftian film flopping at the box office has natural ripple effect going forward.

While it is often churlish to blame a film's poor box-office performance as not being a consequence of its merits but of the nebulous villainy of other factors, the ill-fortune of *Underwater* in both tangible and intangible aspects was considerable. It was the last film to be released under the banner of the venerable umbrella of the 20th Century Fox name, after the acquisition of that studio by the Disney Corporation. The latter is of course famously a family-friendly corporate entity not wishing to be associated with horror, and there is an impression that the film was held in low regard by its new owners, easily demonstrable by its largely unheralded debut in the traditional post-holiday dumping ground for new features in the North American film landscape of January 2020. Adding to its misfortune was a huge delay, especially for a relatively large studio film, between the completion of shooting in May 2017 and the final release, and while this can be indicative of many things it is rarely a positive sign for future success.

For a sci-fi horror action film, the latter of which are particularly noted for casting unknown actors given the low budgets and generally predetermined audience who tend to see such films irrespective of other considerations, the cast was filled with names carrying a certain amount of cachet, including Kristen Stewart, Vincent Cassel, and T. J. Miller. Shortly after production wrapped, the last-named was unfortunately (this term used solely in relationship to audience interest in *Underwater*) caught up in in the #MeToo movement and had his career destroyed as a result, with his behavior alleged to be both odious and criminal. Given his role as the likeable comic relief in the film, this was particularly jarring for audiences aware of such events, and it limited Miller's previously positive utility in marketing. Vincent Cassel is a well-respected and celebrated actor with an impressive pedigree, although with much of his work in French cinema he was simply not very well-known to the English-speaking horror genre community. Even Kristen Stewart was ultimately a negative for the film, although critics commonly singled out her acting for praise in the film itself. Unfortunately, many genre fans unfairly dismissed Stewart for her *Twilight* connection as the co-star in the often mocked modern vampire/paranormal romance franchise. In addition to the ill-starred aspect surrounding *Underwater*, Stewart's immediately previous film in wide release was the financially unsuccessful and hugely divisive remake[10] of *Charlie's Angels* (2019) barely two months earlier. For this role Stewart was nominated for the facetious "She Deserves a New Agent Award" by the Alliance of Women Film Journalists (AWFJ), and *Charles Angels* itself scooped the "Time Waster Remake or Sequel Award."

Background aside, *Underwater* is a hugely claustrophobic and

---

10. A remake of the previous two remake films of the original television series no less.

tense science fiction horror film, with not a single frame occurring outside the titular environment. The premise is simple: in the near future the ongoing deep-water mining operations on the ocean floor of the Mariana Trench are destroyed in an apparent earthquake, the few trapped survivors must make their way in diving suits to a second site to find viable rescue pods, and it becomes apparent that there is some sort of hostile marine life in the water intent on picking the survivors off. The premise is very much a mixture of the classic B-grade science fiction, monster, and disaster films. Indeed, the echoes of other films, in particular James Cameron's *Aliens* (1986) and *The Abyss* (1989), are quite noticeable. This connection of modern films with other predecessors the reader will have seen is a trend in this monograph, reflective as it is of the broader trends in twenty-first-century filmmaking. In modern cinema, drawing as it does now upon over five generations of previous works with study of all aspects of filmmaking taught at the tertiary level, there is always the question of the blurred lines of homage, influence, precedent, genre conventions, borrowings, and direct (or even subconscious) copying. The aforementioned and very Lovecraftian *Alien*, for example, is noted for its striking and original designs by Swiss artist H. R. Giger, who is rightly acclaimed as a visionary and pioneer of the biomechanical art that is now inextricably associated with his name. The iconic set piece image of the "Space Jockey" skeleton is an original Giger creation, being presumed as the pilot of the vessel and which is the first thing encountered in the derelict alien ship. Yet this quintessentially Gigeresque creation is clearly influenced in its very existence by a nearly identical scene of finding the skeleton of an alien captain or pilot in a downed spacecraft in *Planet of the Vampires* (1965).

However, the setup in *Underwater* is in many ways a misdirection. The earthquake serves to rouse the Sleeper of R'lyeh, or possibly the earthquake is in reality just the awakening of Cthulhu, who appears on-screen toward the end of the film. Although the name Cthulhu is not spoken in the film, it is an immediately recognizable and obvious visual representation fitting the general parameters as described by Lovecraft, albeit with a decidedly more brutal rather than corpulent character reminiscent of the kaiju of Guillermo del Toro's *Pacific Rim* (2013), who themselves come from a rift in the depths of the Pacific Ocean. Nor it is mere fan speculation, wishful thinking, or overinterpretation. *Underwater* director William Eubank has confirmed in interviews that it is Cthulhu itself, not merely a Cthulhuesque creation. Additionally, there are several very subtle Easter eggs and foreshadowings inside the movie itself connecting to the broader ideas of the Lovecraft and his mythos.

First, there is a metatextual example. One of the two men briefly glimpsed as they attempt to run to safety down a corridor in an early scene, but end up dying as the pressure wave of water overwhelms them, is actor Gunner Wright. His voice (as a different character) is also later heard on a scrambled message, boding ill for the remaining survivors before they head out. Wright is both the face and voice of Isaac Clarke from the highly successful (both critically and commercially) *Dead Space* video game series, another creation highly influenced by Lovecraft. The Old Gent is even directed referenced, as the mutilated corpse Howard Philips, in *Dead Space 2*. Tian Industries, the company that run the mining operation in *Underwater*, may be more sinister than just a heartless corporation funding the dangerous hadal zone venture. Mythological allusions abound in *Underwater*, with various structures being named as Triton and Poseidon class, while Pontus, the primordial Greek god of the sea present before the rise of the Olympian deities, is a support corporation named on jackets and equipment. Tian (more correctly *Tiān* [天]) is a Chinese word, loaded with meaning and dating in recognizable usage to at least 2000 B.C.E. It can be translated blandly as "sky," but it is more commonly rendered as "heaven," and can also mean a "heavenly deity," or more simply "god." Yet simple translation doesn't convey conceptually the underlying connotations deeply imbedded within Chinese religious thought and philosophy. As but one example, the Mandate of Heaven giving divine right of a ruler in Imperial China is *Tiān Ming* [天命]. Given the actions of the corporation, who it is stated in an opening text montage ignores rumors of strange goings-on at their facility, later rejects outside help with the destruction of its base, keeps the survivors secluded away from questioning, and immediately attempts to restart its operations, it is certainly a reading of their motives that they are cultists using the mining operation as a cover to awaken Cthulhu. It should be remembered that the undying leader of the Cthulhu cult are said in "The Call of Cthulhu" specifically to dwell in the mountains of China. These ideas are, however, more speculative than factual, at least as demonstrated in the film. China is a common corporate or national force in modern Western genre cinema, such as *The Martian* (2015) and *The Meg* (2018). Equally, actor Wright may have just been chosen for less metatextual and more personal reasons: he had previous starred in director Eubank's debut 2011 film *Love*.

Not at all ambiguous is another moment that confirms the intended identity of the monstrous being. At approximately minute 105, as the camera pans over a map pinned up in a locker, the iconic image of Cthulhu as drawn by Lovecraft himself can be very briefly seen. Indeed, the entire film can be interpreted as a very loose adaptation of "The Call of Cthulhu," including some more direct elements. These include the awakening of Cthulhu by accident rather than deliberate means; and although this perhaps runs somewhat counter to the Tian hypothesis noted above, the actual workers we meet in the film are certainly not part of the cult. Other more direct translations from the story include pursuit of the fleeing interlopers, the attempted destruction of Cthulhu via excessive physical force, the results of which are purposefully unknown to the viewer, the traumatized survivors, and the unknown future implications. Additional, less formal connections are present: the monsters in the water are the Cthulhu-spawn, which nest inside its bulk in a deliberately revolting parasitic image that evokes a latent trypophobic nightmare,[11] and in the nihilistic ending the protagonist kills herself deliberately to save her friends and hopefully end the

---

11. The common Suriname or star-fingered toad (*Pipa pipa*) native to South America does actually give birth to its young from its back. Let the google-er beware!

horror they have uncovered. Interestingly, given all the obvious connections to Cthulhu, the original script by Brian Duffield was decidedly more generic in regard to its monster, and with the Tian Company absent entirely. It was director Eubank, bringing in second credited scriptwriter Adam Cozad, who determined the later Lovecraftian course of the film, in particular the extensive two-year post-production in which much of the movie was created with visual effects after principal shooting wrapped:

> I just knew at that point the movie was more mystical; in the way we shot it, in the way there were so many unanswered questions. I knew that the best way to service that was to head towards Lovecraft.
>
> Because we were working on the movie in order, we were able to shift the designs towards a darker, more Lovecraftian thing. When I started submitting designs for the Behemoth at the end, I was basically just telling the artists, "Alright, let's make the Old One. Let's get the boss of all bosses." (Squires)

It has been said, incorrectly, that *Underwater* represents the cinematic debut of Cthulhu. There have been a number of films featuring Cthulhu, or more often featuring either its name or likeness. This includes two simply titled *Cthulhu* (2000 and 2007), the rather improbably titled *Call Girl of Cthulhu* (2014), and the animated *Howard Lovecraft and the Frozen Kingdom* (2016), based on the graphic novel of the same name, which in turn spawned two sequels. "The Call of Cthulhu" has also been directly adapted with admirable faithfulness by the aforementioned HPLHS as a silent period film[12] bearing that name in 2005. Yet in terms of large-scale films made inside the regular Hollywood system and widely released cinematically, *Underwater* represents the first attempt to make Cthulhu the central premise of a mainstream science fiction horror movie hoping to garner large success at the wider box office. Most curiously, the fact that this was the case was deliberately hidden from the audience in marketing. The appearance of Cthulhu at the end of the film

---

12. In Mythoscope!

comes as a genuine surprise, at least so far as anyone going into the movie having only seen the trailer is concerned. This was in line with Eubank's wishes: "In order to make a proper Cthulhu movie, in my opinion, you can't say it's a Cthulhu movie because then the experience of the unknown and the cosmic horror really isn't there" (Squires). While this is aesthetically laudable, it engendered through ignorance a lack of interest from the wider Lovecraft fandom. Hard numbers on such intangible concepts as "buzz" are difficult to assess, but anecdotally I knew of no one who was aware of Underwater as so potentially Lovecraftian, although at the time of its release I was pointed by other Lovecraft fans to far smaller films such as The Void and Wounds. Given the film's lack of box office success upon initial release, this attempt to obfuscate the true nature of the film to add a sensation the audience with a such a revelation may have been the final nail that unintentionally doomed it.

Color out of Space (2020)[13] made no attempt to hide its Lovecraft lantern under a non-spoiler bushel. His name is prominently displayed upon all the marketing as the author, often directly above the title, and the director plans it to be part of a trilogy of Lovecraft-based film adaptations, with the next to be based upon "The Dunwich Horror." The slight change in title is presumably to avoid confusion with other films using the name, such as Die Farbe (The Colour), which as noted is often billed as The Color out of Space outside of Germany, and with spelling to bring it in line with American rather than British usage. Such would not be the only departure from Lovecraft, although the film is remarkably faithful in some facets, as will be shown, although paling in such aspects in comparison with Vu's version discussed earlier.

Color out of Space begins by showing an eerie woodland, with voiceover quoting the opening passages of the Lovecraft tale, and the hydrological engineer who is a main character is shown wearing his Miskatonic T-shirt proudly as he wanders through these woods. Almost immediately he encounters a teenage girl performing a Wiccan ritual, and the jarring pivot away from

13. The film was commercially released in early 2020 but premiered at the H. P. Lovecraft Film Festival in Portland, Oregon, in October 2019.

Lovecraft both textually and thematically is obvious. Setting the trend to come, the remainder of the film is very much a mixed affair as concerns faithfulness to the source material and an admixture of other ideas and influences, although it is largely internally coherent and certainly follows the tale in broad strokes. The Gardner family is infected by the Color, slowly descending into madness and physical transformation, and the end of the film has the Color consuming the last remaining member of the Gardner family and escaping into the void, with the Lovecraftian narration returning to speculate about the potentially contaminated new reservoir.

There are many unusual things about the film, both as a piece of Lovecraftiana and otherwise, that are worth examining. Its release was decidedly heterogeneous, playing in many markets first on the festival circuit, then released in different countries theatrically, on streaming and physical home media at differing, sometimes wildly divergent dates. The production was done in Portugal and was the passion project of director Richard Stanley, who also co-wrote the script. Stanley is infamous for the débâcle that saw him removed as director from the 1996 adaptation of *The Island of Doctor Moreau*, clearly a defining experience that completely derailed the career of the previously up-and-coming filmmaker. The documentary *Lost Soul: The Doomed Journey of Richard Stanley's Island of Dr. Moreau* about the experience is even included on the Blu-ray release of *Color out of Space*. Stanley's own connection with Lovecraft is typically paradoxical of the man, as these two interviews reflect:

> Lovecraft reinterpreted the gothic horrors of the nineteenth century through the lens of early 20th century science, describing a multidimensional universe inhabited by impartial alien deities that symbolised his mechanistic atheism and the vast and formless forces of chaos that determined the true warp and weave of our day to day human lives. (Curzon)

> While I'm a huge Lovecraft fan, I also find that I generally don't agree with all of his ideas. I'm not really an atheist and I'm not a materialist and I'm not a racist and I'm not a misogynist and I find his ni

hilism pretty hard to take. So, I saw much of the movie as being kind of an argument with Lovecraft. (Shapiro)

Stanley was introduced to Lovecraft from an early age by his mother who "was a huge Lovecraft fan"; he later read the tales to her as she suffered from the cancer that ultimately would claim her life. The parallel with the inclusion of the cancer subplot with Theresa Gardner in the film is almost certainly in homage to his own mother (Whittaker). Stanley stated that "cancer and radiation poisoning lies at the core of Lovecraft's original conception. In many respects the manner in which the fictional Gardner family are sickened and destroyed by the unearthly colour closely matches period descriptions in the New York Times of radium necrosis in their coverage of the then current 'Radium Girls' scandal" (Curzon). Such real-life events certainly did find their way into fiction, such as "The Blue Woman" by John Scott Douglas which held the cover privileges in the September 1935 issue of Weird Tales. Indeed, Stanley's cancer subplot ultimately does tie into the thematic underpinning of the uncaringly malign cosmos present in the original story. Therein a brief, deeply human pathos has Nahum Gardiner applying his country folk ideas of Christian morality in an attempt to discover a reason for the inexplicable ills visited upon his family: "It must all be a judgment of some sort; though he could not fancy what for, since he had always walked uprightly in the Lord's ways so far as he knew" (CF 2.384). In the film the cancer is itself a symbol of this uncaring universe, with all daughter Lavinia's spells to protect the family, and her mother in particular, ultimately having no beneficial effect against the Color.

Other homages are more readily apparent. One of the Gardner boys is gender-swapped to Lavinia, the name of daughter of Wizard Whateley and the mother of the abominable Wilbur in "The Dunwich Horror." The section in which the sheriff is unexpectedly taken by a tree and killed by a tree branch down the throat indubitably has resonance with the rape tree of The Evil Dead (1981) infamy, a film series that also references the Necronomicon. The scene toward the end of the film with Lavinia looking into the eyes of Ward giving him visions of a planet filled with writhing tendrils is strikingly reminiscent of a similar scene in writer-director James Gunn's *Slither* (2006), itself filled with Lovecraftian touches and a deliberate homage to many other films. Stanley is patently familiar with James Gunn's work, lamenting that he "hasn't given us *Call of Cthulhu* yet" (Cochrane). Most patent as an influence in *Color out of Space* is John Carpenter's *The Thing* (1982), a highly notable Lovecraftian film already mentioned and much homaged, copied, and borrowed from. Indeed, the aforementioned *Slither* named the sheriff of the town after the character of MacReady in the Carpenter film, and Stanley himself stated, in regard to adaptations of Lovecraft, that "*The Thing* comes a lot closer in tone to the actual stories" (Cochrane). Nor is it just in tone there is a connection to the aforementioned film. The fusing of Theresa Gardner with her son at the head is strikingly reminiscent of the body discovered at the Norwegian camp by the characters in *The Thing*, and the fusing of the alpacas together in the barn echoes a similar scene with the dogs at the base. Even the dog Sam is of a very similar phenotype as the unnamed Norwegian dog that is actually the Thing, and the focus upon Sam and his "acting" is reminiscent of that canine actor Jed in Carpenter's film, one of many notable aspects of the former. This side trend of Lovecraft in connection with the body horror and extreme, visceral practical effects coming to the fore in the 1980s, in particular following on from *Re-Animator* (1985), remains in force in the twenty-first century. This is perhaps most obviously exemplified by the aforementioned *The Void*, which again itself heavily homages *The Thing*, among numerous other 1980s films.

Nor is this trend something the creators of *Color out of Space* are unaware of. Rather, they have leaned into the retro nostalgia. The static that appears on the screen of computers and televisions throughout the film is far more the horizontal/vertical static of the analog rather than the pixilation of the digital. One song in the film, "Cycle" by Su Na, has a decidedly 1980s electronic ambience at times and was recorded to be so in a deliberate decision by the artist on analog equipment. Then there was the highly pointed choice in releasing the film in a limited edi-

tion on that most 1980s of now largely defunct viewing plat-
forms, VHS. A final note must be made of director Stanley referencing his own work, yet in such a manner as to create a
certain consistency with the film at hand. On the wall behind
Benny Gardner's computer are the pasted the cut-out words
"No flesh shall be spared." This phrase actually appears about
the M.A.R.K. 13 robot in Stanley's 1990 sci-fi cult classic film
Hardware, where it is falsely attributed to the biblical verse
Mark 13:20. The actual verse more commonly reads as "no flesh
would be saved" (KJV) or "no one would survive" (NIV). Yet in
Color out of Space this writing is behind the computer that dis-
plays a schematic of the solar system and beyond, whence the
unknown Color originates, and which will indeed spare no flesh.

Mention must next be made of the cast of the film. The star
of the film, at least in terms of the actor's billing, is Nicolas
Cage. An Academy Award winner, as of the second decade of
the twenty-first century his star has waned considerably, although far from entirely, in term of prestige; for example, recently performing as a voice actor in *Spider-Man: Into the Spider-
Verse* (2018), which itself won the Academy Award for Best Animated Feature. Cage as Nathan Gardner is certainly a higher-
profile actor in such a role than most of the generally lower-
budget modern Lovecraft adaptations can boast of. This connection originates with production company SpectreVision, who
had an existing relationship with Cage from producing his generally well-received violent cult revenge film *Mandy* (2018).[14]
According to Stanley, *Mandy* producer Josh Waller discovered
that Cage was a huge Lovecraft fan and gave him the script for
Color out of Space, causing him to reach out to Stanley with a
phone call at four in the morning from a Nevada bar (Shapiro).
When questioned, Cage himself stated:

> I've always admired old science fiction. You know, H. P. Love-
> craft, Robert Chambers' *The King in Yellow*. I love that book.

---

14. Incidentally, both an AWFJ nominee in its year for "Most Egregious Age
Difference Between the Lead and the Love Interest" and another of *Screen
Queen*'s entries for the subgenre of "weird horror."

Lovecraft was inspired by that book, and I admire many of Love-craft's stories. There was something about his writing style that I found visceral, and it appealed to my imagination. (Collins)

Such cachet notwithstanding, Cage is noted for his willingness to appear in any number of smaller-budgeted films, frequently action-oriented and with dark supernatural themes, that often have staggeringly low scores on review aggregator site Rotten Tomatoes. Even less favorably, Cage is also the subject of nu-merous, often unflattering, Internet memes. The relevance of this is seemingly known by the director, and there is an almost certainly deliberate direct visual shout-out to the "My hair is a bird, your argument is invalid" meme that invokes the actor's image with a bird Photoshopped on his head as a denial of an *ad hominem* attack. Curiously, this moment actually illustrates some of the surprising depths the film contains. In the scene in ques-tion the character of Nathan is being subject to such an attack to deny the veracity of his statements about the meteor. More importantly, he is being subjected to ridicule by the city news reporters, who imply he is drunk and place the euphemistic "bourbon enthusiast" as a text descriptor under his name when the interview is broadcast. This updates and reflects the original story, in which:

> Nahum took some blossoms to Arkham and shewed them to the editor of the *Gazette*, but that dignitary did no more than write a humorous article about them, in which the dark fears of rus-tics were held up to polite ridicule. It was a mistake of Nahum's to tell a stolid city man about the way the great, overgrown mourning-cloak butterflies behaved in connexion with these saxifrages. (CF 2.378)

Such hidden depths abound in the film, with some more ob-vious than others. The role of Theresa Gardner is played by Jo-ely Richardson, who has a previously established connection to the Lovecraftian milieu in the sci-fi horror *Event Horizon* (1997). This film, dealing with the horrors beyond our knowledge touched upon by humanity's expanding scientific prowess, was a box office failure upon initial release, but has subsequently de-

veloped a wide cult following and is endlessly referenced in later
works, and with enough cachet that a special collectors' edition
Blu-ray is due for release in early 2021. Another notable actor,
albeit for entirely different reasons, is Tommy Chong. Perhaps
interpretable as a wildly distorted version of Ammi Pierce from
the source material, he is claimed by Stanley as a new figure,
based upon a friend and shamanic figure named Uranie (Vulture). Playing entirely to type as an aged stoner, Chong is a her-
mit and crackpot named Ezra. Interestingly, this intersects with
the heady psychedelia that is one of the most notable aspects of
the adaptation of *The Dunwich Horror* (1970), and Stanley
openly refers to his film as "psychedelic" (Rolph).

Tet the name Ezra is more than just a basic Lovecraftian
nod, as this Ezra fulfills the same role of exposition from beyond
the grave that he does in *The Case of Charles Dexter Ward*,
wherein he is the vengeful jilted fiancé who is determined to ex-
pose the evils of Joseph Curwen. In an eerie scene near the end
of the film, a tape of Chong's voice, integrating direct adaptation of text from the original story, plays slightly out of sync as
Ezra's dead body, killed and infected by the Color, sits in his
chair. Given that this film is a genuine expression of the director's interest in Lovecraft and that very special thanks are made
to people such as Sean Branney and Andrew Leman, founders of
the HPLHS (which is also directly thanked), who have themselves been responsible for numerous adaptations of Lovecraft to
film and as radio plays, this makes a welcome change for the often abysmally bad arrogation of a few Lovecraftian names over
an unrelated horror veneer.

It is instructive to first look further at the more direct translations of the scenes within the original story that make it relatively intact to the screen. The meteorite vanishing before a
thorough investigation can be completed as it had "drawn the
lightning" (CF 2.374) in the storm is referenced both in visuals
and spoken as dialogue. The appearance of the mutated cat
running across the road as Nathan drives home, in one of the
few jump scares in the film, and the horrible mutated things collected by the sheriff connects with the disappearance of the cats

from the Gardner household mentioned in the story, along with the distorted prints of the local animals and the grotesque tale of the queerly altered woodchuck shot by the McGregor boys near the Gardner place. The moving trees swaying to no earthly breeze are also given a manifestation, albeit a decidedly more extreme one, with the killing of the sheriff noted earlier. The insanity of Nahum Gardner is fairly directly adapted, complete with the gesturing and conversing to family members not present to be seen by the sheriff and hydrological engineer, characters who are themselves a condensed and reflective portion of the investigating party led reluctantly by old Ammi Pierce in the original. Nathan even tells them of his eldest boy living in the well, which Nahum does to Ammi in the story. Nathan also now performs Ammi's mercy killing of Theresa on the youngest boy fused to his mother, who has been more conventionally killed in defense of Lavinia's life. The creation of the Blasted Heath by the final departure of the Color is also transposed directly, as is the final narration about not drinking the water of the new reservoir. This is given with a backdrop of a sunset just suggestive enough of the Color to bring it to mind as another (or perhaps even the same) Color-distorted praying mantis flies by the screen as the movie's title appears.

Note must also be made of the color of the Color chosen for the film. A fundamental problem in filmic adaption of Lovecraft is the difficulty in translating his images, designed to be beyond description but successfully crafted with words, negative description, and inside the reader's imagination, to this very visual medium. This problem is of course heightened to extremes with "The Colour out of Space," in which it is styled as follows: "The colour, which resembled some of the bands in the meteor's strange spectrum, was almost impossible to describe; and it was only by analogy that they called it colour at all" (CF 2.373). One simple yet ingenuous solution to showing this Lovecraftian ineffable was to add the Colour as the only color in an otherwise black and white film, as in *Die Farbe* adaption. Stanley was well aware of this paradox, stating: "We realized that we couldn't show the audience something that's completely outside the human spectrum" (Rolph). The approach devised by Stanley to resolve this was to make the Color a signature magenta, something that is a distinct part of all the trailers, posters, packaging, and ancillary marketing. Magenta is an extra-spectral color, and as such is not actually seen by humans on the wavelength of light. Rather, it is understood that our brains instead create a color to fill the space between red and violet light, which we perceive as magenta. As such it seems an oddly appropriate Lovecraftian choice; the similarity with the color chosen by Vu's film is probably not entirely coincidental, and Stanley himself cited *Die Farbe* as a favorite previous adaptation of the story (Van Beck).

Notable on several levels is the character of the hydrological engineer. In a departure from the unnamed narrator of the original tale, *Color out of Space* offers as an addition a name for the main character, in the transparent homage of Ward Phillips. This meta-inclusion of Lovecraft, or patent Lovecraft stand-ins and avatars, in his own fictional universe has an ever-increasing longevity. The original is of course Lovecraft's own dream-self expressed in tales as Randolph Carter, but his friends were quick to add their own versions. Frank Belknap Long's "The Space Eaters" features the weird writer Howard (and his friend Frank!), while Robert Bloch memorably killed his mentor's avatar (with Lovecraft's copious and enthusiastic written blessing) in "The Shambler from the Stars" (*Weird Tales*, September 1935).[15]

But this trend continued long after Lovecraft's death, and authors outside of Lovecraft's friends and correspondents started to incorporate the author into his own works as indicative of reality, with Robert Barbour Johnson's "Far Below" (*Weird Tales*, June–July 1939) being a particularly good early example. This tale, set in a New York subway with a secret force dealing with the ghouls who inhabit the lower tunnels, drew inspiration from the railways accident scene in "Pickman's Model" and references the Old Gent by name, reverentially but cheekily stating that Lovecraft got much of his authenticity from the true tales of ex-

---

15. In truth, Bloch actual killed Lovecraft avatars in several stories. This is merely the most famous.

periences the narrator had imparted to him. Secondly, and to a more difficult issue, the actor playing Ward is Elliot Knight, a British thespian and person of color. Given the controversy that simmers about Lovecraft's known racism, this seems a pointed choice, all the more so given that he is a stand-in for Lovecraft himself. Like directors James Wan's decisions in *Aquaman* concerning Lovecraft as "a talented xenophobe," Stanley seems to be deliberately trying to turn his back on this negative aspect of Lovecraft's character while still wanting to honor his work and legacy. It should be noted that this is all purely metatextual. Knight does a splendid job in the role, and his race is not remarked upon at all in the film.

Few Lovecraft aficionados will have failed to recognize the copy of the Simon *Necronomicon* in connection with the daughter's witchcraft, and this infamous arrogation of Lovecraft's most famous grimoire is too widely known to require further elucidation here. However, the *Necronomicon* in either the published Simon version or Lovecraft's original conception sits oddly ill-at-ease with discussions of Alexandrian or Wiccan magic systems, and this introduction of actual witchcraft as practiced in the real world is a topic that I will return to presently. The book Ward is seen reading outside his tent, again flashed directly on screen to the audience, is "The Willows" by Algernon Blackwood. Lovecraft is on record as praising at as the finest supernatural tale in English literature, and famously stated in "Supernatural Horror in Literature" that "here art and restraint in narrative reach their very highest development, and an impression of lasting poignancy is produced without a single strained passage or a single false note" (CE 2.120), facts Stanley seems well aware of (Curzon).

As might be expected, references are made to some of the other well-known Lovecraft creations. At one point the television shows the seven-day weather forecast for Arkham, incorporating Arkham County, Dunwich, Ipswich, Amesbury,[16] and Kingsport. In fact, the name of the television news company is briefly shown as WARK News, and its logo is the Elder Sign in-

16. An actual town in Massachusetts and the probable source for Lovecraft's fictional Aylesbury.

side a circle, the very branching stick design as drawn by Lovecraft himself. Sharper observers may have noticed the unique T-
shirt designs worn in the film. They are the creations of Liv
Rainey-Smith, who has done numerous woodcuts of Cthulhu
Mythos beings, although the ones shown on screen, "Woodland
Rites" and "Wyrm," are of more traditional mythological aspect,
although still theatrically appropriate. In fact, these choices
seem deliberately to eschew the Lovecraftian designs, and that
makes sense from a metatextual perspective. In a world where
the Mythos is real there would probably not be such designs
flaunted in pop culture ephemera as T-shirts.

Yet the currents run deeper still, in the specific musical
choices made for the film. The music of the film is composed by
Colin Stetson, who also created the score for *Hereditary* (2018)
and the upcoming four-episode 2021 *Uzumaki* anime television
series. The latter is another adaptation of the famously Lovecraftian manga by Junji Ito, previously made into a film of the
same name in 2010, while *Hereditary* is a slow-burning horror
film ultimately about a demonic cult whose largely minimalist
score is crucial to its atmosphere of dread and suspense. A genuinely avant-garde musician with numerous collaborations and
appearances, Stetson's soundtrack for the former film was inspired
"from the sound of water and animals while walking around in
pitch-black night," and he tried "to turn up the silence to the
point where it's not quiet anymore" (Fitzmaurice). It was famously
described in the *New Yorker* as "scored for violins, percussion, a
humpback whale, and bats." Stetson's overall theme for *Color out
of Space* was of "the natural made unnatural" (Vehling). By design
the score for the film pushes toward ultrasound and infrasound.
These are sound waves that are outside the normal range of human hearing, but which at the liminal transitions are sometimes
faintly detectable in other senses, and sometimes associated with
experiences perceived as paranormal, a fact that Stanley is openly
aware of and deliberately drawing upon (Rolph).

The soundtrack to *Color out of Space* is likewise chosen with
a meticulous Lovecraftian eye. Tangentially connected to the
overall thematic ideas are Wormwitch's Two Wolves:

The Hunters
The twisting waft of prophecy
A malediction uttered through
The hollows in the hills

A gift of solar lineage
They descend like falling light
Two bolts collide upon a mortal plane
Two hunters pace beyond the astral gate

This might be dismissed as coincidental were it not for other, more obvious connections. Four of the seven soundtrack songs played in the film are from the heavy end of the heavy metal spectrum, with two in particular being from the extreme subset of the genre, Norwegian Black Metal. This scene (in the parlance of its adherents) is infamous for actually indulging in the type of behaviors that moral guardians have without foundation accused heavy metal of since its inception, including church-burnings and homicide. Yet is worth noting that Norwegian Black Metal has a number of very distinct literary influences, including Tolkien and Lovecraft, as well as a quixotic blend of Satanism, paganism, and various extremes of nationalism. Tolkien tends to be used for his creations, drawing heavily as they do from Northern European mythology, and invented languages: the band Gorgoroth are named for ill-famed locations in Middle Earth, while the stage name of convicted murderer and church arsonist Varg Vikernes of Burzum, which means "darkness" in the Black Speech of Mordor, was Count Grishnackh, an orcish captain (spelt Grishnákh) in *The Lord of the Rings: The Two Towers*. The attraction to the scene of Lovecraft is more the bleakness of his cosmic horror and the perceived disdain for humanity inherent in it, which feeds into the extreme self-centeredness and nihilism that pervade Norwegian Black Metal. They are also one of the few groups that often have members actively espousing and supporting Lovecraft's racism, that most unpleasant aspect of the Old Gent which most readers of Lovecraft repudiate, or at least ignore.

Looking directly at the usage in *Color out of Space*, "Feeble

Screams from Forests Unknown" by Burzum is appropriate by
title alone, but it is in the lyrics of Mayhem's "Watcher" that we
see a deeper connection. While it is a common complaint of
those who do not listen to heavy metal that the lyrics are inde-
cipherable, in Norwegian Black Metal this is by design, the low-
fi quality of many of the recordings being a signature aspect of
the genre evolving out of the seminal *Black Metal* album by
Venom and the lack of financial backing for production. Bands
such as the aforementioned Gorgoroth do not include lyrics in
the liner notes, and the idea is that the only the dedicated fan
will listen to the songs with enough repetition to comprehend
them. So despite the indecipherability the lyrics to "Watcher"
are highly topical:

> Come to my spinal serpent
> Fatal doom in DNA-design
> Result of the ancient covenant
> Outer races made upon mankind
>
> The genesis of human race
> Endless cosmic experiment
> To enslave the supreme self
> Hybrid of alien gene

In addition to thematic resonances with the specific story and
the movie adaptation there is the link between Lovecraft's writings and the pseudo-historical modern mythology encapsulated
under the aegis of ancient aliens. There is a distinct line of connection from Lovecraft to Erich von Däniken, whose 1968 best-
seller *Chariots of the Gods?* is widely considered responsible for
the wider dissemination of the extensively discredited theory, as
examined in Jason Colavito's *The Cult of Alien Gods: H. P. Lovecraft and Extraterrestrial Pop Culture* (2005).

The witchcraft aspect presented in *Color out of Space* presents a particularly curious addition to the source material. It is
worth remembering that Lovecraft's original short story is only
about 12,500 words, a rather modest amount upon which to
hang an entire film and significantly shorter than even a short
screenplay; and some addition is almost certainly necessary to

fill the runtime of a standard theatrical film. As we saw in Vu's 2010 version, the additional framing device of a man returning to find his father who served in the occupation of Germany operates in part to achieve this, as well as giving a natural reason for the changing of location to the filmmaker's country. The esoteric decision-making that goes into such changes between a written work and a film adaptation is often convoluted at best, and driven by factors unconnected with the best interests of a film's narrative, structure, and resultant final presentation at worst.

The choice to make Nathan Gardner an alpaca farmer, presumably to show him as mildly but harmlessly eccentric, is one such curious change. The most obvious reason to add in an element of magic and Lovecraft's most famous fictional grimoire would perhaps be for largely for brand recognition, to add something to the plot that is part of widespread Lovecraft lexicon or the idea of shadowy cults that is, and not without merit, part of the popular perception of his works. Some of this esoterica is purely visual, and could be seen merely as good directorial storytelling and connected imagery. Stanley clearly has an excellent grasp of the nuances and subtleties of his medium; his name as director appears directly over Lavinia's compass in the opening scene. A prime example of this subtle connection inside the film itself would be of the triangle that we see holding Lavinia's hair as she performs the ritual of protection over her mother as we first meet the character. She is first show in close-up from the rear, highlighting this choice, which is later echoed in the triangular window that frames her mother Theresa's office, the locale that ultimately becomes Theresa's prison and scene of her death.

Yet it may be that the application of the logical norms of filmmaking in this instance is incorrect, and esoteric is certainly the best word to describe the choice to add witchcraft as a subplot. It is not the witchcraft of fiction, but rather fictionally using the real-world beliefs of modern adherents of witchcraft, as shown in the Alexandrian/Wiccan dichotomy question noted earlier, or in Lavinia being shown to possess a copy of Aleister Crowley's seminal modern magical tome *The Book of the Law*. Mixing the message, Stanley also states of the sanguinary ritual that Lavinia attempts from the *Necronomicon*: "I wanted to make it clear that those rituals are no protection or any assistance whatsoever when it comes to dealing with the ultra-dimensional threat that's facing the family" (Shapiro). And they are the books "typical of the sort of 'forbidden books' a thirteen or fourteen year old might prize" (Curzon).

The film boasts a most unusual credit, that of Occult, Ritual, and Witchcraft Advisor. The individual in the position so named is Amanda Mariamne Radcliffe, a self-proclaimed psychic, mystic, and ordained bishop of the fringe religion of the French Gnostic Church. Thus aspects such as the ritual performed by Lavinia at the beginning of the film are genuine, in the sense that they are based on real-world witchcraft practice and were genuinely performed. A personal friend of Stanley, Radcliffe is one of the small but insistent group of individuals who believe that Lovecraft was not writing fiction, a trend that started even within Lovecraft's lifetime. Her view on the film and its production is thus, unsurprisingly, far from conventional:

> There were many mystical and magical influences which made their presence known throughout this process. The Color spoke to me in visions and dreams, and through séances with my friend Susan Leybourne—and it made it known to us that it did not want to be portrayed as evil at all—but as beautiful—because it was not evil—but rather, Evolution Out of Place. (Dashiell)

It is a beautiful paradox that the person with the most divergent perspective from Lovecraft's own materialistic atheism grasps best his own perceptive on the cosmic Outside rather than the traditionally malignity that fuels the original tale. In the final scene of the film, standing before the tainted well in a shot framed to look like a person on the scaffold before a hanging, Lavinia, who has presumably been practicing witchcraft (not necessarily as shown by the film) as a prophylactic measure against what is occurring, indeed states of the Color, before her own destruction, that it is "so beautiful." Her posture and attitude with upraised arms as the Color flows into the sky in her final moments likewise speak of adoration and worship rather than fear. Although uncredited as such, Radcliffe does speak in an interview of having actually help write the script.

Nor is Radcliffe alone in her otherworldly attentions. Stanley himself has a deep and abiding interest in the occult. Concerning his aforementioned shaman friend Uranie friend Stanley said:

> He had a French-language copy of what he believed was the Necronomicon and actually celebrated Yog-Sothoth Day and various ritual dates throughout the year. I became very fond of him over the 30 years I knew him. About two years ago, he did an invocation to Yog-Sothoth, one of the Lovecraftian deities, in order to make Out of Space happen. We have it on videotape somewhere. A storm blows up halfway through it. It was all quite light-hearted. (Shapiro)

Sadly, less light-hearted is the death of Uranie from untreated hepatitis C prior to commencement of filming, which resulted in his replacement by Tommy Chong. Among numerous other movies and productions focused on unusual and supernatural aspects, Stanley's documentaries include *The Secret Glory* (2001), a true oddity[17] concerning the search for information on real-life mystic and (co-opted) SS officer Otto Rahn and his quest for the Holy Grail. Stanley himself owns objects he discusses in the documentary, and further talks about his otherworldly experiences in his aptly titled documentary *The Otherworld* (2013), also featuring the aforementioned Uranie. Stanley additionally adapted and directed a Clark Ashton Smith witchcraft-centric tale, "Mother of Toads," for the 2011 omnibus film *The Theatre Bizarre*. This decision was, as indicated by his own account, suggested by a Ouija board, albeit a glow-in-the-dark one from a chain store. As in *Color out of Space*, Stanley gratuitously added the *Necronomicon* into "Mother of Toads." Concerning the latter's filming in the area he moved to, a location that connects directly to his Grail research, Stanley opined:

---

17. Its *IMDb* page notes its first-billed star as Heinrich Himmler.

It was, of course, extremely important for our well being and continued survival in the Zone [note the usage of the terminology from the Strugatsky novel] that the various secret societies and what you might call the invisible and even "supernatural" presences that truly govern the area were on-side with what we were doing. (Richard Stanley, interview)

Such practices were continued for *Color out of Space:* "With the cast, I kept it to just rituals to keep the shoot safe and to make certain that there was no negative blowback to anyone involved. For this reason, we ended up doing the banishing ritual at the beginning of the movie" (Shapiro). This seems to have paid dividends from Stanley's perspective, with the director noting in the shoot that "we were helped by a lot of good luck with this movie . . . As we would be setting up a shot, automatically, a creepy mist would start to come in through the trees and the wind would start to come up in just the right way" (Rolph).

Other additions to the film not present in the original tale are far more Lovecraftian in a traditional sense, unencumbered by ties to modern mystic beliefs and ideas of secrets truths. There is a very Lovecraftian consistency of tentacles and tendrils. The clearly contaminated praying mantis (itself a probably deliberate choice given the name) that emerges from the well has multiple globular eyes and more mauve or purple tentacles, distinct against its own Color magenta, emerging from its mouth. These match the tendrils of a more purple hue inside the magenta of the flowers blooming about the property. When the Color first truly emerges from the well it does so as a mass of questing tentacles. As mentioned earlier, as the Color prepares to depart the well and Lavinia goes out to join the cascade the character of Ward Phillips gazes into her eyes and sees a glimpse of a nightmarish world, presumably whence the Color originates. It is all in the hues of the Color itself, the very ground writhing in a mass of tendril or tentacles. The vision appears to sweep as if through the ribcage of a colossal fallen beast, and huge white worms, perhaps referencing the bholes[18] of Lovecraft's creation

---

18. Dholes in older editions of Lovecraft's work, due to a misreading by August

and their undulations in the nightmarish ossuary of the Vale of Pnath. The viewer is then drawn up to a peak with an asymmetrical U-shape forming a crowning point framed against a halo of a planetary body and shapes that seem to represent devices or creations made by sentient beings. It is never explained, aside from the terror it induces in Ward, and is a rather deft touch in seeming to offer information yet ultimately not illuminating the mysteries any further.

This harkens back a curious piece of imagery earlier in the film when, as the meteor initially approaches and crashes, the youngest Gardner boy is clutching a stuffed dinosaur and looking up another. This double imagery as a reference to the Cretaceous-Paleocene extinction event seems to be deliberate, and may be seen as a metaphor for the annihilation of the Gardner family, or just obliquely referencing extinction from the uncaring hand of the cosmos. Yet given the huge skeletal shapes of the alien world of the Color one might be tempted to see that the destruction of the Gardners is part of a far larger cycle that was significantly more destructive in a previous visitation. Adding to the ambiguity, in the vinyl release of the soundtrack the internal cover of the record proper is an alternative version of the image Ward sees of the peak with the uneven crown and planetary halo. In this there is clearly a Cyclopean, hunched humanoid figure with two extruding growths coming from its shoulders in the attitude of one resting on a throne to which it may form a part. Whether this is concept art, an alternate version unchosen for the film, or simply another interesting vision inspired by the film is unclear, but is certainly worthy of note in passing.

Another aspect of the film, which may easily go unnoticed by a casual viewer upon a first watch, is the alterations with the natural flow of time that seem to be occurring. These are not for the most part explicit, but it seems clear that the standard linear time progression is not happening in its accustomed fashion about the Gardner residence or in reference to its residents. Mentions are made of having to do the task of feeding the al-

---

Derleth. Dholes are "undoubtedly one of the most confusing problems in Mythos scholarship" (*Cthulhu Mythos Encyclopedia* 80).

pacas, which is clearly not done, yet we the viewers have clearly seen the character of Benny doing the task earlier. In the film Benny is equally baffled, although his portrayal as a typically disordered stoner prevents the viewer from focusing on this chronological dislocation. The attempts to utilize telephones are often not unsuccessful, but rather distorted and often frightening, the calls being in two different places in space and time. Journeys seemingly take greater or lesser time for different characters depending on where they are, and the ripening of the tainted fruit and blooming of tainted vegetation seem to take place overnight, from an outside perspective. In the final scenes in the house Ward sees the Gardner family sitting in the lounge, hearing dialogue from earlier in the film, perhaps reflecting a reality that Nathan Gardner had been experiencing earlier when questioned by Ward and the sheriff. Ward is then attacked by Nathan himself, who was clearly killed in a previous scene. All this adds a distinct hint of the weird and unsettling, especially insofar as it is never foregrounded nor explained.

Color out of Space is a perfect exemplar of a straight Lovecraftian adaptation to film in the twenty-first century. It is based upon one of his original works and follows the plot and certain specific beats and moments of the story to a degree that even with an unrelated title would be instantly recognizable. Yet it is also infused with Lovecraftian artefacts from his other works, like the name change of the gender-swapped Gardner child to Lavinia and the presence of the *Necronomicon*. Likewise, it mixes in, to various degrees, aspect of creations that are an outgrowth of Lovecraft's work and blends these descendants back into the original narrative, such as the repeated homage of *The Thing* and genuine spiritual beliefs erroneously associated with a mystical truth of Lovecraft's work. Like the aforementioned *Star Wars* and *Star Trek* franchises, Lovecraft's works and the Cthulhu Mythos have varying degrees of accepted canon, retconned works, divergent storylines, divided fan bases, and most importantly a layer of pop cultural expectation and understanding about them that differ from the actual facts as present in the works themselves. "Beam me up, Scotty" is never uttered in *Star Trek*, Vader never said "Luke, I am your Father" in *The Empire Strikes Back*, and Lovecraft never refers to Cthulhu as a being innately connected with the water, yet these ideas are widespread due to memetic mutation and later arrogations. The perception that something is a certain way in the collective popular memory is as influential as the reality. That Greek and Roman statuary was actually brightly colored with paint is immaterial; it will meet with rejection if shown to a modern audience in that form. In *Color out of Space*, this blending of Lovecraft's actual work, creations based upon his works and ideas, and perceptions of his work demonstrates how the ideas he has created are so deeply woven into the fabric of the ongoing horror landscape, and how his creations continue to draw those seeking to emulate or adapt them in ever-widening concentric circles out from the long-stilled quill of the Providence Master of Horror.

Works Cited

Bolf, Samantha. "Nothing Like Lovecraft: An Interview with Jeff VanderMeer." *The Liberator*, theliberatormagazine.com/2017/09/24/nothing-like-lovecraft-an-interview-with-jeff-vandermeer/

Brooklyn Horror Fest. "Sea Fever." *Brooklyn Horror Film Festival*, brooklynhorrorfest.com/program/sea-fever/edate/2019-10-24/

Chand, Neeraj. "Guillermo Del Toro Will Fight to His Grave to get *At the Mountains of Madness* Made." *Movieweb*, movieweb.com/at-the-mountains-of-madness-movie-guillermo-del-toro/

Coberly, Bill. "The Call of Leviathan: Mass Effect and Lovecraft." *The Ontological Geek* (5 March 2013), ontologicalgeek.com/the-call-of-leviathan-mass-effect-and-lovecraft/

Cochrane, Glenn. "Interview with Director Richard Stanley— *Color out of Space*." *Stack* (3 May 2020), stack.com.au/film-tv/film-tv-interview/interview-with-director-richard-stanley-color-out-of-space/

Collis, Clark. "Why Nicolas Cage Went Crazy for the Horror Film *Color out of Space*." *Entertainment Weekly*, ew.com/movies/2020/01/23/nicolas-cage-color-out-of-space-interview/

Curzon. "Interview: Richard Stanley." *Curzon*, www.curzonblog. com/all-posts/2020/3/6/interview-richard-stanley

Dashiell, Mad. "Interview: Amanda Mariamne Radcliffe." *Ain't It Cool News* (22 January 2020), www.aintitcool.com/color-out-of-space-occult- witchcraft-supervisor-82729/

Elliot, Dave, C. J. Henderson, and R. Allen Leider. *A Field Guide to Monsters.* New York: Hylas Publishing, 2004.

Fitzmaurice, Larry. "The Most Terrifying Movie of the Year, *Hereditary*, Has Colin Stetson to Thank." *Pitchfork* (7 June 2018), pitchfork.com/thepitch/colin-stetson-hereditary-score-interview/

Guglielmo, Connie. "'Annihilation' Director Alex Garland Chats with CNET about the Upcoming Film." 9 February 2018, www.youtube.com/watch?v=nYhT5Ey42gg

Harms, Daniel. *A Cthulhu Mythos Encyclopedia.* 3rd ed. Lake Orion, MI: Elder Signs Press, 2008.

Harn, Darby. "*Lovecraft Country*: 10 Hidden References You Missed in Episode 1." *Screen Rant* (25 August 2020), screenrant.com/lovecraft-country-episode-one-pilot-references-easter-eggs/

H. P. Lovecraft Film Festival. "Cold Skin." *H. P. Lovecraft Film Festival* (August 2018), hplfilmfestival.com/films/cold-skin

Infamous Horrors. "Sea Fever Review." *Infamous Horror*, www.infamoushorrors.com/2020/04/22/sea-fever-review-a-pitch-perfect-creature-feature/

Joshi, S. T. *S. T. Joshi's Blog*, 16 May 2014. stjoshi.org/news 2014.html

———. "Jeff VanderMeer: An Aesthetic Catastrophe." In *21st-Century Horror: Weird Fiction and the Turn of the Millennium.* Seattle: Sarnath Press, 2018.

Kiernan, Caitlín R. "From Cabinet 34, Drawer 6." In Stephen Jones, ed. *Weird Shadows over Innsmouth.* London: Titan Books, 2005.

Kermode, Jennie. "The Romance of the Other: Xavier Gens on Feminism, Colonialism and the Challenges of Filming *Cold Skin*." *Eye for Film* (30 April 2018), www.eyeforfilm.co.uk/

feature/2018-04-30-interview-with-xavier-gens-about-cold-skin-feature-story-by-jennie-kermode

Kermode, Mark. "2007: A Scorching New Space Odyssey." *The Guardian* (25 March 2007), www.theguardian.com/film/2007/mar/25/sciencefictionspecial.features

Lane, Anthony. "'Hereditary' Delivers a New Kind of Horror." *The New Yorker* (18 June 2018), www.newyorker.com/magazine/2018/06/18/hereditary-delivers- a-new-kind-of-horror

Leeson, Chloe. "'The Beach House' Is a Lovecraftian Trip That Won't Give You Any Answers." *Screen Queens* (6 July 2020), screen-queens.com/2020/ 07/06/review-the-beach-house/

Lindberg, S. E. "*Lost Worlds*—Clark Ashton Smith: Review." www.selindberg.com/2020/06/lost-worlds-clark-ashton-smith-review.html

Lovecraft, H. P. *O Fortunate Floridian: H. P. Lovecraft's Letters to R. H. Barlow*. Ed. S. T. Joshi and David E, Schultz. Tampa, FL: University of Tampa Press, 2007. [Abbreviated in the text as *OFF*.]

———, and Clark Ashton Smith. *Dawnward Spire, Lonely Hill: The Letters of H. P. Lovecraft and Clark Ashton Smith*. Ed. David E, Schultz and S. T. Joshi. New York: Hippocampus Press, 2017.

Miller, Liz Shannon. "*Star Trek: Picard* EP Akiva Goldsman Explains the Season Finale's Biggest Twists." *Paste* (26 March 2020), www.pastemagazine.com/tv/star-trek-picard/episode-10-explained/

Miska, Brad. "Fresh Look at Lovecraftian Horror 'Cold Skin.'" *Bloody Disgusting* (11 January 2018), bloody-disgusting.com/images/3477934/fresh-look-lovecraftian- horror-cold-skin/

Navarro, Meagan. "Keeping Secrets: Diving into the Folklore and Myths Behind 'The Lighthouse.'" *Bloody Disgusting* (21 April 2020), bloody-disgusting. com/editorials/3613569/keeping-secrets-diving-folklore-myths-behind-lighthouse/

Newby, Richard. "Why Horror Movie 'The Beach House' Hits So Close to Home." *Hollywood Reporter* (10 July 2020), www.hollywoodreporter.com/heat-vision/why-beach-house-hits-close-home-1301697

Norris, Duncan. "Lovecraft and *Aquaman*: An Unlikely Mating." *Lovecraft Annual* No. 13 (2019): 189–203.

Purdom, Clayton. "A Brief History of *The Zone*, the Sci-Fi Idea That Swallows Everything." *AV Club* (17 October 2019), www.avclub.com/a-brief-history-of-the-zone-the-sci-fi-idea-that-swall-1838901974

Reilly, Kaitlin. "In Armie Hammer's *Wounds* Cockroaches Are Just Half the Horror." *Refinery29* (19 October 2019), www.refinery29.com/en-us/2019/10/8588074/wounds-armie-hammer-horror-movie-explained

Richard Stanley Interview. unfilmable.blogspot.com/p/richard-stanley-interview_13.html

Rolph, Ben. "Richard Stanley on Faithfulness to H. P. Lovecraft & Psychedelics of 'Color out of Space.'" *Discussing Film* (25 April 2020), discussingfilm.net/2020/04/25/richard-stanley-on-faithfulness-to-h-p-lovecraft-and-psychedelics-of-color-out-of-space-exclusive-interview/

Schager, Nick. "*The Lighthouse* Director Wades through the Mysterious Ending of His Nautical Nightmare." *Esquire* (18 October, 2019), www.esquire.com/entertainment/movies/a29504100/the-lighthouse-ending-explained-director-robert-eggers-interview/

Shapiro, Lila. "How Nic Cage and a Ouija Board Brought Richard Stanley Back to Set." *Vulture* (13 February 2020), www.vulture.com/2020/02/richard-stanleys-return-thank-nic-cage-and-a-ouija-board.html

Squires, John. "'Underwater' Director Shares Creature Concept Art and Talks about How He Got THAT Monster in the Movie." *Bloody Disgusting* (15 April 2020), bloody-disgusting.com/interviews/3613015/underwater-director-shares-creature-concept-art-talks- got-monster-movie-exclusive/

Tallerico, Brian. "The Beach House." *RogerEbert.com* (9 July 2020), www.rogerebert.com/reviews/the-beach-house-movie-review-2020

Van Beek, Anton. "Interview: Richard Stanley on Cult Horror *Color out of Space*, His Love of H. P. Lovecraft, and Working with Nic Cage and Alpacas ..." *Home Cinema Choice* (10 June 2020), www.homecinemachoice.com/content/interview-richard-stanley-cult-horror-color-out-space-his-love-hp-lovecraft-and-working-nic

VanderMeer, Jeff [@jeffvandermeer], 9 November 2015, twitter.com/jeffvandermeer/status/663574661058265088

———. [@jeffvandermeer], 17 July 2016, twitter.com/jeffvandermeer/status/754674019174060032

———. [@jeffvandermeer] 4 July 2018, twitter.com/jeffvandermeer/status/1014182230695055367\

———. *Annihilation*. London: Fourth Estate, 2014.

Vaughn, Adam. "Interview with 'The Beach House' Director Jeffrey A. Brown." *Film Festival Today* (9 July 2020), filmfestivaltoday.com/interviews/interview-with-the-beach-house-director-jeffrey-a-brown

Vehling, Aaron. "The 'Natural Made Unnatural': Colin Stetson Discusses His 'Color out of Space' Score." *Vehlinggo* (1 February 2020), vehlinggo.com/ 2020/02/01/colin-stetson-space-interview/

Vishnevetsky, Ignatiy. "What *Annihilation* Learned from Andrei Tarkovsky's Soviet Sci-Fi Classics." *AV Club* (24 February 2018), www.avclub.com/what-annihilation-learned-from-andrei-tarkovsky-s-sovie-1819005171

Vlk, Kevin, "Annihilation. Alex Garland. Talks at Google." 23 February 2018, www.youtube.com/watch?v=w5i7idoijco

Whittaker, Richard. "Fantastic Fest Interview; Richard Stanley Sees *Color out of Space*." *Austin Chronicle* (19 October 2019), www.austinchronicle.com/daily/screens/2019-09-19/fantastic-fest-interview-richard-stanley-sees-the-color-out-of-space/)/

How to Read Lovecraft

A Column by Steven J. Mariconda

Part 5: Playing in Deep Time; or, The Game of Writing and Reading

As it has been at least twelve months since our last column, a recap will be helpful. *Our premise:* Lovecraft approached writing weird fiction in the spirit of play, and to know *How to Read Lovecraft* it pays to understand the rules of the game.

Lovecraft's sense of play is apparent not merely in his writing style, but also in his fictional style and themes. The concept of "play" is a little slippery, but we can characterize it with a set of motivations and cognitive elements including the following:

> It is non-literal and mentally distinct from reality.
>
> It is self-determined and self-directed.
>
> It is undertaken with an engaged yet unstressed mindset.
>
> It has structure or rules created by the participant(s) rather than imposed by necessity.
>
> Its focus is upon enjoyment of the process rather than the outcome.

As a consequence of two factors—heredity and environment, especially his difficult family circumstances—the young Lovecraft developed a unique approach to play. This manifested itself between the ages of four and seventeen, first with an indoor theater using tiny figures and backdrops, later with an exterior play railyard, and finally with an elaborate landscaped village ("New Anvik"). In these settings the young Lovecraft created tableaux—figures and props with which to play—and devised lengthy, multi-episode scenarios enacted over an extended duration. My thesis is that we find a similar approach in Lovecraft's fiction, and that we as readers can benefit from this insight and engage with the work in a more enjoyable and enlightening way.

Lovecraft wrote at remarkable length about his boyhood activities to certain correspondents, and the information he provides strikes one as both candid and precise. Of his youthful play he said:

> About the only childish things I disliked were [. . .] aimless activities. Anything with a coordinated interest (i.e., something like a plot element) gave me the keenest delight. [. . .] My mode of play was to devote an entire table-top to a scene, which I would proceed to develop as a broad landscape. [. . .] I had all sorts of toy villages with small wooden or cardboard houses, & by combining several of them would often construct cities of considerable extent & intricacy. I was always consistent—geographically and chronologically—in setting my landscapes as my infant store of information would allow.[1] (Letter to J. Vernon Shea, 8 November 1933; JVS 186–87)

He continued this until he was sixteen or seventeen, and, as he elaborated, he developed a distinctive approach to the *scope* of his play:

> My mode of play was to construct some scene as fancy—incited by some story or picture—dictated, & then to act out its life for long periods—sometimes a fortnight—making up events of a highly melodramatic cast I went. These events would sometimes cover only a brief span—a war or plague or merely a spirited pageant of travel & commerce & incident leading nowhere—but would sometimes involve long aeons, with visible changes in the landscape & buildings. Cities would fall & be forgotten, & new cities would spring up. Forests would fall or be cut down, & rivers (I had some fine bridges) would change their beds. (Letter to J. Vernon Shea, 8 November 1933; JVS 187)[2]

I draw attention to the unusual phrase "long aeons," which is as Lovecraftian as they come, and points us to what has come to

---

1. Throughout, the italics are mine, and the presentation of quoted material has been slightly edited for clarity. Quotations from Lovecraft's fiction and letters may be found in their respective Hippocampus Press editions.

2. Oddly, Lovecraft repeats the locution "mode of play" only a few lines after its first use in this missive to Shea (see prior quotation). Apparently, the writer is suffering a case of epistolary exhaustion—the letter occupies more than 42 pages of printed text (*Letters to J. Vernon Shea* 169–212).

be called the Lovecraft Mythos.[3] In other correspondence, Lovecraft the author explained how he had tried in his Mythos to create the "vague coherence" of a sequence of traditional lore. In the description of his childhood approach to play above, then, we may see foreshadowed the persistent settings of the Mythos (Arkham, Innsmouth, Dunwich), its vast scope (both geographical and chronological), its familiar personages (Cthulhu, Alhazred, etc.), and its props (the *Necronomicon*). Many of Lovecraft's stories contain sequences of events that hang loosely together: in "The Shadow out of Time" (1934–35), for example, the narrator is cast into the body of one of the extraterrestrial Great Race of 250 million years ago, and subsequently recounts his episodic adventures in a tropical precursor to Australia:

> . . . [Th]e visions included vivid travels over the mighty jungle roads, sojourns in strange cities, and explorations of some of the vast dark windowless ruins from which the Great Race shrank in curious fear. There were also long sea-voyages in enormous, many-decked boats of incredible swiftness, and trips over wild regions in closed, projectile-like airships lifted and moved by electrical repulsion. Beyond the wide, warm ocean were other cities of the Great Race, and on one far continent I saw the crude villages of the black-snouted, winged creatures who would evolve as a dominant stock after the Great Race had sent its foremost minds into the future to escape the creeping horror. (CF 3.401)

In fact, certain critics have gone so far as to see the various tales that use the apparatus of the Mythos (estimates on the number vary depending on the criteria, but it is perhaps two or three dozen stories) as mere installments of a longer saga. Pioneering Lovecraft scholar George T. Wetzel even proposed that "the Mythos stories should actually be considered not as separate works but rather the different chapters of a very lengthy novel" (79).

---

3. The phrase "long aeons" indicates that as early as age eleven or twelve, Lovecraft had adopted the cosmic worldview that helps make his fiction unique. The contemporary term "deep time," which "denotes vast, extremely remote periods of (natural or other) history—distant and extensive spans of time that are almost beyond the grasp of the human mind" [Riggs 47], is a useful construct here.

This episodic or loosely coupled character of the Mythos is also prefigured by early play habits: "In about a week or two I'd get fed up with a scene & substitute a new one, though now & then I'd be so attached to one that I'd retain it longer. . . . There was a kind of intoxication in being lord of a visible world (albeit a miniature one) & determining the flow of its events" (letter to J. Vernon Shea, 8 November 1933; JVS 188).

Anyone familiarity with Lovecraft's biography will affirm that he was a child prodigy, but it is nevertheless a testament to his native intelligence that his play was so sophisticated at an early age. While Lovecraft's basic path of imaginative development follows the outlines formulated by psychologist Joost Meerloo, his progress far outstripped the norm. Citing English behaviorist John Cohen, Meerloo states that a gradually expanding conception of time is a distinctive feature of cognitive development from infancy onwards:

> The baby lives entirely in the present, unable to look into the past or future. Slowly consciousness begins to extend backward and forward in time. The infant is unable to relate a current event to occurrences more than a month back, or ahead. Ideas of "morning" or "night" come to most children at about the age of four. Understanding of one's own age comes at about five years; of "today," "yesterday" and "tomorrow" at about six years, and of clock time at about eight years. Temporal aspects of history are almost meaningless before the age of eleven when orientation toward the passage of time begins to be appreciably enlarged. The inability to appreciate causal sequences that stretch beyond the time span of the particular age has important pedagogical implications in regard to the effects of rewards and punishments in learning. (47–48)

The Synchronology out of Time

This is quite abstract, but one fascinating bit of ephemera may be of tangible help in getting inside the boy Lovecraft's mindset of play. Regarding his epic play scenarios, Lovecraft said:

> [M]y data (culled from stories, pictures, questioning of my elders, & a marvelously graphic historic device called "Adams' Synchronological Chart" [which I still have]) was of a distinctly

juvenile kind & extent. Sometimes I would try to depict actual historic events & scenes—Roman, 18th century, or modern—& sometimes I would make everything up. (Letter to J. Vernon Shea, 8 November 1933; *JVS* 187–88)

Adams' Synchronological Chart of Universal History
(here split into three parts)

Sebastian C. Adams's *Synchronological Chart of Universal History* outlines the evolution of mankind from Adam and Eve to 1871 (the chart's first publication). It is a 23-foot chart visualizing the flow of 6,000 years of history. The Adams Chart was first produced as a series of chromolithographic panels; it went through many editions and was published both as a scroll and in a foldable book form. With it came a narrative "Key" by the published John E. Colby, proclaiming that "Through the Eye to the Mind," the user would be enabled to:

trace the rise, progress and fall of nations; to clearly outline the world's great epochs and eras; and to definitely place eminent men, marked events, and the succession of rulers, in time, in the same manner and just as easily as he traces on the school map the courses of streams, bounds states and continents, and locates mountains, lakes and cities; and, as places of the same longitude are intersected by meridians on the map, so the contemporaneous events of the whole world throughout all historic time can be seen by simply tracing each of the fifty-nine century[4] columns, or its decades, across the face of the chart. (5–6)

In *Cartographies of Time: A History of the Timeline,* Daniel Rosenberg and Anthony Grafton describe the Adams Chart as "a great work of outsider thinking and a template for autodidact study; it attempts to rise above the station of a mere historical summary and to draw a rich picture of all history" (172). Using timelines, maps, flow charts, and family trees, the Adams Chart incorporates settlements, countries, empires, and civilizations around the world, from Babylon, Sparta, and China to Italy, Russia, and Wales. Vertical lines mark intervals of years.

Lines of Time versus "The Indeterminate Now"

I do not mean to imply that *Adams' Synchronological Chart* is the kernel of the Mythos—Lovecraft was clear that he adapted the idea from Lord Dunsany. Rather, it is fascinating artifact of how Lovecraft's mature imaginative mindset grew from his boyhood activity of play. Regarding his conception of time, whose foundation was established in this play, Lovecraft wrote:

I agree with you regarding [Oswald] Spengler's distinction betwixt the "Faustian" or modern Western sense of infinity (which begins with a clearer idea of, & interest in, one's orientation in time & space) & the classical localism & lack of a time-sense. [. . .] His pointing out of the modern time-&-space consciousness as opposed to the Hellenic indifference to long cycles and sequences [. . .] gave me almost a shock, because it revealed so

---

4. The wording here recalls Lovecraft's "Nyarlathotep" (1920): "He said he had risen up out of the blackness of twenty-seven centuries, and that he had heard messages from places not on this planet" (CF 1.203).

great a streak of the non-classical in myself, who have always felt so closely akin to the Graeco-Roman as opposed to the me-diaeval. (Letter to Fritz Leiber, Jr., 15 November 1936; *Letters to C. L. Moore and Others* 273)[5]

So the simple, linear "left-to-right" progress of time as show in the Adams Chart would be jettisoned, as Lovecraft matured and began toying with similar ideas in his adult fiction. Michael North, in *What Is the Present?*, his monograph on "deep time," notes that the ancient world, the use of a simple timeline to pre-sent history was superseded by "synchromatic tables, *parallel* columns of important events, counted down according to the Greeks, the Romans, and sometimes the Asian or North African worlds beyond" (76). Rosenberg and Grafton have shown that such tabular, parallel histories were the dominant graphical form used to visualize the passage of time well into the contemporary period:

> Though the purpose of such tables was to provide a sort of Ro-setta stone for the *translation of one timeline into another*, what they tended to expose was the *incoherence of the timeline as a metaphor.* ... What the tables showed ... was that for the greater part of human history, there were multiple times run-ning *simultaneously* and thus *multiple historical presents.* Or, to put it more accurately, *the notion of a historical present as a single synchronizing point* to which all could refer *made no sense.* (79)

Thus, as the product of Lovecraft's nascent play, the Mythos reflects a more complex conception of time; linear time is re-placed (consistent with modern notions of indeterminacy) by a kaleidoscopic array of simultaneous, illusive images. Lovecraft characterized the Mythos is as "a kind of shadowy phantasmago-ria which may have the same sort of vague coherence as a cycle of traditional myth or legend" (letter to Harold S. Farnese, 22 September 1921; *SL* 4.70). For his fictional protagonists, the

5. For Oswald Spengler's definitions of his Faustian or epic concept of time, see *The Decline of the West*: "the Classical [concept of time consists of] the near, strictly limited, self-contained Body; the Western [Faustian concept of time is] infi-nitely wide [time] and infinitely profound three-dimensional Space; the Arabian [concept of time consists of] the world as a Cavern [dome of the heavens]" (174).

Mythos—whose history reaches infinitely into the past—has intruded into the "historical present" (more simply, the *now*).

Unborn . . . Boy . . . Man . . . Dead . . . Unborn . . .

Lovecraft had a strong feeling of the "eternal now" as a boy and continued to feel the indeterminacy of time as an into adult. Boyhood and adulthood had an element of *simultaneity* for him, and consisted essentially of a single point in time.

> It is as if my fascination with the idea of time had had some effect on my personality, so that *all the years I have lived or shall ever live are as a single point in my consciousness*. Curious, anyhow—whether or not linked with any lifelong phantasy-wish of being able to rove at will through the aeons. . . . [O]nce in a while my age strikes me as a huge, secret joke. For *I am actually the same person that I was in 1900 & kindred years*. I still feel the feelings of 1900, & retain the essential perspectives. (Letter to J. Vernon Shea, 8 November 1933; JVS 193)

It seems Lovecraft the child is very much present in Lovecraft the mature author. Regarding the view of the "eternal now" or historical present, Michael North inquires

> This version of epic time is a kind of constant in European histories, so old as to seem almost perpetual itself. . . . But it is worth asking . . . whether the [historical present] time scheme . . . is *all present* or *no present at all*. [Russian sociologist Georges] Gurvitch maintains that . . . the epic tradition always projects *the present into the past*. In its attempt to ensure the stability of things, these [i.e., Spengler's Faustian] societies *make the past endure* by *dissolving the present and future in it*. (74)

Or as Lovecraft put it to correspondent J. Vernon Shea, in a more perplexed and impressionistic—and Lovecraftian—way:

> Time . . . time . . . space-time—it doesn't take an Einstein to make it a confused chaos! Am I moving through it, or is it flowing past me—or are there infinite *I's*, each eternally coëxisting in one simultaneous eternity? Un-born . . . boy . . . man . . . dead—flash—flash—flash. . . . Hell, but I wish I could get on paper some hint of the mystery of time & personality! (JVS 194)

And knowing how to read Lovecraft, we can safely say, he *did* get
it on paper. Wait—it sounds just like a Lovecraft story: "Clocks—
time—space—infinity—" ("Hypnos" [1922]; CF 1.331).

Works Cited

Adams, Sebastian C. *Adams' Synchronological Chart*. New York:
    Colby & Co., 1881. Composite digital facsimile available at Da-
    vid Rumsey Historical Map Collection, www.davidrumsey.com
    /luna/servlet/detail/RUMSEY~8~1~226099~5505934:
    Composite—Adams—Synchronological-. Accessed 06/2021.

Colby, John E. *Key to Adams' Synchronological Chart of Universal His-
    tory, 4004 B.C. to 1881 A.D.* New York: Colby & Co. [c. 1881].

Cohen, John. "Analysis of Psychological 'Fields.'" *Science News*
    13 (1949): 145–58.

Gurvitch, Georges. *The Spectrum of Social Time*. Tr. Myrtle Ko-
    renbaum. Dordrecht, Netherlands: Reidel, 1964.

Lovecraft, H. P. *Letters to C. L. Moore and Others*. Ed. David E.
    Schultz and S. T. Joshi. New York: Hippocampus Press, 2017.

———. *Letters to J. Vernon Shea, Carl F. Strauch, and Lee
    McBride White*. Ed. S. T. Joshi and David E. Schultz. New
    York: Hippocampus Press, 2016. [Abbreviated in the text as
    JVS.]

Meerloo, Joost. *The Two Faces of Man: Two Studies on the Sense
    of Time and on Ambivalence*. New York: International Uni-
    versities Press, 1954.

Riggs, Peter J. "Contemporary Concepts of Time in Western
    Science and Philosophy." In Ann McGrath and Mary Anne
    Jebb, ed. *Long History, Deep Time: Deepening Histories of
    Place*. Canberra: ANU Press, 2015.

Rosenberg, David, and Anthony Grafton. *Cartographies of Time:
    A History of the Timeline*. Princeton: Princeton Architectural
    Press, 2010.

Spengler, Oswald. *The Decline of the West*. Tr. Charles Francis
    Atkinson. London: George Allen & Unwin Ltd., 1932.

Wetzel, George T. "The Cthulhu Mythos: A Study." In S. T.
    Joshi, ed. *H. P. Lovecraft: Four Decades of Criticism*. Athens:
    Ohio University Press, 1980.

Reviews

H. P. LOVECRAFT. *Letters to Rheinhart Kleiner and Others.* Edited by S. T. Joshi and David E. Schultz. New York: Hippocampus Press, 2020. Reviewed by Ken Faig, Jr.

Every Lovecraft scholar or fan will need to acquire this volume, even if he or she already owns the earlier-published *Letters to Rheinhart Kleiner* (Hippocampus Press, 2005), curated by the same editors. The 2020 volume runs 544 pages as compared with the 298 of the 2005 volume, and adds correspondents Arthur Harris, James Larkin Pearson, Winifred V. Jackson, Arthur Leeds, and Paul J. Campbell. The linking theme is of course amateur journalism. The narrowest of these qualifications as an amateur journalist is probably that of Arthur Leeds, through his participation in the Kalem Club in 1924–26. All the other correspondents have solid credentials as amateur journalists, as evidenced by their publications listed in the bibliographies assembled by the editors. Of these correspondents, Kleiner, Pearson, and Jackson were all poets. The editors print samples of the work of all the correspondents, not just the poets.

Of the poets, Kleiner was clearly the closest to Lovecraft. He was one of the few amateur journalists to visit Lovecraft at 598 Angell Street, and unlike the slightly rumpled W. Paul Cook, who was nearly turned away at the door, the debonair Kleiner was welcomed by Mrs. Lovecraft, who even considered that his pipe-smoking habit might be "soothing" for her son. Lovecraft shared with Kleiner information concerning his life, his writing, and his dreams that he shared with no one else, which probably explains why the letters to Kleiner are quoted so copiously by Lovecraft's biographers and expositors. Lovecraft and Kleiner bantered back and forth in verse over attractive young ladies they had seen, and Kleiner thereby elicited from Lovecraft some deliciously humorous poems. Lovecraft could share with Kleiner comments concerning sexuality that are difficult to find elsewhere in his correspondence. He found Charles Isaacson's writings "obscene," while he felt that a letter sent to him by Elsa Gidlow's friend Roswell George Mills was fit only for the garbage heap—although he asked Kleiner to return it to him. Lovecraft's and Kleiner's poetical banter appears to presume a shared, none too diluted heterosexuality, an interesting counter (if words can provide any evidence) to later speculation that Lovecraft may have been a closeted homosexual.

Did Kleiner and Lovecraft eventually drift apart, as evidenced by the falling-off of their correspondence? Correspondence is a habit, and naturally Kleiner and Lovecraft had little occasion to correspond while they both resided in Brooklyn and were participating in the weekly meetings of the Kalem Club in 1924–26. After Lovecraft's return to Providence, Kleiner lost his longtime employment and had to make many adjustments in his life. Lovecraft's focus in his later years was the fantastic, and it was only natural for the new legions of weird fiction fans to supplant some of his older correspondents who did not share any strong interest in the fantastic. In his next-to-last letter to Kleiner, dated 20 November 1936, Lovecraft announced the publication of his book *The Shadow over Innsmouth* by William L. Crawford. Writing even later, on 7 January 1937, his final words to his old friend were: "Yesterday & today I've been loafing around in a dressing-gown & dumping down on the couch every hour or two." He complained of "grippe," "diffused nausea," "sleepiness," and "pervasive general weakness."

Within the amateur journalism hobby, the name of Winifred V. Jackson was often linked romantically with Lovecraft's: Sonia Greene is said to have boasted that she "stole" Lovecraft away from Jackson. Jackson, some fourteen years older than Lovecraft, met him as a member of Boston's Hub Club. Perhaps some female amateur journalists who had cast their eyes upon Lovecraft felt that the death of his mother on 24 May 1921 opened an opportunity for them to replace her in his affections. What Mrs. Jackson thought when Lovecraft sent her a snapshot of his mother with his letter of 7 June 1921, history has not recorded. The winner in the marital competition, Sonia Greene, first met Lovecraft at the National Amateur Press Association convention in Boston in July 1921. Other potential candidates have been less noted. Myrta Alice Little (subsequently Myrta Davies) rented a home and cooked an entire New England dinner for Lovecraft. She was a near-contemporary of his, but perhaps he ultimately preferred a more motherly partner: Sonia Greene was seven years his senior. While both Greene and Jackson collaborated with Lovecraft on fantastic stories (Mrs. Jackson under the pseudonym "Elizabeth Berkeley"), only Jackson shared with Lovecraft a strong interest in the fantastic, as evinced in some of her poetry. Sonia Greene felt that Lovecraft's interest in the fantastic derived mostly from his "loneliness."

A surprising adjunct to the Jackson correspondence file is a letter from George Julian Houtain to Lovecraft dated 16 September 1921, which solicits contributions for his magazine *Home Brew*. I do not know that any other letter from or to Houtain survives. Of the letters printed in the present volume, those to Arthur Harris and to James Larkin Pearson survive in the form of the original holograph manuscripts, owned by Brown University and Wilkes Community College (Wilkesboro, North Carolina), respectively. All the other letter files printed here survive primarily in the form of transcripts, most notably the Arkham House transcripts and transcripts of the letters to Jackson made by R. H. Barlow. (The letters to Kleiner have a secondary source, the extracts originally printed in Hyman Bradofsky's *Californian* for Summer 1937 under the title "By Post from Providence.") However, it is not accurate to say that no relics of Lovecraft's holograph letters to Kleiner are known to survive. The editors reproduce samples of illustrations drawn by Lovecraft for the letters to Kleiner on pp. 49, 55, and 160. August Derleth probably had these pages photographed for potential use as illustrative material. In fact, the illustrations reproduced on pp. 55 and 160 were ultimately used in a montage for the dustjackets of *Selected Letters* (Arkham House, 1965–76). The *Selected Letters* jackets include at the lower right hand corner a drawing from the back of a periwigged correspondent signing his name "H. Lovecraft"—a drawing not reproduced in the present volume unless I have missed it. Perhaps this drawing came from another correspondence file. Derleth is known to have had other illustrations from Lovecraft's letters photographed.

It is notable that of Lovecraft's major amateur journalist correspondence files, Kleiner, Moe, and Morton all survive primarily in the form of the Arkham House Transcripts. These files all passed through Arkham House for transcription, but the fate of the originals is not known. While it is possible that the files perished after being returned to their owners, that fate seems unlikely to me if the owners had any idea of their potential value. However, we need to remember that work by Lovecraft did not always command the attention and the prices it does today. In the 1940s Samuel Loveman purchased for $500 Frank Long's file of letters from Lovecraft—a file that L. W. Currey subsequently obtained at auction at Sotheby's for something under $50,000 and subsequently offered for sale for $150,000. The fact that Kleiner, Moe, and Morton all died relatively early—in 1949, 1940, and 1941, respectively—may be correlated with the disappearance of their files of original Lovecraft letters. Even today, bundled or boxed letters uncovered as part of an estate run the risk of being discarded unless properly identified. I for one hope that at least some of these files will eventually come to light and become available for publication. Even given the richness of the letters to Kleiner, Moe, and Morton as published by Hippocampus Press, I feel confident that the original letters, if recovered, would yield additional insights. Joshi and Schultz have done much to complete the record of Lovecraft's writing, but I hope that there will remain tasks for Lovecraft scholars and editors in the year 2100 and beyond.

There is no question that the Lovecraft correspondence that Joshi and Schultz have published with Hippocampus Press is a far advance beyond the Arkham House *Selected Letters*. Of the correspondents covered by the present volume, Arthur Harris, James Larkin Pearson, Arthur Leeds, and Paul J. Campbell were not even included in *Selected Letters*. Winifred V. Jackson was represented by a single letter. Only the Kleiner file had a rich representation in *Selected Letters*. I take this information from S. T. Joshi's *An Index to the Selected Letters of H. P. Lovecraft* (Necronomicon Press [second edition], 1991). When Joshi and Schultz complete the publication of the Lovecraft letters with Hippocampus, I hope they will add a separate index volume. All the Hippocampus letters volumes published to date have thorough indexes, so presumably the editing of a separate index volume would only involve an amalgamation of files. For myself, I hope Hippocampus (or some successor publisher) will eventually publish a searchable electronic edition of the full surviving Lovecraft correspondence. Of course, we should note that the Brown University Library has already made available on its website electronic images of all the Lovecraft manuscripts it owns.

The editors are to be commended for the rich biographical information they provide in their introduction for each correspondent. They have done real research, and not just grabbed the "low-hanging fruit." In addition, they have found photographs of each correspondent to commence each section of the volume. They have done a particularly impressive research job for Paul J. Campbell, who was well known in the amateur journalism hobby of his day but is nearly forgotten today. Campbell provided a refuge for Lovecraft's close friend W. Paul Cook in the difficult years between the death of his wife and his ultimate recruitment to join Walter J. Coates's Driftwind Press in North Montpelier, Vermont. Cook apparently did not retain any of his letters to Lovecraft. He would probably have maintained that the general public ought not to be reading any of Lovecraft's private letters. If Cook had had his way and only a single selection of Lovecraft's best stories (and perhaps *Fungi from Yuggoth*) been published, perhaps we would not witness Ray Rickman's calling Lovecraft a "vicious racist" and the attempts to block the placement of the statue that Lovecraft's fans wished to donate to the City of Providence. However, for myself, I would gladly relinquish this alternative universe for the Lovecraft letters, despite their occasional infelicity for modern readers.

Having devoted a few words to Kleiner and Jackson, I offer a few comments about the other correspondents. Arthur Harris, a British amateur, corresponded regularly with Lovecraft over the years 1915–37—perhaps an average of two or three letters per year. Lovecraft's letters to Harris concerned themselves not only with the amateur journalism hobby but with a wide range of topics, including history and architecture. Lovecraft had the talent to "listen" to his correspondents, and to slant his letters according to their interests.

The letters to Leeds reflect a common interest in the outré, and the editors even print a supernatural story by Leeds. The letters and postcards to him reflect the ease of two old friends' speaking to each other through correspondence. Leeds was only a few years older than Lovecraft, and the two men could recall such things as the melodies that were being sung in their boyhood years.

Like Lovecraft, James Larkin Pearson was a poet. He had ample printing equipment and printed a 400-page collection of his own poetry. The letters to Pearson are quite formal; clearly, the two men were not as simpatico as Lovecraft and Kleiner. Lovecraft's letter to Pearson dated 3 August 1919 makes abundantly clear that he had no sympathy with his correspondent's religious beliefs: "Naturally I cannot share your belief in the Hebrew Bible, since to me it is only one of many similar collections of Oriental maxims, history, laws, poetry, & legends." Lovecraft doesn't even pause to praise the beautiful English prose of the King James Bible, which so influenced the prose style of his idol Lord Dunsany.

Co-editor Schultz has done his usual fine design job with the present volume. The margins (especially in the gutter) are ample, the font is sufficiently large and dark, and the overall aesthetic effect is pleasing. I think that deferring notes to the ends of the letters avoids the cluttered look that would have been produced by footnotes on every page. The editors have done able work with the annotation and have avoided "throwaway" notes devoted to material known to most readers, while identifying some very obscure persons, places, and events. Readers unfamiliar with any abbreviation used should resort first of all to the list of abbreviations on p. 32.

If I had any quibble to pick with a very fine book, it would be the failure to list all the illustrations. The photographs of correspondents that commence each section of the book are by no means the only illustrations you will find in these pages. Don't fail to have a look at Rheinhart Kleiner's bookplate on p. 376, or at Paul J. Campbell's gushing oil well on the preceding page. There's a second photograph of Mrs. Jackson on p. 449, with her hair lighter and piled up on the top of her head. I've already remarked on the drawings by Lovecraft in his letters to Kleiner printed in this volume that were also featured on the dust jackets of *Selected Letters*. Since Arthur Harris was interested in architecture, Lovecraft drew for him a sketch of his new dwelling at 66 College Street (p. 284) and sketches of different types of colonial roofs (pp. 298, 299). Willis Conover was one of the first to capitalize on the illustrations that Lovecraft drew for his letters, in *Lovecraft at Last* (Carrollton-Clark, 1975). Reproduced illustrations help to draw the reader into the experience of the original recipient.

"Morton is a problem!" Lovecraft proclaimed in the same 25 November 1915 letter to Kleiner that contained some of his complaints about Charles Isaacson's writing. Of course, Morton is a perfect example of how Lovecraft could be good friends with someone largely opposed to him ideologically. The ever-vigilant editors cite Morton's "'Conservatism' Run Mad" in Isaacson's *In a Minor Key* no. 2 (1915): 15–16. The piece itself can be found in the appendix to *Letters to James F. Morton* (2011). In any event, the two men later became fast friends. Lovecraft's letters were his way of maintaining an extensive circle of friends and acquaintances from the comfort of his own study. Yes, his letters sometimes contain remarks that, in the light of changed cultural circumstances, are offensive to many. But Lovecraft always modulated his epistolary remarks to reflect the interests and the sensitivities of his correspondents. I like to think that their common interest in Providence history and architecture could have made possible a friendship between Lovecraft and Ray Rickman had their lives intersected. I don't think Lovecraft would have slighted Rickman because he is a Black man. Perhaps Rickman would have had occasion to amend his opinion of Lovecraft as a "vicious racist"—at least enough to eliminate the modifying adjective.

In any case, I advise Lovecraft scholars and fans not to miss the new, expanded *Letters to Rheinhart Kleiner and Others*. You will have a better appreciation for Lovecraft the man, and his views, after reading this volume.

H. P. LOVECRAFT. *Letters to Family and Family Friends*. Edited by S. T. Joshi and David E. Schultz. New York: Hippocampus Press, 2020. 2 vols. 1104 pp. $60.00 tpb. Reviewed by Darrell Schweitzer.

The volumes of H. P. Lovecraft's letters can now fill a quite large shelf. I confess that my frequent habit is to get a volume down over breakfast or at other odd times and read just a few letters, approximating the experience of receiving correspondence from the Old Gent, but if you go through such books cover to cover, you initially have the impression of reading the same story over and over again. We all know the basics: early contacts with amateur journalists, a widening social circle, marriage to Sonia (but in the absence of her letters from him, which she burned, not much about the courtship), the New York sojourn turning into an "exile," the triumphant return to Providence, then travel, the major journeys to Quebec, Charleston, and Florida and prolonged stays with the Barlow family there, the deteriorating relationship with *Weird Tales*, increasing involvement with early fandom; and then the typical correspondence volume fades out about the end of 1936 as Lovecraft's illness begins to overwhelm him.

But each of these correspondences is in its own way quite distinctive. In the letters to R. H. Barlow (*O Fortunate Floridian*), we see Lovecraft at his best, as friend and mentor, almost a fatherly figure to the young Barlow. In the letters to Robert E. Howard there we see that the two have much in common, but the letters almost turn into a slugfest in the great "Civilization vs. Barbarism" debate. In those to James F. Morton, there is a great deal of exposition of ideas and philosophy, and a rather calmer sort of controversy. The letters to Derleth are a bit more detached, as Derleth is so heavily preoccupied with professionalism in writing.

And so on. *Letters to Family and Family Friends* begins with letters to his mother, mostly written while she was in the hospital in her last years, but the bulk of the contents consists of letters to his aunts, Lillian D. Clark and Annie E. P. Gamwell. This gives a very strong emphasis in some areas, with evasions in others. For one thing, he only wrote to his aunts when he was not living with them, of course, so many of these letters are from his New York period, or from his travels. His letters to his mother give us a glimpse of the early, still poorly socialized Lovecraft, with low self-esteem. He regards himself as disfigured because of his ingrown whiskers, which he would apparently pick out with a needle. A new suit "made me appear as respectable as my face permits." His voice is "a monstrosity." When he attends an amateur meeting in 1921, he is very surprised at how well it went. Someone tells him he is a natural speaker.

These are some of his most personal letters, but unlike those to Morton or Wandrei or many others, there is very little exposition of ideas in them. His elder aunt, Lillian Clark, seems more interested in weird fiction—or at least he is more likely to recommend that she read Blackwood or Machen—but he does not expound aesthetics or philosophy very much here. As a compensation we get some of his very best travel writing. One thinks of that half-joking suggestion Avram Davidson made years ago that if Lovecraft had worked for the government during the Great Depression, he could have written guidebooks that would have been classics. Yes, he could have. The great strength in these letters is their vividness. Lovecraft is doing his best to share the actual experience of his explorations of Philadelphia or New York or Charleston or St. Augustine. Present-day inhabitants of those cities may enjoy trying to follow Lovecraft's footsteps, and discovering what remains of what he saw nearly a century ago. (There seems to have been many more colonial survivals, even rusticity, in parts of lower Manhattan than there is today. Much of what he describes in Philadelphia is still famil-

iar and carefully preserved for tourists.) His account of St. Augustine is particularly elaborate, possibly topped only by his
book-length account of Quebec; a complete history of the city
from its foundation by the Spanish in the sixteenth century up
to 1930. He must have sat in a library looking all this stuff up,
all for the benefit of just two readers, the aunts. This is the pure
"gentleman amateur" in Lovecraft, writing for the satisfaction of
doing so, with no thought of a larger audience, even if he has
put more effort into the result than do many journalists, or, indeed, guidebook writers.

At times he can be surprisingly evasive. He seems to have
sprung his marriage to Sonia on his aunts as a complete surprise,
writing only after the momentous act had already taken place.
You can imagine Lillian Clark puzzling over the letter of 9
March 1924, noting that for once, despite his "Grandpa Theobald" persona already being in place (Lovecraft was short of thir-
ty-four at this time), he addresses her by name, rather than as
"My dear Daughter," then goes on for several thousand words of
this sort of persiflage:

> With congeniality so preponderant, and having such a vital
> bearing on the progress, activity, and contentment of those
> concerned, one might well wonder why some permanent pro-
> gramme of propinquity was not arranged over a year and a half
> ago. Radical events, however, do not develop hastily; no matter
> how sudden their conscious and immediate planning, or their
> final occurrence may seem to be. You know Theobaldian re-
> serve, Theobaldian conservativism, Theobaldian adherence to
> the old order of things until some *deus ex machina* roughly de-
> scends to override all indecision [. . .]

And so on for three pages of solid, tiny type. Gradually the hints
become clearer, then Lovecraft makes the announcement, and
offers a pause for recovery from the shock. By the end of the
same letter he is proposing that his aunts leave Providence and
come live with him in New York, where he has already taken up
residence. ("You—and this is already an irrevocable dictum of
fate—are going to live here permanently.")

This may seem high-handed and presumptuous, but it is also extremely revealing. At the same time Lovecraft felt the need to take a leap out into the world and become a full-fledged adult (with what looked like good prospects for employment), he was also trying to rebuild the lost paradise of 454 Angell Street, with the extended family all under the same roof, even if now, of course, he would have a somewhat different position in the household than he did as a child.

It was not to be, of course, and soon the New York experience began to go sour. On page 339 we find the famous "pounding the walls" passage that is so often quoted out of context. Lovecraft is defending his need to cling to old possessions—pictures, books, items of furniture etc.—that he had from Providence:

> I am unable to take pleasure or interest in anything but a mental re-creation of other and better days [. . .] so in order to avoid the madness which leads to violence & suicide I must cling to the few shreds of the old days & old ways which are left to me. [. . .] When they go, I shall go, for they are all that make it possible for me to open my eyes in the morning or look forward to another day of consciousness without screaming in sheer desperation & pounding the walls and floor in a frenzied clamour to be waked up out of the nightmare of "reality" to my own room in Providence.

Even Charlotte Montague in her otherwise useful *H. P. Lovecraft: The Mysterious Man Behind the Darkness* (2015) gets this wrong (p. 105 of her book). No, Lovecraft *wasn't* screaming and pounding on the walls, which at the very least would have gotten him ejected from his Clinton Street apartment, if not carried off to a madhouse. He was expressing his misery in a rather over-the-top manner and suggesting that he *might* end up doing those things if he lost all connections to his Providence past.

The great advantage of publishing these letters at such length is that we get full context, even when Lovecraft is at his worst, as in the infamous (and often quoted) letter to Aunt Lillian of 11 January 1926, which is more or less a tirade against, not just other racial and ethnic groups, but *everybody* except maybe Frank Belknap Long, for being too modern, too affected, too "foreign," etc. You know this one: ". . . loathsome Asiatic hordes trail their dirty carcasses over streets where white men once walked . . . It is not good for a proud, light-skinned Nordic to be cast away alone amongst squat, squint-eyed jabberers with coarse ways and alien emotions whom his deepest cell-tissue hates & loathes as the mammal hates & loathes the reptile . . ." What context shows us is that this is *outburst*, not part of a debate, as such discourse might have been in letters to James F. Morton or Rheinhart Kleiner. It is not clear that Aunt Lillian held such views herself, or at least that she held them as strongly; more likely she knew her nephew well enough to know not to argue when he was like this. By the end of that same letter he has calmed down and is talking about a new overcoat, reading Bulwer-Lytton, and searching for an all-night restaurant.

New York did bring Lovecraft's always-present racism to the surface, to the extent that some modern readers might desire trigger warnings, although certainly these volumes are not for the beginning Lovecraft devotee. First you have to get past the constant and commonplace use of the n-word, as if it is just another noun, no more unusual than *horse* or *pigeon*. Context shows him using it in quite cheerful, otherwise pleasant passages, such as when he describes the inner courtyard of Philadelphia's City Hall as inhabited by pigeons and lazy n******s, blind to the possibility that those idle Black people might have been the unemployed, or else just taking a moment of leisure. Elsewhere he remarks on the "unpleasing proximity of African habitations" to a colonial section of New York, or, worse yet, the African-American quarter of Cleveland being a "gorilla-peopled jungle." In New England he does not overlook the "hovels of Italian and Portuguese swine." And so on.

But there are also lots of positive points to these letters too. I have noted the travel descriptions. He discusses his career and writing, though not in such depth as he might with, say, Clark Ashton Smith or Robert E. Howard. But on page 410 he makes the surprising statement that he proposes to write interplanetary fiction, which of course he never did, except in collaboration with Kenneth Sterling in "In the Walls of the Eryx." We also get sometimes appalling glimpses of the increased poverty of his last years. In 1936, while Annie Gamwell was in the hospital recovering from what no gentleman could ever mention (a mastectomy), he wrote to her *every day* in the form of a diary, as if he is trying, through correspondence, to share his life with her. He was already residing at 66 College Street at this point, but subsisting on canned provisions from 10 Barnes, some of them ten years old. The cocoa has gone bad and acquired an "earthy" taste, but he forces himself to use it anyway. Fortunately the canned bread is still edible. At one point he has an extra quantity of milk that must be used up, and so is reduced to "meals" of milk and crackers. Fortunately the orange juice for "dessert" would have been enough to save him from scurvy.

What we otherwise see in the diary portions is how his life went, day by day. He would rise late, read the newspaper, perhaps "wrestle" with his extensive correspondence, and perhaps undertake errands. There is very little mention of remunerative work. He attends lectures at Brown University on various subjects. Life must have been quite precarious. We can appreciate how those two fat checks he got from *Astounding Stories* in 1935 must have been life-savers.

A particularly pleasing discovery at the end is a series of letters to Marian F. Bonner, a friend of Annie's. At first Lovecraft is just an intermediary conveying good wishes back and forth, but he seems to have particularly warmed to Ms. Bonner (a neighbor). His letters to her are soon filled with delightful whimsy about cats, including carefully drawn letterheads from the Kappa Alpha Tau fraternity. She has become a regular correspondent. The letters continue well beyond Annie's recuperation and cover literature, ideas, colonial history, and even a few self-deprecating remarks about his on work ("Now and then the magazine *Weird Tales* drags out some early atrocity I have long since repudiated . . . I thank the dark gods Nyarlathotep and Yog-Sothoth that relatively few civilized persons ever see *Weird Tales!*"). In his last letter to her, 9 December 1936, he congratulates her for finding a copy of Margaret Murray's then-influential

The Witch-Cult in Western Europe.

Finally there are four letters *to* Lovecraft dated 1894–99 from his grandfather, Whipple V. Phillips, who addresses him as "Skimper" and "Punky," nicknames that, fortunately, did not stick. What is remarkable in the first of these is that Grandpa Phillips could write a full-page letter to a four-year old and expect it to be read.

The actual excellence of the editing and apparatus of these volumes hardly needs be remarked on. As usual there are introduction, thorough notes, bibliography, and index all up to the high standard we have come to expect from the team of Joshi and Schultz.

H. P. LOVECRAFT. *Letters to E. Hoffmann Price and Richard F. Searight.* Edited by David E. Schultz & S. T. Joshi. New York: Hippocampus Press, 2021. 486 pp. $25.00 tpb. Reviewed by Martin Andersson.

After H. P. Lovecraft died, August Derleth and Donald Wandrei were bold enough to envision a one-volume selection of letters by their friend, who even then was recognized as a master epistolarian by the narrow circle of his correspondents. Over the decades, this project grew into *five* volumes. But the present reviewer is confident in saying that not even that brave and visionary duo could have imagined in their wildest dreams the present Hippocampus Press project of getting the *entirety* of Lovecraft's extant and available correspondence into print, which, when finished in the not too distant future, will run to *more than twenty* volumes.

This ambitious and much-needed project has now reached Lovecraft's letters to two colleagues, E. Hoffmann Price and Richard F. Searight. Price and Searight were both writers with an affinity for the weird, but there the similarity ends, and this contrast creates a dynamic that contributes to making the present volume such a delight to read.

E. Hoffmann Price (1898–1988) was clearly a very colorful character, as evidenced by his own writings and by others' descriptions of him: a West Point graduate and a veteran of the

Great War, a traveler and a prolific writer of pulp fiction and valuable memoirs of the pulp era, an astrologer and a "boozing Buddhist" (as an acquaintance of the present reviewer jocularly described him). He had the unique distinction of being the only person who met all three of the great *Weird Tales* triumvirate—H. P. Lovecraft, Robert E. Howard, and Clark Ashton Smith—in the flesh. Lovecraft himself described him as follows in a letter to J. Vernon Shea, written after his first encounter in person with Price:

> Price is a remarkable chap—a West-Pointer, war veteran, Arabic student, connoisseur of Oriental rugs, amateur fencing-master, mathematician, dilettante coppersmith & iron worker, chess-champion, pianist, & what not! He is dark and trim of figure, not very tall, & with a small black moustache. He talks fluently and incessantly, & might be thought a bore by some—although I like to hear him rattling on.

Lovecraft and Price first met in New Orleans in 1932, when Robert E. Howard, himself unable to join them, telegraphed Price to notify him of Lovecraft's visit to the city. This first meeting, lasting for more than *twenty-five hours* of non-stop conversation, is the stuff of legends.

In correspondence, Lovecraft is at his best when his correspondent challenges him in some way, and this explains why he valued Price as much as he evidently did—indeed, as he noted in a letter of 1932 to Robert E. Howard: "As a matter of fact, all my favorite major correspondents are persons with whom I differ on some subject or another—usually many subjects—so that my long letters always tend to fall more or less into the debate class." As a writer, Price was resolutely professional, carefully analyzing potential markets and then writing what would sell, with little consideration for artistic merit, whereas Lovecraft was his complete opposite. This makes for a scintillating discussion of aesthetics versus commercialism that is just as thoughtful and penetrating as the debate on civilization versus barbarism that Lovecraft and Howard engaged in, even though Price's side is not reproduced in the present volume for reasons of space.

(Lovecraft did keep Price's letters to him, but in sheer wordage they dwarf the Lovecraft side of the correspondence, which is nevertheless of considerable size; Price was also in the habit of dashing off typed postcards the way some modern-day people dash off text messages on their cellphones—without much after-thought or content—so that much of it makes for rather repetitive reading. Those who are interested can easily find Price's letters to Lovecraft online at the Brown Digital Repository.)

A particularly delightful detail in these letters is Lovecraft's greetings and signatures, playing humorously on Price's interest in the Orient. Thus, a letter can open with "Subterrene Mosque of Eblis, Night of the Darting Flames, Dear Malik" (Lovecraft's playful nickname for Price was Malik Tawus, after the Peacock Angel of the Yazidi religion) and end with "Beatitudes of Yog-Sothoth upon thee!" followed by an illegible scrawl meant to give the impression of Sanskrit, Arabic, or some imaginary language.

Richard F. Searight (1902–1975) had ambitions to write pro-fessionally but never achieved the necessary success in the pro-fessional market, in spite of his talent for fiction as well as poetry; instead he worked as a telegraph operator, bookkeeper, and public accountant. When trying to break into the weird pulps, he was recommended by Farnsworth Wright of *Weird Tales* to contact Lovecraft regarding the latter's revisory services, which he did in August 1933. However, Lovecraft never took on Searight as a client, because, as he noted in his letter dated 31 August 1933, the occasional shortcomings of Searight's sto-ries "are matters of subject-matter rather than technique." But they stayed in touch, with Lovecraft occasionally commenting on Searight's writings in a non-professional capacity (the way he did with his younger correspondents such as Robert Bloch and Duane Rimel). In January 1934 Lovecraft commented upon "The Sealed Casket," for which Searight had created the imagi-nary Eltdown Shards (analogous to the *Necronomicon*), which Lovecraft himself later cited in "The Shadow out of Time" and "The Challenge from Beyond."

Their correspondence (previously published by Necro-nomicon Press in 1992 as *Letters to Richard F. Searight*) rapidly branched out into other topics, such as colonial architecture, Lovecraft's travels, and Searight's growing family, in which Lovecraft took a sincere and delighted interest. The letter dated 15 April 1936, will provide an example:

> Thanks immensely for the view of the young Sea-brights—which shows up well under a magnifying glass. The Crown Prince looks like a very promising & prepossessing young man, well worthy to carry on the traditions of his ancient line! And so he has three teeth? Bless my soul, but how the young do grow! Before I realise it he'll be writing fiction—or at least listening to stories told by his sire & probably inventing imaginative variants of his own.

(Searight's son Franklyn did indeed become an accomplished writer of weird fiction; a selection of his stories was published in 2007 by Hippocampus Press as *Lair of the Dreamer*.)

In these two correspondence cycles, Lovecraft displays the depth and wide range of his erudition, his keen sense of analysis, his pungent wit and humor, his playfulness and his seriousness, and the warmth that marked him in his final decade. It is also interesting to note how Lovecraft presents himself to his correspondents (not just Price and Searight). Each of them got their own personal image of Lovecraft, which when put together indicates the complexity and depth of the being that was Howard Phillips Lovecraft—a complexity and a depth that cannot be captured in any other way, particularly in this age of online superficiality and brevity.

As always with the Hippocampus Press letter series, the letters have been meticulously edited and annotated by Messrs. Schultz and Joshi. Elucidating references in Lovecraft's letters frequently requires large amounts of detective work, which the editors have honed into a skill over the years. They deserve especial praise for the list of nicknames (of which Lovecraft was inordinately fond) preceding the letters section, and the glossary of frequently mentioned names at the end of the book. An appendix of rare texts, such as Price's recipe for curry and a small sampling of Searight's poetry, rounds out the volume.